DE PROPRIETATIBUS LITTERARUM

edenda curat

C. H. VAN SCHOONEVELD

Indiana University

Series Maior, 30

IVOR ARMSTRONG RICHARDS

Photograph by Gyorgy Kepes

POETRIES

THEIR MEDIA AND ENDS

by

I. A. RICHARDS

*A collection of essays by I. A. Richards
published to celebrate his 80th birthday*

edited by

TREVOR EATON

1974

MOUTON

THE HAGUE · PARIS

LIBRARY OF CONGRESS CATALOG CARD NUMBER: 73-93947

Printed in The Netherlands by Mouton & Co., The Hague

IVOR ARMSTRONG RICHARDS

Born at Sandbach in Cheshire on 26th February, 1893, I. A. Richards has had a long and distinguished career. So diverse have been his interests and achievements that it is difficult deciding to which of these priority should be assigned. He first made his mark as co-author with C. K. Ogden of *The Meaning of Meaning*, a pioneering work in semantics. This book, published in 1923, in still regarded as a classic. Having tackled the complexities of the sign-situation, Richards turned his philosophical mind in other directions. With his *Principles of Literary Criticism* (1924) and *Practical Criticism* (1929), he established himself as the most penetrating literary theorist of the century. His approach to the problems of literature was influential in the founding of the New Criticism, just as his joint efforts with Ogden led to the development of Basic English and the establishment of Orthological Institutes all over the world – Richards was himself Director of the Chinese branch from 1936-1938. Meanwhile, Richards was devoting himself to practical criticism. His contributions on Coleridge are perhaps the best known, but he also became involved in re-presenting the writings of Plato, as part of a design to make Hellenocentric culture available to those with small Latin and less Greek. This development – given his background of philosophy and psychology – led naturally to his tackling problems in education, notably as to the sequencing of first steps and use of depictive language, set forth in *English Through Pictures*, Books 1 & 2, and in *Design for Escape*. His broad and humane attitudes towards education may best be seen in *Speculative Instruments* (1955), and in the present volume. Finally, he made his reputation as a poet. His first book of verse *Goodbye Earth and Other Poems*, published in 1958, when he was in his late sixties, was followed in 1959 by *The Screens and Other Poems*. Recognition of his poetic talent was swift: in 1962, he received the Russell Loines Award for Poetry and the Emerson-Thoreau Medal in 1970. *Internal Colloquies,* the collected poems and plays, appeared in 1971.

 His wide-ranging and successful intellectual quests have been matched by his academic appointments. He became Lecturer in the English Faculty at Cambridge in 1919, and was elected to a Fellowship at Magdalene College in 1925. From Cambridge, he went in 1929 as Visiting Professor to Tsing Hua University, Peking, where he stayed two years. He moved on to Harvard University, remaining there, having been made a University Professor, until his retirement in 1963: a glance at his list of publications since that date will remind us that this was retirement only in name. In 1974, he returns to the country of his birth, and to Magdalena College, his *alma mater*, where he first met C. K. Ogden, and where in the second decade of the century it all began.

T.E.

FOREWORD

They are like strangers, more admired and less favored.
All this is true, if time stood still; which contrariwise
moveth so round, that a froward retention of custom
is as turbulent a thing as an innovation.

Francis of Verulam, *Of Innovation*

The terms of the title are in the plural, because *Poetry* is to *poems* as *Life* is to *living beings*. We can make endless progress in studying organisms. Meditation on what Life is has not been – for many – of much help. *Media* is in the plural for somewhat different reasons. If we say that the medium of poems is language (or words) we gain little by that – unless we go on and consider what words may be: as types and as tokens; as speech dispositions and acts; as auditory patterns and images; as script, actual or imaged, . . . all these taken in their relationships as types and in their manifold interplay as tokens, again plural. It may be that poetries, along with all else, have some ultimate goal. But the way of useful speculation as to that seems to require the finest discrimination we can attain to of subordinate ends serving, each in its place, as means. And there is a further reason for using such plurals. They encourage us in an empirical approach. The singular formulation may readily tempt us to suppose we are in possession of generalizations when we may be only toying with tautologies.

In putting together a selection of pieces: essays, broadcasts by radio and TV, lecture scripts and notes written at widely separated dates and for diverse audiences, the impulse to tinker with them is strong. They could soon become chiefly patches and solderings. It has seemed best to leave them for the most part as they were.

In a bookful as much concerned as this with the casualties of communication: with how messages at destination may fail to accord with messages at source, and with the waste of effort entailed, trial use of special devices, as hoped-for partial remedy, should need no apology.

I am accordingly here continuing the experimentation with specialized
ˢʷquotation marksˢʷ or (ᶦinverted commasᶦ) begun in my *How to read
a Page* (1943). These are no more than a compact meta-semantic means
of indicating to the reader that (as we both know) there may be something tricky, noteworthy, queer, special, (ʳPickwickianʳ) about the way a
word or phrase is being used and, further, of making a start towards
suggesting what the particular use (the semantic peculiarity) may be. A
table of these special ᵗmeta-semantic markersᵗ is printed for convenience
of reference following the table of contents.

It is my belief that few readers will have difficulty in understanding –
sufficiently well – what these superscripts are trying to do. They may
however wonder whether the experiment is worth the trouble. But
ˀunderstandingˀ is, after all, the major concern throughout this selection.
Insight into its varieties and improvement in the conduct of our pursuit
of them is what the book attempts to promote. Surely it would be a hide-
bound or a timid linguistic engineering that would shrink from trying out
any device which may possibly help. But to be tested such suggestions
must be both experimented with and reflected upon. Since *How To
Read a Page* no one has, so far as I know, reported or commented on
outcomes of either. We may suspect that interestingly strong resistances
are at work if a proposal towards a refinement in meta-semantic
notation receives no overt notice through some 30 years.

Naturally I have speculated about this silence. One possible explanation would have little or nothing to do with any merits or demerits of
such devices: their service to their purpose. It would point rather to
variations in the degree of concern for the purpose. Those curious about
intellectual history are often uneasily aware of tides and currents, un-
accountable ebbings and flowings in the attention that topics can attract:
fluctuations, these, as puzzling and as important in their outcomes as
fashions. Probably in all studies or subjects these vogues may be remarked. What may be a dominant concern in one decade may be almost
entirely neglected in the next. Intense activity may be followed by quies-
cence without any sufficient reason anyone can suggest. The spotlight
has moved elsewhere and there is nothing as yet to be said about the
why's and wherefore's of the change. The topic may not have been in
the least exhausted, sometimes important new developments may have
been just opening up. No matter: suddenly the focus of interest shifts,
the hunt pursues other prey. Literary and philosophic "movements"
provide the most striking examples of these seemingly random variations. Indeed the phrase *THE MOVEMENT* in its very vagueness

sums the situation up. Those most involved are commonly as much as anyone at a loss to explain why one sort of work is *in* the movement and another not.

But perhaps readers have merely felt that no such new devices are needed, that current resources are adequate, that any fit reader will always see what a competent writer is doing? To this I would reply that the more reflectively I examine my own phrasing in the process of composing my sentences, the more grateful I am for help in clarifying for myself (and suggesting to others):

whether we should be taking a word to have a safely settled sense (in the context), technically or otherwise determined;

whether we are engaged in a meta-semantic inquiry as to what a word may do, does here, and should do;

whether we are using a word for lack of one more appropriate (sailing misapprehensions;

whether we are using a word for lack of one more appropriate (sailing with a jury-rig, stop-gapping, throwing it to the addressee to guess correctly what is meant);

whether we are treating a term derisively, amusedly or seriously;

whether the sentence is to be taken as skating . . . as swimming . . . as diving;

whether, in brief, we are to be *literal,* or, in some fashion, *figurative* – both of these terms being admittedly in need of further elucidation.

Nevertheless, with these devices, as with some other proposals made in these pages that are also awaiting welcome, I may be wise to appeal to Bacon's shrewd words that serve as epigraph to this Foreword; and to add that I have seen enough confusion, frustration and incapacitation due to neglect of these and other differences or to sheer lack of awareness of their possibility and importance, not to wish devoutly for the development of some better technique than *writers* have had available for the heightening of these "just-how-does-he-think-he-is-saying-it" discernments.

As I have written this, the contrasts between *writers'* and *speakers'* resources will, I hope, have been brought to mind. Through rhythm, stress, intonation, pausing . . . a speaker (even without the aid of gesture and facial expression) can clear up much that the most careful and crafty writer has to leave to his readers' sagacities. Anyone turning his Lecture Notes into an Essay finds himself dealing with a string of such problems. What must be done, at point after point, to make his written words not lose too many of the nuances they might have if suitably spoken. (Sometimes the safest thing to do is forcefully to remind the reader that it is a speech he has to imagine – rather than paragraphs to peruse.) So too, anyone who does much studied reading aloud has the chance to learn something of the reciprocal lesson: how to use oral utterance to translate, without betraying, the bare signalling of the marks on paper. And this, of course, is every actor's task.

Looking my selection over it comes home to me that its prime theme is the mutual aid that the media can offer to one another, the way in which they can train one another to improve their separate and joint efficacies. For well-understood reasons, social, economic, and techno-logical (our unparallelled accelerations in change), a catastrophic decline in the fundamental arts of saying things well has been occurring and is likely to continue. The schools, to which unprecedently heavier tasks are increasingly assigned, are quite unable to do anything commensurate with the need. The traditional models and controls that served as channels have been broken down and nothing that can take their place has yet come into being. That there is a Literacy Crisis begins to be re-cognized – though its dangers are still much underestimated. But it is not realized that failure to learn to read and write adequately is only one aspect of the situation. The illiteracy that is spreading is a more *general* disability; it is not a matter only of not managing reading and writing, but of not managing utterance and comprehension, of mishandling the communications without which reasonable standards of humane coop-eration cannot be long upheld. Reading and Writing – within our in-creasingly de-traditionalized urban agglomerations – are decisive be-cause they are our most powerful means of developing these abilities: to convey and to understand. They are, in the present world, NECES-SARY for what they can do towards safeguarding society, keeping its crime and insanity within bounds.

As yet the media have been of only incidental service. Much of their use, indeed, must be counted among the technological causes of the decline of Literacy (in the over-all sense of capacity to communicate). That they could be used to supply a suffficient remedy I have argued at length elsewhere. It has been demonstrated that suitably designed se-quences building mutual control between eye and ear can do what is needed. May it be done soon enough! But this requires better and more widely diffused understanding of how meanings are developed and con-veyed, clarified and heightened – as well as contaminated and degraded. In recurrences of hope that understanding may be improved the various pieces which follow were written.   I. A. R.

EDITORIAL NOTE

Although I. A. Richards has had a profound influence upon my own thought and attitudes throughout the last decade, it was not until June last year that I met him. He was giving a lecture at Birkbeck College. During this address, to illustrate a point he was making, he spoke of his own earliest memories, evoking a vivid image of the infant I. A. R., a Victorian baby, *speculating,* in the Latin sense of the word, within his cot. He has been *speculating* ever since, and has instructed countless others in this art. Ivor Armstrong Richards is one of the outstanding intellectual men bequeathed to us by the Victorian era. When, at Birkbeck, he announced to me his intention of climbing, at the age of seventy nine, the odd Alp or two, I found it easy to believe that this figure will, even in the twenty-first century, still be seen surveying the view from the summit.

The essays in this book have, apart from a few exceptions, been published severally in various journals and monographs. Professor John Paul Russo, at present engaged in compiling an exhaustive bibliography of Richards' works for the O.U.P. Festschrift honouring Richards in his eightieth year, has kindly drawn up the following particulars. The list gives details of previous publication and, where appropriate, should be regarded as acknowledgement of permission to reprint.

1. "Functions of and Factors in Language", *Journal of Literary Semantics*[1] (1972).
2. Forthcoming. Appearing as an article in *The 73rd Yearbook of the National Society for the Study of Education* (Chicago, Illinois).
3. "Jakobson's Shakespeare: The Subliminal Structure of a Sonnet". Review of Roman Jakobson, *Shakespeare's Verbal Art in "Th' expence of Spirit"* (The Hague, Mouton, 1969). *Times Literary Supplement* 28th May, 1970.
4. "The Sense of Poetry: Shakespeare's 'The Phoenix and the Turtle' ", *Daedalus* 87 (1958). First broadcast in the winter 1957-58 season

of WGBH-TV, Boston.

5. First broadcast in the winter 1957-58 season of WGBH-TV, Boston.

6. "The Interactions of Words", *The Language of Poetry*, edited by Allen Tate (Princeton, Princeton University Press, 1942).

7. First broadcast in the winter 1957-58 season of WGBH-TV, Boston. Subsequently printed with the same title in *Master Poems of the English Language,* edited by Oscar Williams (New York, The Trident Press, 1966).

8. First broadcast in the winter 1957-58 season of WGBH-TV, Boston.

9. "Coleridge's Minor Poems: A Lecture Delivered in Honor of the Fortieth Anniversary of Professor Edmund L. Freeman at Montana State University on April 8, 1960" (Missoula, Montana, 1960).

10. Comprises an essay (a), and a review (b): (a) "Coleridge: The Vulnerable Poet", *Yale Review* 48 (1959); (b) "An Angel's Talk", a review of S. T. Coleridge, *The Friend,* edited by Barbara E. Rooke, *The Collected Works,* Vols. I and II (Princeton, University Press, 1969), *Listener* 25 September 1969.

11. Unpublished. Written in 1971.

12. Forthcoming. Appearing as an article in *The Uses of Literature,* edited by Monroe Engel (Cambridge, Mass., Harvard University Press).

13. "Sources of our Common Thought: Homer and Plato", *The Great Ideas Today 1971* (Chicago, Encyclopedia Britannica, Inc., 1971).

14. Broadcast BBC Radio, 14 September 1959 and published in the *Listener* 17 September 1959. Not to be confused with the essay of the same title published in *Speculative Instruments* (1955).

15. Unpublished. Written c. 1964.

16. *Nation,* 18 July 1934.

17. Unpublished lecture. Professor Russo's photostat copy is dated 20 October 1942.

It is hoped that, as well as formally celebrating I. A. R.'s 80th birthday, these writings will provide an up-to-date and unified account of his poetics.

I take this opportunity of thanking Mr. G. Thomas, of Ham Street, Kent, who helped me with the reading of proofs, and Miss Mabel Sculthorp, Director of the Language Centre, University of Kent at Canterbury, for help and encouragement.

Ashford, Kent, 1973   T. E.

TABLE OF CONTENTS

Ivor Armstrong Richards V
Foreword VII
Editorial Note XI
Key to Meta-semantic Markers XV

1. Factors and Functions in Linguistics 1
2. Powers and Limits of Signs 17
3. Linguistics into Poetics 39
4. "The Phoenix and the Turtle" 50
5. Reversals in Poetry 59
6. Interinanimations of Words 71
7. "The Exstasie" 85
8. "The Garden" 95
9. Coleridge's Other Poems 112
10. The Vulnerable Poet and *The Friend* 128
11. Poetry as Paideia 146
12. Literature for the Unlettered 149
13. Sources of our Common Aim 165
14. Poetry as an Instrument of Research 215
15. What is Saying? 222
16. What is Belief? 234
17. The Ever-new Discovery 242
Index 250

KEY TO META-SEMANTIC MARKERS

w——w   indicates that the word —- merely as that word in general — is being talked about. The marks are equivalent to "the word". For example, ^{w}table^w may mean an article of furniture or a list.

r——r   indicates that some special use of the word or phrase is being referred to. The marks are equivalent to, "Please refer to the place in the passage we should have in mind here." For example, ^{r}Nature^r for Whitehead is not Wordsworth's ^{r}Nature^r.

?——?   indicates that our problem is, What does this word say here? (Not whether anything it seems to say is acceptable or not.) The marks are equivalent to "Query: what meaning?" There is no derogatory implication. Most $^?$important$^?$ words are, or should be, in this situation.

!——!   indicates surprise or derision, a "Good Heavens! What-a-way-to-talk!" attitude. It may be read $^!$shriek$^!$ if we have occasion to read it aloud.

t——t   indicates that the expression is a technical term.

sw——sw   specialized quotation mark meaning that what may be said with the word or phrase is not necessarily as we will ordinarily take it.

1. FACTORS AND FUNCTIONS IN LINGUISTICS

I propose to examine minutely a famous formulation summarizing what language does and relating this systematically to the means through which language does it. Six basic functions are there cursorily described and a corresponding scheme of six fundamental factors is put forward. This clear and succinct account is that offered by Roman Jakobson in his concluding statement: "Linguistics and Poetics", closing the Conference on Style[1] held at Indiana University in Bloomington, April 17-19, 1958. The subject matter of the passage is clearly of central importance to literary semantics, amounting to a draught constitution for that study. It is condensed enough to justify and reward unusually close attention even at some cost in tedium.

The techniques tried out in this examination may also deserve explicit description and systematic exploration. This can set out from Jacobson's reminder[2] of Pierce's seemingly revolutionary doctrine of the *Interpretant:* "For us, both as linguists and as ordinary word-users, the meaning of any linguistic sign is its translation into some further, alternative sign, especially a sign 'in which it is more fully developed' as Pierce, the deepest inquirer into the essence of signs, insistently stated." Such translation into other signs of the same language, such RE-WORDING, to use Jakobson's label, will be the means here employed. The aim is to gain as deep, as wide, as full an awareness of WHAT WE ARE DOING as possible, as many-angled a set of views of that as we can. The three paragraphs we so consider were addressed to an audience composed of linguists, psychologists, literary critics, and theorists in literary criticism. Such diversity among their approaches may be expected to entail difference between their interpretations. And naturally the high compression

[1] Reported in *Style in Language*, edited by Thomas A. Sebeok (New York and London: Technology Press of M.I.T. and John Wiley and Sons Inc., 1960). See pages 353-358.
[2] "On Linguistic Aspects of Translation" in *On Translation*, Reuben A. Brower (ed.), pp. 232-233.

of the account makes it, at first glance, seem to many readers somewhat cryptic. It thus poses a finely exacting challenge to sympathetic exploratory paraphrase, gloss, and commentary.

We will be returning to Pierce's doctrine. But let us first give a preliminary reading to Jakobson's three paragraphs.

I will then offer a number of RE-WORDINGS (intra-lingual translations). I do so not in the least to suggest that Jacobson's sentences are in any need of change. Or of explanation, except in so far as any attempt to bring out the meanings of a discourse entails experimental change and comparison with possible alternative phrasing. My hope is to focus attention upon the process of making out meanings and thereby to raise the question: Are not procedures in this crucial activity capable of far more systematic development than has in general hitherto been attempted? As I weigh these various re-wordings I will take occasion to point out, as explicitly as I can (1) the types of control under which choice of the alternatives is being made; (2) the principles guiding the comparings that occur; (3) details of the discriminative process. The version[3] will be followed by a commentary organized under these three headings: 1. Control; 2. Principles; 3. Detail.

Language must be investigated in all the variety of its functions. Before discussing the poetic function we must define its place among the other functions of language. An outline of these functions demands a concise survey of the constitutive factors in any speech event, in any act of verbal communication. The ADDRESSER sends a MESSAGE to the ADDRESSEE. To be operative the message requires a CONTEXT referred to ("referent" in another, somewhat ambiguous, nomenclature), seizable by the addressee, and either verbal or capable of being verbalized; a CODE fully, or at least partially, common to the addresser and addressee (or in other words, to the encoder and decoder of the message); and, finally, a CONTACT, a physical channel and psychological connection between the addresser and the addressee, enabling both of them to enter and stay in communication. All these factors inalienably involved in verbal communication may be schematized as follows:

CONTEXT
MESSAGE
ADDRESSER ——————— ADDRESSEE
CONTACT
CODE

[3] As John Hollander perceptively remarks, "It is usually assumed from the start that, keeping an original text in mind, there is going to be *something* queer about a version of it, whether a French version, or a shortened one, or a version leaning strongly toward the views of Professor von Braun, or even a garbled version". "Versions, Interpretations, Performances", in *On Translation*, Reuben A. Brower (ed.), p. 221.

Each of these six factors determines a different function of language. Although we distinguish six basic aspects of language, we could, however, hardly find verbal messages that would fulfill only one function. The diversity lies not in a monopoly of some one of these several functions but in a different hierarchical order of functions. The verbal structure of a message depends primarily on the predominant function. But even though a set (*Einstellung*) toward the referent, an orientation toward the CONTEXT — briefly the so-called REFERENTIAL, "denotative", "cognitive" function — is the leading task of numerous messages, the accessory participation of the other functions in such messages must be taken into account by the observant linguist.

(After four intervening pages)

Now that our cursory description of the six basic functions of verbal communication is more or less complete, we may complement our scheme of the fundamental factors by a corresponding scheme of the functions:

REFERENTIAL

EMOTIVE   POETIC   CONATIVE

PHATIC

METALINGUAL

RE-WORDED VERSION

Language has many different things to do. Before going into ?poetic? work we must say what place this has among the other sorts of work it does. We need a short, over-all account of the conditions which come together whenever anything is said. There must be:

(1) an ADDRESSER (someone directing, sending)

(2) a MESSAGE (what is sent) to

(3) an ADDRESSEE (person or persons to whom the message is sent).

For this to work out there must be:

(4) a CONTEXT (something the addresser is thinking of, talking about; which the addressee can think of, more or less, as the addresser does)

(5) a CODE (system of sounds, marks, related to parts that can make up messages) and this must be fully or in part the same for 1 and 2

(6) a CONTACT (physical and mental conditions which let 1 and 2 come into and keep in communication).

CONTEXT

MESSAGE

ADDRESSER ——————— ADDRESSEE

CONTACT

CODE

Each of these six conditions has chiefly to do with a different sort of work that language does. Though there are these separate angles from which we can look into language, few if any messages do only one sort of work. Language can do different things not through each side having only one sort of undertaking but through different organizations in which the sides may control or be controlled by one another. The structure (make-up) of a message depends, firstly, on the chief thing it is doing. It is true that, for many messages, their most important work is to represent the context; even so, the other things they may be doing must be noted by anyone wishing to see what is going on.

(After four intervening pages)

Having given a short outline of the six sorts of work language does, we may add a parallel picture of these:

	REFERENTIAL	
EMOTIVE	POETIC	CONATIVE
	PHATIC	
	METALINGUAL	

COMMENTARY

1. *Control*

The character of this version, it will be evident,[4] has been governed by a wish to make its message simple, non-technical, and accessible to readers unaccustomed to learned language. In view of the importance for all users of language of what Jacobson's summary has to say, some study of how such things can be said so as to be maximally intelligible to all interested persons, no matter what their scholarly training and experience may be, should need no apology. As will be seen below, alternative versions of Jacobson's sentences can be given that are more penetrating, illuminative, and precise than these in Everyman's English. But most of those – for the ADDRESSEES that this version has in view – would hardly be more readily comprehensible to them than the original.

---

[4] Those familiar with the literature of language-control will recognize that it is written in a limited English (Everyman's) deriving from Basic English, keeping to the Basic English Word List (except for a very few additions, of which CAN and MUST are typical) but using selected verbs appearing as nouns (or within them) on that List.

One of the most fundamental axioms or assumptions (^{r}constitutive factors$^{r\,5}$ if you like) of literary semantics is here being illustrated. For any ^{r}speech event or act of communication^r the character and resources of the Addressee(s) is plainly of first order importance. [6] Most Addressers will of course feel divided loyalties: all the six factors have their claims, and rivalry and conflict often arise. Fidelity to the Context (a dual term always, covering both what-is-talked-of and what-is-being-said-about-it); to the Contact (let us not lose the Addressee's attention; may we be audible or legible!); to the Message itself (let us not say too much or too little); to the Code (due respect for the dictionary, for usage, for linguistic decorum, for keeping verbal resources up); and to the Addresser too (concern for his proper interests and/or image): all six, in degrees varying with the situation and occasion, have to be satisfied. Between them, and through clever compromises, they CONTROL the how of our utterances.

I will juxtapose here for convenience in comparing Jacobson's two depictions and my own yantra – a diagram cross-section of a type-specimen Message. For two related explanations of it, see *Speculative Instruments*, "Toward a Theory of Comprehending" and *Poetries and Sciences*, "How does a Poem know when it is finished?", p. 110.

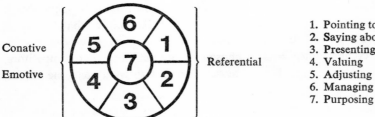

Conative

Emotive

Referential

1. Pointing to
2. Saying about
3. Presenting
4. Valuing
5. Adjusting
6. Managing
7. Purposing

The centrality of 7 is important: 1, 2, 3, 4, 5, 6 are its means. So too with the work of 6 – controlling the often conflicting endeavors of 1, 2, 3, 4, 5. Activity 3 has to do with realizing or not what the utterance is doing.

[5] ^{r}...^{r} A specialized quotation mark meaning "Refer to a passage in which word or phrase has above appeared". Here the reference is to line 4 of the Jakobson excerpt. Specific directives can evidently be added to the r mark.
[6] Others than the Addressees may be also concerned. The bystander, the possible critic, the detached observer frequently, and rightly, can take part in the shaping of the utterance.

2. *Principles of our comparings*

Plainly enough, bookfuls might be poured out under this heading. The mention of compromises met above points to a leading Section. No living sentence can do all that it might have done. Something has been given up for something in its framing. (Sentences within Logic, Mathematics, purely expository Physics ... etc. are exceptions. Perhaps we should not call them living? Their Addressees are ideal recipients, qualified by specifiable ability and training.) The comparing of any feature with any possible alternative proposed for it is a weighing of gains and losses.

We can go further. Whether it is already selected or merely considered for selection, what any feature in any utterance is (or can do) comes to it from its relations to the possible alternates. It is what it is (can do what it can do) by NOT being any of a number of other possibles. This principle rules throughout – from minimal ᵗdistinctive featuresᵗ[7] on up through all the varieties and hierarchies of linguistic units – up to paragraphs and chapters in discourse.[8] Comparing is taking account of, or participating in, this oppositional texture of being. Wittingly or unwittingly, we select in all that happens in and to us. The degree in which we may be said to SELECT actively or to be, screen-wise, passively selective, varies and there are frequently cases in which what we are consciously trying to do differs greatly from what is brought about. In any case selection entails likeness-with-difference in what is present when we choose one course rather than some rival. COMPOSITION indeed is competition.[9] What is chosen pushes past the other competitors, as being more compatible, more consonant, with what has gone before,

---

[7] ᵗ...ᵗ A specialized quotation mark meaning: "the expression is a technical term and as such is anchored to definitions and specimens which should strictly limit how it is used". See Jakobson and Halle, *Fundamentals of Language* (Mouton, 1956), p. 59.

[8] See Jakobson and Halle, *Fundamentals of Language*, p. 60. "Any linguistic sign involves two modes of arrangement. (1) Combination. Any sign is made up of constituent signs and/or occurs only in combination with other signs. This means that any linguistic unit at one and the same time serves as a context for simpler units and/or finds its own context in a more complex linguistic unit. Hence any actual grouping of linguistic units binds them into a superior unit; combination and contexture are two faces of the same operation. (2) Selection. A selection between alternatives implies the possibility of substituting one for the other, equivalent to the former in one respect and different from it in another. Actually, selection and substitution are two faces of the same operation." CONTEXT here has a different use from CONTEXT (p. 2) above. The two are distinguished below (pp. 9-11).

[9] I have twice recently found myself to have written COMPETITION in place of COMPOSITION (ETI for OSI).

with what is, at the moment, directive, and with what is divined as being likeliest to come. In brief, composition is purposive, it is seeking what will suit later developments (as it tries to foresee them) as well as paying for promises entered upon by what it has already done.

All this is, of course, deeply familiar to us all. What we want x FOR determines which x we use – in any course of action in which we are alert enough, vigilant enough, awake enough, for USE and CHOOSE to become equivalents. The rest is habit, the acquired mechanical, a conserving, though sometimes potentially disastrous, legacy from past choices. This is true universally in behavior. Not surprisingly it rules most evidently in verbal composition – the most typically purposeful of our activities.

Whenever two or more candidates for selection are being compared our consideration of any one of them influences and is influenced by our considerings of the others. At every point, for example, my Everyman's Version seems simpler, and more obvious and less ambiguous, than it otherwise would, BECAUSE IT IS BEING COMPARED WITH JAKOBSON'S SENTENCES. It takes from them a continuous stream of decisions through an inter-related sequence of choice-points. It is being guided (its readers too) by Jakobson's original decisions. And they, too, I hope and believe, will seem in the comparison more lucid, more penetrable, kinder to the teeth, than they would alone. They convey more and penetrate further – unless I am mistaken. But I have to remember as I write this that I have just been through the elaborate process of composing an Everyman's Version (EV), involving me in multiple comparings of Jakobson's phrasing with a wide variety of candidates for substitution. In fact, I have been reading him with an unusual degree of attention and weighing against one another several ways of taking him – imagining too, as fully as I can, YOUR possible re-weighings, my Addressees, who will of course include here Jakobson himself, and what sort of a showing as a reader I may be making. These comparings, if reported explicitly enough, entail a good deal of showing up of the reader. Among the principles guiding comparings may be proposed, as highly desirable, constant assistance from a modicum of reflective doubt.

3. *Details of the discriminative process*

The six words selected by Jakobson as names for his six factors, for which the rest of the passage is serving as explication, mark the cardinal points (the pivots or hinges) on which the account turns. On how selectively (choosily) we take these six our understanding of it depends. They are, together with ᵗFUNCTIONᵗ and ᵗFACTORᵗ themselves, being ᵗtechnicalizedᵗ (fixed as to their senses) in this passage – and in the four brilliant pages of explanation and exemplification developed between the two diagrammatic schemes. This process of technicalization by which these terms are related to one another and the two schemes put into parallel order repays further exploration and description. We could hardly find a better example, or type-specimen, showing how systematic treatment is made possible.

The six names of the factors and the six names of the functions are retained in my Everyman's Version, though FUNCTION and FACTOR are replaced by substitute phrases. The Metalingual purpose (ʳpre-dominant functionʳ) of the passage requires this. What it is primarily doing is ˢʷtelling us howˢʷ [10] these words are here being, and will hereafter be, used. That we should know this is essential if what will be said with their aid in ensuing paragraphs is to be rightly understood. Let us see here all we can of how this ʳtelling us howʳ is done.

There are two main means of metalingual elucidation: exposition and exemplification. We can either offer the Addressee DEFINITIONS or place before him INSTANCES of what we are referring to, chosen as especially revealing the characteristics we want him to note. Both these, we may note, are predominantly conative in function. Our definitions will usually look like statements of fact made in the indicative mood. But ʔessentiallyʔ [11] they are disguised imperatives or prayers or optatives: commands, or hope-generated invitations to the Addressee to behave with terms in certain ways rather than in others. [12]

As usual here, this ʔessentialʔ is as much a reinforcement of the conative intent of the sentence as it is a furthering of the referential task: to describe, that is, what we ˡreallyˡ [13] do in definitions. This ʔessentiallyʔ is, it is to be noted, an illustration of our second mode of metalingual clarification. To use Pierce's terms it is a token of that TYPE of procedure. And, while we are thinking of Pierce, we may

[10] ˢʷ. . .ˢʷ. Specialized quotation marks meaning that what may be said with the word or phrase (step warily) is not necessarily as we will ordinarily take it.
[11] ʔ. . .ʔ Specialized quotation mark meaning that the enclosed term needs metalingual questioning.
[12] For a fuller discussion of this position, see my *Interpretation in Teaching*.
[13] Shrieks suggesting that such use of the words may be absurd (a jointly emotive and conative gesture). We may indeed fairly question (so I read the last sentence of Jakobson's second paragraph) whether, with many sentences, two or more functions may not rightly be considered to be co-equally in control.

pause to consider further the ʳitʳ in Jakobson's quotation from him with which we began.

Not only may any ʳfurther, alternative signʳ into which a sign may be translated be ʳmore developedʳ (or less developed: to enlarge the field of Addressees, the signs used in the Everyman's Version are on the whole LESS developed than those in Jakobson's original) but they may be developed in different directions to bring out different possibilities, (potentials) in the meaning. Corresponding to Jakobson's two parallel schemes, six such potentials, or vectors may be proposed. An alternative sign may affect:

(1) The Addresser-Emotive component (Factor-Function) that is, it may make the utterer's concern clearer or less clear, more noticeable or less.

(2) The Addressee-Conative component. That is, it may make what is being attempted through the utterance more evident or less.

(3) The Context-Referential component. That is, it may make what is being spoken OF and what is said ABOUT it more ʳseizableʳ or less.

(4) The Code-Metalingual component. That is, it may show better or worse (by its explications or through its examples) how terms are being used.

(5) The Contact-Phatic component. That is, it may bring and keep the parties in touch more successfully or less. (ʳInsistenceʳ, incidentally, often switches the Addressee off. Pierce might have had more students earlier if he had not tried so hard to gain and hold them.)

(6) The Message-Poetic component, with which we come to the chief point that Jakobson has it at heart and in mind to make: the point to prepare for and frame which he has drawn this outline of the other factors and functions. It is also the point which Addressees in general may be least likely to take in without confusions.

To guard against these, some further attempts to provide alternative signs, ᵗrewordingsᵗ, developing especially the Context-Referential and the Code-Metalingual components will be in place. Jakobson rightly remarks that the nomenclature of 'referent' is ʳsomewhat ambiguousʳ. It is. But so too is that of 'context' and that of 'code' and those of 'message' and of 'meaning' themselves. There are topics for which it often seems that any terms which may be introduced to deal with them become quickly infected with ambiguity whatever precautions are taken. And of these topics, that which we approach through this cluster of related verbal signs has some claim to be rated the most virulent of all promotors of confusion. It is as though the SIGNATA themselves here are especially corruptive – an impression perhaps due to their being so ʳinalienably involvedʳ in whatever attempts we may make to order them.

Some of the sources of these ambiguities are not hard to point out. The difficulty rather is to keep and protect in our usage the distinction we have observed: "Observe the 'No Smoking' Sign!" This is a case where knowledge is not necessarily virtue. Noting an injunction and doing accordingly need not be the same thing. To take these terms in turn: ʳREFERENTʳ: "that which is being thought of, spoken about, that on which truth tests depend". Such a definition looks straight enough – until we observe that ᵗreferentᵗ, so defined, is dual: both a bare denotation (extension) AND the character being ascribed to it. The truth test takes account of both. Has the referent in fact the character ascribed? That is a question. Two translations arise: Is the ʳreferentʳ what would be, were it as the statement represents it as being? Or is it what would make that representation true, if true, and false, if false? The trouble can be detected WITHIN, I believe, every attempt either to give some account of it or to account for it.

CONTEXT links this trouble with at least two others. Any attempt to describe how we come to know anything through experience, become able to refer to it, think of it, talk of it, point to it, etc., has somehow to connect present thinkings of, pointings to, etc., with past originative occasions. Through one nomenclature or another it has to take account of recurrence. Perhaps I may best recur to a past attempt of my own to deal with a chief ambiguity.

A word, like any other sign, gets whatever meaning it has through belonging to a recurrent group of events, which may be called its context. Thus a word's context, *in this sense*, is a certain recurrent pattern of *past* groups of events, and to say that its meaning depends upon its context would be to point to the process by which it has acquired its meaning.

In another, though a connected, sense, a word's context is *the words which surround it in the utterance*, and the *other contemporaneous* signs which govern its interpretation.

Both senses of 'context' need to be kept in mind if we are to consider carefully how interpretations succeed or fail. For clarity we may distinguish the second sort of context by calling it the *setting*. It is evident that a change in the setting may change the context (in the first sense) in which a word is taken. We never, in fact interpret single signs in isolation. (The etymological hint given by *inter* is very relevant here.) We always take a sign as being *in some setting*, actual or supplied, as part of an interconnected sign-field (normally, with verbal signs, a sentence and an occasion). Thus, insufficient attention to the accompanying sign-field (the setting and occasion) which controls the context (recurrent groups of events in the past) is a frequent cause of mistaken understanding. But equally, no care, however great, in observing the setting will secure good interpretation if past experience has not provided the required originative context.

(Preface to *Interpretation in Teaching*, London, 1937, p. viii.)

For further details I must refer to *The Meaning of Meaning* (1923), more specifically to Appendix B, "On Contexts", in that volume: a formulation in which Frank Ramsey, when still a boy at Winchester, took an active part.

Two other ingredients should be noticed in considering how CONTEXT has acquired its present equivocal role in semantics.[14] O.E.D. enters: "Concretely, the parts which immediately precede or follow any particular passage or text and determine its meaning" (cf. ʳsettingʳ above), adding that there are transferred and figurative uses. It is one of these to which Malinowski gave extended currency in his Supplement to *The Meaning of Meaning*: by introducing *"context of situation*, if I may be allowed to coin an expression which indicates on the one hand that the conception of *context* has to be broadened and on the other that the *situation* in which words are uttered can never be passed over as irrelevant" (p. 306). He followed this up, two pages later, with "It is obvious that the *context of situation*, on which such a stress is laid here, is nothing else but the *sign-situation* of the Authors". They, however, were not so sure of that, and would rather stress the metaphor of weaving behind the word. The immediate situation within which the utterance occurs is principally important because through this the required linkages with past experience are activated. It is these linkages which weave into one vast web all the illimitable possibilities we cover so calmly with the word 'meaning'. The contexture which structures this web is not one of events or objects (except in very special senses[15]). It is a knitting together of what Pierce christened TYPES, instances of which are what he called TOKENS. He takes this nomenclature from the printed page.

[14] A third may well be a doubt whether Emotive and Conative functions are not mediated as fully through Contexts as the Referential. See Jakobson's discussion on page 354 of *Style in Language* and his comment there on "Saporta's surmise". We would however still have to find a means of distinguishing Referential from Emotive and Conative components in a message.

[15] Two of these are Pierce's *Immediate Object* and *Dynamical Object* which correspond to the two senses of ʳreferentʳ touched on above. "We have to distinguish the *Immediate Object*, which is the object as the Sign itself represents it ... from the Dynamical Object, which is the Reality which by some means contrives to determine the Sign to its Representation". (From "Prologomena to an Apology for Pragmaticism", *Monist*, 1906, quoted in Appendix D of *The Meaning of Meaning*, p. 280, where the passage from the same article on the type-token distinction will also be found.)

There will ordinarily be about twenty 'the's' on a page, and, of course, they count as twenty words. In another sense of the word 'word,' however, there is but one word 'the' in the English language; and it is impossible that this word should lie visibly on a page, or be heard in any voice, for the reason that it is not a Single thing or Single event. It does not exist; it only determines things that do exist. Such a definitely significant Form I propose to call a *Type* . . . this or that word on a single line of a single page of a single copy of a book, I will venture to call a *Token*.

For our present purpose, the taking account of some ambiguities of the word CONTEXT, what is most needed is a sustained act of realizing imagination of the extent and degree to which words as TYPES are interconnected. It is not hyperbolic but literally the case that every word we can use is related, either directly or mediately, through one or other chain of links, with every other word in our vocabulary, and potentially every occasion in our past of passive and active use of any word, as Addressee or Addresser, can enter into the guiding contexts of present and future use. Ordinarily there need be little or no awareness of these influences, though occasionally the normal veil is in part, for a moment, lifted. It should be added further that these connexities are far from fixed and static. Later experience can shift them, it may develop them or impair and seemingly obliterate them. Typically, as we learn more about a matter or come to think differently of it, our contexts, the references we make, are changed. And since any Message is what it is thanks (in part and among the other factors) to its Context, we should not be surprised if Messages are inherently hard to identify and if communications are normally defective. Full and complete reproduction at the destination of what was selected at the source is no more than an ideal, a mathematical fiction. We don't expect to meet in this life points or straight lines or circles. No more should we hope for perfect understanding. The wonder is that Messages are so often conveyed so well.

The term MESSAGE too has its troubles. Chief among them is confusion with the Signal. A Message is a Meaning selected from the limitless possible field through (among other factors) the operation of a subsystem of references, its Context. It is conveyed (more or less) by use of a Signal. This, we should realize, is an entity of quite another order of being. In speech, the Signal consists of sounds and pauses; in writing, it is made up of marks on a ground. These are physical events. For good reasons they are among the most fully and exactly observable events that can be found. That is why they are so useful in communication. With suitable apparatus, high enough magnification, sensitive enough recording, we can carry the identification process further with them than any need can call for. The contrast with Messages could hardly be stronger. This Essay has been one long attempt, far from successful I fear, to help in the identification of some fourteen central meanings of linguistics. Few literates with normal sight, facing a properly printed sentence, are uncertain whether they are reading CONTACT or CONTEXT: the differences between them can be described as precisely as we please. Who, however normal his intelligence, will be quite certain where CONTACT ENDS AND CONTEXT TAKES OVER, or whether this emphasized word-group makes any sense, or how to settle such a question? None the less, as we shall shortly see, we have to try.

On the cover of the paperback edition of the second printing, 1965, of *Psycholinguistics*, edited by Charles E. Osgood and Thomas A. Sebeok (Indian University Press), appears the middle part of that word – *ycholinguist* – out of focus and eye-strainingly distorted. I take it that the designer of the cover had been reading the opening pages and was making a valid and witty comment on the outcome. For there, in the course of defining the subject, message and signal are as openly and as thoroughly confused as could be. On page 2, after mentioning "at least two communicating units, a SOURCE UNIT (speaker) and a DESTINATION UNIT(hearer)" the authors continue:

Between any two such units, connecting them into a single system, is what we may call the *message*. For purposes of this report, we will define message as that part of the total output (responses) of a source unit which simultaneously may be a part of the total input (stimuli) to a destination unit. When individual A talks to individual B, for example, his postures, gestures, facial expressions and even manipulations with objects (e.g., laying down a playing card, pushing a bowl of food within reach) may all be part of the message, as of course are events in the sound wave channel.

and on the opposite page, as explicitly, an identification of the two is attempted.

Microlinguistics (or linguistics proper) deals with the structure of messages, the signals in the channel connecting communicators, as events independent of the characteristics of either speakers or hearers. Once messages have been encoded and are "on the air", so to speak, they can be described as objective, natural science events in their own right. In an even stricter sense, the linguist is concerned with determining the *code* of a given signal system, the sets of distinctions which are significant in differentiating alternative messages.

Turning the page over, we find "Psycholinguistics is that one of the disciplines studying human communication which is most directly concerned with the processes of decoding and encoding".

This is surely very odd behavior, probably best accounted for by what is said in the closing paragraph of the preface:

The actual thought and discussion of each topic was so thoroughly shared within the seminar that it would be difficult if not impossible to properly assign either credit or responsibility as the case might be. Therefore, we wish the reader to view this report as truly a joint product. We also hope the reader will keep in mind that this represents the result of only eight weeks' work. It is an exploratory survey of an interdisciplinary area, not a scholarly exposition of well-mapped territory.

Can one help being reminded of the definition of a platypus as an animal designed by a committee? I must return however to contexts and contacts. The chief thing we have to do is to unscramble them and keep them, if we can, unscrambled. It is not easy. The topic strongly invites, indeed tempts, us to mix them up.

Messages are generated by Contexts; they are conveyed by signals. Messages are living. They are animated instances of meaning, determinations from the context field; the signals which convey them are dead. My thinking, doubting, wondering at this moment is living activity; so is the nerve-muscle-joint process guiding my pen as I compose my Message. But the motions of the pen itself are inanimate, as are the configurations its point is tracing on the paper, the signals. The typist, the printer, the library, etc. put the page before you. As you read the inanimate lines of print, a living activity of thinking, doubting, wondering ... despairing perhaps ... arises in you. That is the Message coming into being again. It was not in the pen or on the page. So too with a speaker: ʳhis postures, gestures, facial expressionsʳ, actions and the rest, together with what his voice does ʳin the sound wave channelʳ ... anything that videotape can take down: all that is signal, merely. Not until it is interpreted by some living recipient does anything that should be called the Message appear. It is essential to a Message that what forms in the Addressee (or other recipient) should be of the same order of being with what has formed in the Addresser. He may get it all wrong (and often does) but there is an IT. The two apparitions are both meanings. But a sound track and a system of meanings are not things of a sort, able to agree or disagree. The distinction between Message and signal (Context and physical channel) is indeed a PONS ASINORUM in linguistics. This point is discussed at length in my essay "The Future of Poetry", first printed as Appendix to *The Screens* and later included in *So Much Nearer*.

I have lingered and labored with this point because Jakobson's central terms in his two schemes: MESSAGE and POETIC, and the correspondence between them he points out, are the heart of the passage we are examining. His own formulation (on page 356) is:

We have brought up all the six factors involved in verbal communication except the message itself. The set (*Einstellung*) toward the message as such, focus on the message for its own sake, is the POETIC function of language. This function cannot be productively studied out of touch with the general problems of language, and, on the other hand, the scrutiny of language requires a thorough consideration of its poetic function. Any attempt to reduce the sphere of poetic function to poetry or to confine poetry to poetic function would be a delusive over-simplification. Poetic function is not the sole function of *verbal art* but only its dominant, determining function, whereas in all other verbal activities it acts as a subsidiary, accessory constituent. This function, by promoting the palpability of signs, deepens the fundamental dichotomy of signs and objects. Hence, when dealing with poetic function, linguistics cannot limit itself to the field of poetry.

The key phrase here is ʳverbal artʳ (they are my italics). A ʳmore developedʳ translation and analysis of this paragraph would nearly double the length of this essay. Even the sentence in which ʳverbal artʳ occurs invites many pages. However, we may here postpone explication and be content with exemplification, with one of Jakobson's most gem-like and compelling illustrations:

The political slogan "I like Ike" /ay layk ayk/, succinctly structured, consists of three monosyllables and counts three diphthongs /ay/, each of them symmetrically followed by one consonantal phoneme / . .l. .k. .k/ . . Both cola of the tri-syllabic formula "I like/Ike" rhyme with each other, and the second of the two rhyming words is fully included in the first one (echo rhyme), /layk/-/ayk/, a paronomastic image of a feeling which totally envelops its object. Both cola alliterate with each other, and the first of the two alliterating words is included in the second: /ay/ /ayk/, a paronomastic image of the loving subject enveloped by the beloved object. The secondary, poetic function of this electional catch phrase reinforces its impressiveness and efficacy.

In conclusion, may I point to the impressiveness and efficacy of the work done by the Poetic function in his two schemes themselves, and in their coordination. They constitute paronomastic images of communication: their symmetries, horizontal and vertical, are, to use one of his favorite expressions, particularly palpable: CONTEXT-CONTACT-CODE (the alliteration framing the MESSAGE); EMOTIVE-CONATIVE (their rime hinting at how the first prepares for the second); REFERENTIAL-METALINGUAL (the outer rime framing again the central function). POETIC (the ʳdominant determining function of verbal artʳ) having its own rime with

PHATIC: the means, up through all levels, from "Hullo!" to *Hamlet,* to the CONTACT, the meeting of minds, which is the least alienable condition of all that language may attempt to do. Can we find a better example of verbal art in the POETIC function helping us more unexpectedly?

2. POWERS AND LIMITS OF SIGNS

I. SPECIAL USES OF LANGUAGES

Our starting point can be Roman Jakobson's admirably forthright formulation:

'For us, both as linguists and as ordinary word-users, the meaning of any linguistic sign is its translation into some further alternative Sign, especially a sign "in which it is more fully developed" as Peirce, the deepest inquirer into the essence of signs, insistently stated. [1]

Jakobson's opening qualification here is highly significant: both as distinguishing linguists [2] from ordinary word-users, and as indicating that there are also other-than-ordinary, or special, USES of Language.

Educators, Teachers, Learners

Among these – and there may be many – some are of particular importance to educators, to teachers, and, above all, to learners. They concern the educator as being the over-all student of the acquisition, development, and degeneration of meanings, their transmission, cultivation, up-keep – all the 'agronomic' aspects. These include the pathology of meanings and the principles of remedial treatment, not to mention the problems of conservation and pollution. In view of the growth patterns of our present de-traditionalized urban agglomerations, (the megalopolitan trend) these last may well be thought of utmost consequence.

---

[1] "On Linguistic Aspects of Translation", in *On Translation*, edited by Reuben A. Brower (Harvard University Press, 1959), pp. 232-233.
[2] In the sense here, 'students of how languages work' rather than 'speakers of more than one language'; it is well to avoid the awkward and somehow slighting term LINGUISTICIANS. It would be interesting to inquire into how this disparaging tinge arises. Is it from the word's rhyme group: beauticians ... dialecticians ... morticians ... metaphysicians?

These special uses concern the teacher, particularly in his capacity as the conveyer, the authority, the exponent and representative of what he teaches, the deputy, moreover, increasingly called on to replace traditional sources of values as these are, sources and values, progressively disabled and destroyed. QUA teacher his particular use of language must, or should be, peculiar. He is not fulfilling his special functions if it is not. And the learner's use of language, that too, if he is really a learner, is correspondingly or reciprocally peculiar – he is (or should be) a recipient, an inverse to the teacher as conveyer.

It is easy, I well know, to misrepresent the points I have been trying to make and to mistake necessities in the process of communication for mere accidentals of manner: tricks of pontification and affected docility that are no more than maladies – most incident to the classroom, I admit. The essentials of this communicative situation are that the teacher speaks as an addresser possessing knowledge to an addressee who does not possess that knowledge. It is these essentials that unavoidably make their uses of language peculiar or extraordinary. These are no matter of postures which may be put on or dropped: pomposity on one side, submissiveness on the other. They are inherent and inescapable, factors in the structure of the operation taking place.

What the teacher conveys may, of course, be DOUBT. To have called it knowledge, as I have just done, may have been misleading; but what he has to convey is a knowledge of doubt, of a degree of uncertainty. And in a further way – equally to be guarded against – to talk here of KNOWLEDGE may occasion or invite misconceivings. What is conveyed in teaching must not be supposed to be purely, or even primarily, cognitive; it may be and often is primarily conative or affective. Commonly what has to be communicated is a POSITION in which cognitive, affective, and volitional components are distinguishable with difficulty, if at all. One of the teacher's chief tasks then is to present the position in a fashion which will enable the learner both to reproduce it and to begin that exploration of it which is the reason why it has been offered. The point, the very heart, of that exploration may well be to make out how these components are related in the message: how feeling, will, and thought combine to do its work. It would be a gross misunderstanding of communication theory which equated its information with data or factual content.

In thus THEORETICALLY distinguishing from ordinary use, the educator's, the teacher's and the learner's special, other-than-ordinary uses of language, it is no less necessary than usual to insist that to distinguish is NOT to separate. Any user of language may – from moment to moment – come into a situation imposing upon him some special use. The educator's duties constantly require in him a clinical, evaluative attitude towards meanings and the transactions they mediate. But we can, most of us, find ourselves at any moment in a situation in which we have to be educators. So too, we may, almost all of us, have to teach. And certainly we do, all of us, have to learn. What special use is requisite is determined by the character of the situation governing the communication.

Other Special Uses

We may widen and confirm our reflections upon ?uses? of language at this point by asking what may be some of the other special ?uses? of language. (We are trying, clearly, to find a sense for ʷuseʷ which will be serviceable, and further examples may help.) Among those that may be suggested the following seem to merit particular notice.

1. The playwright's special use: he has two sets of addressees. Each sentence he pens has one or more of the DRAMATIS PERSONAE as its addressee(s). And yet, the play, as a whole, has an audience, to which, in a necessarily somewhat changed sense, it is addressed. Again, in a somewhat changed sense, much of this applies to the actors. With these two distinctly special uses of language we can put some diplomatic and political utterances. The speaker may have his constituents, his party, his own nation, as addressees in the ordinary sense; he is talking to them. But, in addition, what he says and how he says it, his utterance, may be being shaped by how, as he supposes, other audiences (at the highest level, the Foreign Offices of the world, say) will take his remarks. The skill shown by so many in handling such situations is indeed notable. It is a skill which is being threatened by contemporary trends, by the de-traditioning mentioned above, since it is dependent to no slight degree on the influence of good models and that influence is being increasingly cut off.

2. To some extent the place of good models is being taken by another category of special uses of language: those that in our days have enjoyed such a, probably unexampled, sophistication and expansion, those of ADVERTISEMENT. That the use of language – and its cooperating media, to which we shall return – in advertising is truly a special use (in the

sense of USE we are in these paragraphs trying to clarify) will, I believe, be little questioned. In the script, lay-out, video, employed, whether on the page or on the air, the controlling motive is generally acknowledged and recognized. It is sales. On the other hand, a main, a key principle of successful design (in no very Machiavellian sense, but in the ordinary honest sense of direction of selected means to conscious ends) is that the controlling motive should be hidden behind one or other of a number of motives more likely to be influential with the addressees. Need I detail them? The Propagation of Truth, benevolent eagerness to help, neighbourly impulses to convey good news to especially esteemed recipients, pardonable vainglory in unbelievable accomplishments, in Heaven-sent 'break-throughs' toward the relief of human ills, offerings of sympathetic understanding to the neglected, the arousal of generous indignation against mishandlings, innumerable diverse wheedlings and cajoleries of every sort of vanity, appeals to all the status fears as well as to all the cunningly detected anxieties of those inferiority complexes. But why go on? My probable reader will have many other such attention-getting gimmicks within his recollection. My point is simply that such dressing up, such disguisal of the prime motive of utterance does constitute a special USE (in our sought-for sense) of language. It is true that an Ad. may openly confess its prime aim, sales. But it will be using this confession in the hope of winning its addressees over into purchase. The distinctive feature of advertisement, I suggest, for this sense of the term, is disguise of the essential aim. Here again, the situation in which the communication is occurring is what is determinative of the special use.

Probably, indeed all but certainly, seeing what media are now available, never before have such vast proportions of the human race had their attention, their feelings, their wishes, hopes, fears, etc., solicited by such percentages of disguised appeals, by such cunningly masterful efforts to persuade them. No doubt many of the ablest advertisers have the best intentions. There is a famous and frequented road that is so paved. And perhaps the ability levels maintained in the Advertising business as a whole would be found, (if reliable measures were devisable and available) alarmingly higher than those evidenced in the literary professions, both creative and critical. But such remarks will rightly be thought invidious, I refrain here from pointed reference to the teaching profession, though recent attempts to enlist advertisers to help out with the literary crisis may be recalled by some.

3. With these sad thoughts in mind, it is appropriate to consider the adjacent territories in which this same use of language, marked by disguisal of the prime purpose by other ostensible aims, can be observed to rule. They include, evidently, much political discourse, all sorts of personal seductions, much social ritual – "Thanks yous", and so forth – and not a little that is somehow still being called 'literature' in one of the old high senses of the word. Until very recently, the courts and the police were still enabled to defend the market from what its upholders like to talk about as "porn". People have often believed that it is society that is threatened. This is probably a misestimation of the mind's self-defensive and recuperative powers. What does need protection is SHELF-SPACE in book stores and outlets. And, above all, literary standards, sanity and sagacity in the conduct of meanings. These degradations have not, I believe, yet had any sufficient semiotic study. Perhaps George Steiner only, among literary critics and semioticians, has shown the acumen, independence, and courage to remark on how much damage they can do or to point out what sorts of damage it can be.[3]

As a sewage inflow can distort the ecology of a river (or an antibiotic wreck the enzyme system in the mouth on which its powers of taste depend) so the flood (it has been that) of porn into the display shelves and the cinemas, has not only displaced invitations more needed by the growing mind and much more useful, but, analogously, the contents of this bedizened pulp and film have narrowed, crudified, dulled and blunted a public percipience which was too under-cultivated already.

To balance such losses, such deteriorations in meanings, against any possible gains in freedom (in some worthy sense), in improvement of people's potentials and securities of control – that, as I said earlier, is the educator's business: essentially to be able to weigh just such things is his professional qualification, though not a few of the ?educators? I have known would have been much surprised to hear it. To develop his own powers and those of his charges in such discriminations should be his prime endeavor. He and his advisers: critics, linguists, moralists ... are ignorant of their tasks if they do not acknowledge this. They need not (nor should they) often openly claim such awesome duties; but

---

[3] George Steiner, *Language and Silence* (New York: Atheneum, 1970), pp. 68-77: "Night Words, High Pornography & Human Privacy". For example, "The present danger to the freedom of literature ... is not censorship or verbal reticence. The danger lies in the facile contempt which the erotic novelist exhibits for his readers, for his personages, and for the language."

if they are to know what they are doing they must in their hearts admit that it is so.

That most of what they have to judge does indeed border on the Adman's province in its disguisal of designs cannot be doubted. The banners the march-by carries may bear fine words: "Honesty", "Frankness", "Truth", "Exposure", "Openness", "Down with Hypocrisy . . . with Taboo . . . with Modesty . . ." and the rest of them. Those who finance and run the racket know better. There may still be a very few among the products which do not deserve the accusation that quest for sales is being camouflaged as love of nature, frankness in confession, or something of that sort, but, if there are such, they are lost, buried beneath the rest. It should be added that the other-than-verbal signs – from the pictures in the Ads to the covers of the pulp – deserve study by semioticians and educators almost as much as the verbiage. But to DEPICTION I will be returning.

4. A fourth special use of language that may be suggested is that of poetry. I use this word here in Jakobson's sense:

In poetry, verbal equations become a constructive principle of the text. Syntactic and morphological categories, roots, and affixes, phonemes and their components (distinctive features) — in short, any constituents of the verbal code — are confronted, juxtaposed, brought into contiguous relation according to the principle of similarity and contrast and carry their own autonomous signification. Phonemic similarity is sensed as semantic relationship. The pun or to use a more erudite, and perhaps more precise term paronomasia, reigns over poetic art, and whether its rule is absolute or limited, poetry by definition is untranslatable. Only creative transposition is possible: either intralingual transposition — from one poetic shape into another, or interlingual transposition — from one language into another, or finally inter-semiotic transposition — from one system of signs into another, e.g. from verbal art into music, dance, cinema, or painting.[4]

This distinctive use of language flickers in and out of most verbal communication, of course. It occurs in varying degrees and in various relations to the other functions of language – as it serves them and/or calls on them to serve it. How much of advertising, of political sloganry ("I like Ike"), etc., is applied poetry – poetic means diverted to other than poetic ends – will hardly need pointing out. It cannot be a healthy society in which the majority of susceptible people meet poetic language not in the service of the high aims of poetry – the unacknowledged legislation of mankind – but in the pursuit of gain of one kind or

---

[4] Op. cit. p. 238.

another. Such barrages of suspectable messages are propitious neither to poetry nor to sane living.

II. TRANSLATION INTO ALTERNATIVE SIGNS

These attempts to discriminate special uses – another might be the mathematician's and others, those of liturgists and of some metaphysicians – send us back to ordinary use of language. One somewhat hopeful way of clarifying this may be to consider more strictly and seriously what Jakobson reports, in the first quoted passage. Taking "ordinary word-users" as the linguistic sign it there is, can we approach its meaning nearer by "translation into some further alternative sign" through which the meaning in question can be "more fully developed"? The first problem here turns on the phrase: ⌐IS its translation¬. The word *is* here marks, I take it, an ellipsis, itself calling for expansion, calling for a sign in which its own meaning is more fully developed. What should our expansion be? When we have settled that, we will be readier to answer questions about "its translation". The most helpful "further, alternative sign" among those that occur to me is, I think, 'can be clarified by'. I find myself loth – through a resistance which hardens as I experiment – to accept a reading that takes *is* more literally: e.g. 'is nothing other than', 'is, in fact, actually' and such.[5] Perhaps this resistance reflects possibilities in the reading of "its translation" – to which we may now turn.

In common with very many other words ending in *-tion*, TRANSLATION may represent either a process of translating or the product that is the outcome of the process.[6] I take it to be the process which is being talked of here, not the product. This probably is the cause of my difficulty in taking *is* more literally. With TRANSLATION as product, I seem to see less clearly how any one such outcome could be said to be the "meaning of a linguistic sign". But with TRANSLATION as a process of weighing, comparing, amending, adjusting possibilities of interpretation, selecting, testing etc., etc., I seem to find myself much nearer to a viable view. As process, TRANSLATION allows for the flexibility, the adaptability, the

---

[5] See my *Interpretation in Teaching* (London: Kegan Paul, 1937 now Routledge, and New York, Humanities Press, 1973), Chapter 18, "The interpretation of *IS*" and Chapter 19, "Some senses of *IS*". Also, my *How to Read a Page* (New York: W. W. Norton & Co., Inc., 1942), pp. 162-173.

[6] *How to Read a Page*, pp. 135-137.

manifold resource of most of the meanings I have had dealings with. Figuratively, the process view offers us cells cooperating; the product view, merely bricks in a wall.

Three kinds of translation

A related set (system, rather) of ambiguities with TRANSLATION seems worth exploring here. Jakobson neatly presents (p. 233)

three kinds of translation ... to be differently labeled:
(1) Intralingual translation or REWORDING ...
(2) Interlingual translation or TRANSLATION proper ...
(3) Intersemiotic translation or TRANSMUTATION ... an interpretation of verbal signs by means of signs of non-verbal sign systems.

His essay in *On Translation* is largely devoted to bringing his extraordinary range of knowledge to bear on (2). I confine myself to (1) and (3).

Relatively little explicit analytic discussion of the organization of non-verbal sign systems has, until recent times, been available. (1) and (2), being more accessible, have pre-empted attention. It is easier to talk about our words than about the other-than-verbal signs which may very likely be our necessary means of comparing and controlling what our words are doing.

We must recognize that Peirce's doctrine, along with its encouraging positive aspects, has a negative interpretation which can be grimly forbidding. Many have taken it as denying that we can do more in exploring our meanings than switch from one phrasing to another and on again to yet others. Positivists, Behaviorists and their Nominalist allies, who make it a point of conscience to enact and obey self-denying ordinances in matters such as the occurrence and use of concepts and of images – visual, mobile, tactile, kinaesthetic, gustatory, olfactory and the rest – have seemed to wish to empty the mind of all but verbal equivalences and to substitute word-play for thinking. But SUBSTITUTABLE and EQUIVALENCE, along with COMPARE and CONTROL, are terms whose meanings are as explorable as they are important. Human education indeed might well be described as learning how to explore them.

The key question is: "How do we decide whether an expression is or is not equivalent to, substitutable for, able to replace ... another?" If we answer: "By comparing", we have then to try to say what we are comparing with what and how we do it. And, as we do so, we have again to decide whether or not our account is ?satisfactory?, ?sufficient?, ?able to explain the facts?, ?intelligible? . . . and so on. These expressions again we have to compare (bearing in mind our account of comparing). We see why Peirce held that interpretation is a conversation without an ending.

Non-verbal sign systems: public and private

What are we comparing? Not the expressions alone – apart from their meanings. But these meanings they have: what is our mode of access to them? Must we not have other means than just our phrasings through which to focus our attention on them and, as we say, make them out? Here is where our non-verbal sign systems come in, supplying us with (theoretically illimitable) cultivatable resources for noting within ourselves, to ourselves, how the meanings we are comparing are alike or unlike, require, preclude, supplement . . . in general are related to, one another. The meanings compared are relations within the over-all fabric of sign systems.

The non-verbal sign systems are of two orders: public and private. If we ask ourselves what corresponds to a nod or shake of the head or a face we would like to pull, on occasions when we must give no sign of what we think, we will have these two orders conveniently present for comparison. There are batteries of such questions we may ask ourselves (without necessarily 'putting them into words') that similarly can destroy any contention that thinking is nothing but internal speech. What is a forgotten name which you know is none of those suggested? How do you know what you have to say before you know how you will say it? What is a plan before it is begun to be worked out? Or any movement before it is made? When we recall, moreover, modern accounts of the signaling systems which control cell-growth and cooperation in the body, to try to substitute sub-vocal speech for thinking looks absurd. The point is that we are beginning to have better ideas about how we think, about what thinking must be like.

Nonetheless, if we are ready to let parapsychology go on crying in the wilderness, we only communicate with others through public signs, verbal and non-verbal. With ourselves we have only too many modes of communing. We do talk to ourselves and more than a little; but guiding and controlling these internal colloquies too is THOUGHT: a capacity to compare meanings.

Along with a re-conception of thought should go a more developed idea of meanings. It is not surprising that meanings – through the last fifty years – have been variously out of favour in psychology and in linguistics. Doctrinaire dogmatisms apart, much of the recurrent head-shaking and shoulder-shrugging over ⌐meaning⌐ has sprung from a fair recognition of its enigmatic status. The forbidding side of Peirce's view represents a wish to replace meanings by more examinable fabrics – unduly limiting them, to "further alternative verbal signs" and over-looking the indispensable cooperations and constant support of the non-verbal sign-system components. His fundamental insight, however, – that the meaning of any sign consists in its relationship to other signs – retains all its value.

This relationship may extend very far. As any word may be con-ceived as related, VIA the words most immediately connected with it, to all the other words in the language, so some at least, of the non-verbal sign-systems have, span by span, an analogous though less extensive and inclusive connexity. Consider what the composer is doing in the auditory field and what relationships his phrases may have to other possible phrases. For each phrase, its relationships, at that point within the setting of the composition, are its musical meaning. Compare too what the tennis-player is doing in the optical-motor-kinaesthetic-tactual field. His strokes too can be thought of as having meanings – their re-lationship, rich and subtle or poor and crude, to his other possible strokes.

Two kinds of association

These relationships are highly complex. If we think of them as associa-tions we risk making them seem too mechanical, and must remember that all activity is purposive. Throughout there is selection and control of means by ends. Jakobson performed a fine service to theory of meanings when he reminded linguists[7] that there are traditionally two kinds of association: (1) by SIMILARITY-OPPOSITION and (2) by CON-TIGUITY. These operate in collaborative rivalry. A meaning is what it is through (1) what it is like and unlike and (2) where it is in its setting. A term with no opposite or a term by itself alone would be meaningless. X is HERE through not being THERE. And it is THERE through not being HERE. But without an X to be here or there, no meaning arises. (It may be worth adding that a number of what look like very important but

[7]   R. Jakobson and M. Halle, *Fundamentals of Language* ('s-Gravenhage: Mouton & Co., 1956), pp. 60, 80, 81.

unhappily insoluble problems seem to arise through forgetting this. But that does not make them less painful or important. The theological troubles of omniscience and omnipotence are the prime examples, linked as they are with the nature of defect. Evil seems a very high price to pay for the possibility of good.)

III. DEPICTION

Our most variously powerful non-verbal sign system is depiction: our iconic use of visual signs. Many of its aspects naturally parallel those of other signs. Thus a depiction, e.g. a visual image, may occur in degrees of vividness and presence varying from hallucinatory strength to the faintest, minimal, rudimentary sketch or indication – WITHOUT, in some respects at least, loss of efficacy. So a sentence, heard in the mind's ear, can be reduced to a mere fragment, barely of a syllable, without losing meaning adequate to the occasion. Depiction too has, very evidently, its private and its public sectors. Consider how we decide whether a portrait is or is not 'a good likeness', or whether any drawing is or is not 'right'. We evidently have our internal means (not necessarily confined to more or less veridical visual images) by which to check (control: etymon, CONTRA, 'over against' what is on a ROLL) the meanings that public signs may offer us. Depiction has not as yet received anything like the attention and study it deserves – either in semiotic or in theory and practice of education. In semiotic, to consider how depictions work can serve as valuable CONTROL over accounts of how verbal language works. The metaphor by which we call depiction a 'visual language' is deeply instructive. In education, what depictions can do and how they do it are, both of them, among the largest relatively untapped resources the educator might command.

The TYPE-TOKEN distinction

It is fitting that the semiotic of depiction should itself use depictions: with which to distinguish and hold clear for study the cooperative factors in depictive communication. Let us begin with a

SITUATION (SIT)		PICTURING (PIC).
SITUATION (SIT)	and a	PICTURING (PIC)

Here the *capitals v small capitals* contrast represents C. S. Peirce's TYPE v TOKEN distinction.[8]

Graphic and depictive notations

In the last two sentences (SENTENCES, SENs) the graphic contrast between Caps and small caps (between C and c) represents the semiotic distinction (between an instance, c, and that of which it is an instance, C). In these SENs both verbal and non-verbal signs are cooperating in a way which deserves fuller exploration than can be attempted here. What I have called a GRAPHIC contrast is not DEPICTIVE, for it will not do to describe C and c, as picturings of C and c (otherwise the indispensable distinction between a picture and that of which it is a picture would lapse). On the other hand, in $\underline{\text{SEN}}$, $\underline{\text{PIC}}$, $\underline{\text{SIT}}$ . . . the line under SEN . . . and over SEN . . . can properly be regarded as a depictive sign of the relationship between TYPE and TOKEN, between what is instanced and instances of it. As with all signs it can be read in various ways (varying with the setting and purpose: the 'sit'). Thus it may be indicating just this token status, or it may be going further and telling us that our dealings with Ts are mediated only through Ts (TYPES being known to us and dealt with by us only through TOKENS; no TYPE being seen or smelled or touched or even thought of except through TOKENS of it). In other words, TYPES have to be carried by TOKENS; what occurs, being timeless and placeless, must be represented by datable, locatable occurrings. And this division line may be read (in yet another sense: VERBALIZED, WORDED) as 'over', or as 'is conveyed by' and so on.

Inevitably, in using such a line we are inviting an immensely powerful system of meanings: those deriving from the $\frac{\text{numerator}}{\text{denominator}}$ relationship to intervene, if and when they can. I mention this to illustrate the point made above that any meaning has to defend itself from interpretations not relevant. Indeed its resistances to these usually define what it is. There are exceptions to this. One is exemplified by the fact that a depiction, say, of the relation of a point to a line:

[8] *Collected Papers of Charles Sanders Peirce*, ed. by Charles Hartshorne and Paul Weiss (Cambridge, Mass., 1933), IV, par. 527. Also see Ogden and Richards, *The Meaning of Meaning* (New York: Harcourt, Brace & Co., Inc., 1923), pp. 280-281.

if taken strictly as concerned only with their positions on a plane, is definite in ways in which no verbal transmutation of it normally can be. All we can do, in words, is to indicate and approximate. That is why architectural depictions are so useful. No verbal description can take their place. And any builder's performances based on them will depart, less or more, from what they depict. But this definiteness attends only while they are being regarded as visual statements of relations between items on a plane. Let them be taken as PICTORIAL representations of objects in space and they become as open to misinterpretation as any verbal description could be.

Such a notational device and the semiotic reflections it prompts can help to protect us (1) from confusions between TYPES and TOKENS and (2) from confusions between 'what is said' and 'our ways of saying it'. Both must – as far as possible – be avoided, if we are to trace successfully the powers and limits of depiction and of its cooperations with verbal signs.

Three modes of exploring situations

As Jerome Bruner has usefully reminded us, we have three modes of exploring situations:

1. by performances: fingerings, trials, searchings etc., ENACTIONS, (ENS)
2. imagery: iconics, simulations: DEPICTIONS (PICS)
3. verbalizations, SENTENCES (SENS)

Relationships between these three are endlessly neglected in actual classroom practice. For example, a teacher who has not thought about and is not then thinking about what may be happening in the learners' minds, can invite very persistent confusions through careless handling of her enactions and depictions of such very important verbal distinctions as that between *on* and *off*. With a ball and a table and a floor, the prime physical relationship from which all the manifold metaphorical meanings derive (and on which they depend) can in a few minutes be planted, germinated and developed. In as little a time endless unclarities can be created by careless handling and disregard of timing and pausing. *To* and *from*, *up* and *over*, *in*, *on*, and *at*, (*at* a point, *on* a wall, *in* a room: *at* eight, *on* the first Monday *in* 1973) . . . all our fundamental means of control over space relations and motions, as we represent them in language, can be blurred, and an immense additional burden imposed, by an unaware and stupid teacher. This is one of the reasons why well-designed films, sufficiently tested and criticised, are so valuable in the teaching of such keys to a command of English. Probably only through the alerted attention their design requires can better cooperations between ENS, PICS, SENS and SITS be developed and set to work.

An example here will clarify the terms in the discussion. Let the SITUATION be that in which a child is attempting to find out how writing works by comparing the following two SENTENCES:

     This is a man.
                         This is a hat.

Each SEN is accompanied by a maximally simplified undistractive PIC, placed in contiguous relationship with the SEN. The SENs themselves are contiguous. They are so placed, on the page facing the child, that the parts of them that are similar and the parts that are dissimilar are as manifest as can be. On the blackboard and on the walls of the room the two SENs appear again in different writing and print. In some of these, sameness and difference are indicated by difference of script:

This is a man.
This is a hat.

The accompanying depictions are also varied.

Before the child is a typewriter with all but the following keys covered with blank paper disks: *a hi mn st* (on an electric typewriter all but these seven keys can be inoperable). It will be noticed that these letters are minimally confusable: the differences between them overpower the samenesses. Not one of them is a reversed form of another (as *n* and *u*, *b* and *d*, *p* and *q*) or is an incomplete form of another (as *c* and *e* may be of *o*).

If the keyboard is in Capitals, the child is shown how to depress and lock the shift. He then experiments with the 7 lettered keys, noting that each yields on paper a replica of what is on the key. In this he is comparing an enaction with its outcome. He goes on to compare two or more ENs with their outcomes. In these comparings the joint operation of similarity-difference and contiguity is at its clearest.

He now passes to attempting to reproduce the two SENs. They will have been said TO him (and BY him and others) in a variety of voices (SEN1, SEN2, SENn) all tokens, differing one from another, of the same SEN. Thus continually, one aspect of the over-all SITUATION being explored is kept active – the relation of graphic forms to speech sounds

– but NOT in such a way as to occult the more important relation of the seen word to its enactable and depictable meanings.

The first word here to be tackled will be *This*, followed immediately by what may be perceived as a part of *This*, namely *is*. The exercise in comparings continues as *a* appears again within *man*, but surrounded by differents: *m* and *n*, between which the difference is one which is uncommonly visible and significant: that between 2 and 3 (II and III), two lollipops or three.

From letter to word to $\frac{\text{SEN}}{\text{PIC}}$ thence to $\frac{\text{SEN}}{\text{PIC}}$ (via the other scripts and depictions on the walls), so the sequence of comparings should proceed, but it will do so (if, as we should, we let it) in a see-saw or pendulum fashion. The letters on paper at the very start of the enaction (at EN,) are being compared with the letters on the keys. But, after that, typed letter on paper is compared with letter in the model word on the blackboard as, later, the typed word, as enaction product, is compared with the word in the model SEN. In almost all learning the control of part by whole and of whole by part is, or should be, reciprocal. In advancing from our initial pair of SENs to such pairs as

This hat is his hat.		His hat is in his hand.
That hat is her hat.	or	Her hat is on her head.

The cooperations of PIC with SEN may go as much from SEN (now being read) to PIC as from PIC to SEN. In general, we may note that SIT's form enclosure series. An over-all problem "How does writing work?" is approached via a series of smaller problems whose solving contributes towards its apprehension.[9]

IV. EXPLORATORY ACTIVITY

In passing now to a general account of exploratory activity the relationship between the SIT and the ENS, PICS, and SENS has first to be described. Normally the SIT, which is an event in which the percipient IS

---

[9] For the detail of the design of the instructional sequences this example has been referring to, see I. A. Richards and C. M. Gibson, *English Through Pictures* (Books I, II, III) (Pocket Books, New York, Edition published 1972) and *First Steps in Reading English* (Pocket Books, N. Y., 1957). Information on cassettes, filmstrips, sound motion pictures, television programs, and other teaching aids for use with these texts, is available from Educational Services, 1730 Eye St., N. W., Washington, D. C. 20006 and from Language Research, Inc., 134 Mt. Auburn Street, Cambridge, Mass. 02138.

taking part, an occurrence to him, is in large measure RE-cognized. It is being taken as an instance of a SIT whose character is predominantly familiar, though it may, of course, be much mistaken. How to deal with it is, accordingly, more or less grasped, though there will also be fringes of uncertainty, and it is as attempts to adjust these that exploratory activity via EN, PIC, SEN . . . develops. What ENs occur: handlings, pokings, turnings, approachings . . . take place as representatives of ENs by which they are guided and controlled. Similarly, PICs that assist (images say, of what something may look like if turned, e.g.) derive from PICs. And the SIT, as it is being apprehended, has been represented by other SITs before. While this sort of EN, PIC exploration proceeds, it may be accompanied by verbalization (sub-vocal or not). The explorer may be talking to himself or to a companion: "Let's see how it looks this way", "Try the key upside down", "Don't push it quite so far in", and so on. Through all this, influences from unimaginably many and various former ENs, PICs, SENs, ordered through the relations between their ENs, PICs, SENs, are attempting to bring the SIT home under its appropriate SIT.

All this, as the formation, growth and control of concepts, has, for millenia, been familar ground to educators, though perhaps in recent times, the consequences for it of communication have been somewhat neglected. We are too ready to think of a concept as existing merely in the mind of the conceiver. But any one person's concept is properly to be regarded as itself a representative: depictable too in our notation as $\frac{\text{CONCEPT}}{\text{CON}_1\ \text{CON}_2\ \text{CON}_n}$. Learning can thus be conceived as the taking over in the individual of an order towards the apprehension of which he is progressing. (There is a pathological side, of course, on which I must not dilate here.)

We have not yet entered upon the major complexities, however. We have to recall that these cooperating items: from the SIT down through all the ENs, PICs, SENs that are joining in its exploration, are, each and all of them, what they are through their relationships of similarity-difference and contiguity to their neighbours and rivals, – those that may be competing for a hand in the job. It is this interplay which gives signs their power and makes the wholeness and sanity of acts of clear, self-controlled and just discernment so impressive.

For a fuller discussion of the rationale of these recommendations see Baker, Barzun, and Richards, *The Written Word* (Rowley, Mass.: Newbury House Publishers).

This saving connexity, this consistency, is maintained, we have suggested, through the relationships among the TYPE systems. For every small caps item that takes part there is a Capital, in virtue of which it acts and to which it appeals. Its relations to its fellow small caps components in the comprehending of the situation, is governed, in short, by the order that has been attained among the types. All growth in cognitive abilities comes about through improvement in that. We may cite Coleridge: "I call that *genuine* knowledge only which returns again as power." The prime difference between a mind which 'knows what it is doing' (in the laudatory sense) and one which doesn't is in the organization of its type-systems.

Principles of Useful Depiction

Against some such background as has been sketched let us now consider a few of the principles that govern reasonable use of depiction for instruction.

(1) Mutual dependence of signs. Since similarity-difference and contiguity are jointly ruling throughout, what any depictive sign can do depends on others: like it and unlike it in the percipient's experience, AND cooperative with it in the situation. No depictive sign (any more than any verbal sign) carries its meaning inevitably within it. What it can mean, for the addressee, turns on what other signs have meant for him and on what other present coactive signs can mean.

(2) Due sequence in design. Reverse or displace the order of the steps and relatively little of significance can develop. Sequence in depiction can therefore be of decisive importance. The designer of a course of instruction can do far more than use illustrations as attention-getters, cues and incidental entertainment. By sequencing them aright he can construct series of invitations to intelligent exploration, in which depictions stand in opposition and contiguity relationships to one another and in which earlier SITUATIONS intelligibly PREPARE for instructive COMPARISON with those that follow. Such designing is, of course, most desirable and most feasible in the beginning phases of learning in a new field: in Beginning Reading and in the entering and early stages of a Second Language. In these it is possible to use depiction to conduct a learner's insight through the fundamental discriminations upon which his grasp of how the scriptal notation and how the new language works. There is a reasonable order to be shown him here (as there is for early

stages in geometry) and pictures are the ideal means through which to
do so. Unfortunately, at present it is in these very fields that current
use of depiction can be seen at its least enlightened. It is primarily
DISTRACTIVE, which is worse than putting powdered-glass in the sugar.

(3) Cultivation of insight. The prime aim in depiction is to invite and
guide INSIGHT into how representation VARIES WITH the situation represented. What the learner is attempting to acquire is increased command over a system of representation. In this, the last thing he needs
and the thing he should most be spared is being dragged away to attend
to something else, something allegedly AMUSING or DIVERTING. (Educators could find in the derivations of these two words the strongest
reasons against current practice.) It is the growth of this insight, not
any product of the drilling in of stimulus-response routines or habit-
formation, that leads to advance in skill and power. In all this the role of
controlled depiction is, as yet, only in its initial phase of development.
The most familiar example is the graph and it is worth noting that
GRAPH, in this sense, 'a line or system of lines symbolizing variations of
occurrence or intensity', is a word still less than a hundred years old.
Educators should acquaint themselves with what has in the present
decade been made possible in the field of Computer Graphics and how
compact, forceful and illuminating can be its representations of data
otherwise complex beyond any imagining. That the most striking ap-
plications so far have been to urban and megalopolitan problems is not
surprising. If we add what seems likely to happen in three-dimensional
photography, for example, the new powers for the cultivation of insight
that are becoming available in teaching – from elementary levels up –
are truly astounding. It is hard not to be hopeful. They may make the
triumphs of antibiotics, say, look like a minor advance. But they
will require, of course, judicious handling.

(4) Elimination of distraction. Simplification and the strict elimination
of irrelevances and potentially distracting elaborations are conditions
for efficiency in depictions. Their styling should be under the control
of the designer of the instruction sequences, not left to Publisher's art-
editor or to the artist, who are in this field very much at the mercy of
fashion. It should be remembered that a depiction is a sign calling for
interpretation of a situation. Normally it will be (notably in BEGINNING
Reading or a Second Language) predominantly cognitive. Variations
in its components that are not SIGNIFICANT – that do not contribute to
the interpretation of a situation, are to be avoided, as over-likely to be

distractive. The learner is learning, above all, to discern what is significant, what varies with what, and he should, in early stages of his task, be protected from accidental occasions to go astray. He should certainly not be Pied Piper'd away into nonsense. It should be remembered too that these early steps are his best, perhaps his only, introduction to method of inquiry. They can establish in him his standards as to what to expect; they can and should plant, in fact, the very seeds of his conceptions of order and of reasonable procedure. Ought we not indeed to do our best to put before him good models? What he is learning is the essential technique of science, how to look for what VARIES WITH WHAT in a given setting, how to observe this under the joint control of similarity-difference and contiguity.

This principle of cooperation between likeness-unlikeness and neighborhood operates universally. I began by taking the phrase "ordinary word-users" and looking for 'special users of language' to put into opposition with it. Very likely Jakobson as he wrote was simply opposing ordinary word-users to linguists and it will be useful to consider some of the relevant contrasts here more closely. They bear very directly on what educators, teachers, and learners should and should not be trying to do — especially in their directives, in their instruction, and in their work with language.

The linguist knows, in the sense of being able to state, discuss, support or refute them, innumerable things about languages which the ordinary word-user does not, in that sense, know. The ordinary user may be an admirable word-user (even a Shakespeare) without any of that knowledge. He has another sort of knowledge of the language, a know-how with it, which serves him in its place. Furthermore, there is little or no evidence that the linguist's knowledge would necessarily help the ordinary word-user, if he had it. People can have a great deal of linguistic knowledge and yet be inferior word-users.

V. THE ART OF CONSCIOUS COMPARING

There is, however, one branch of special linguistic knowledge which can help everyone, though it is not enough just to have it; we must learn to use it. This branch has no safe and handy name, but it can be readily described. It is the art of conscious comparings of meanings and of the explicit description of them through linguistic signs.

The lack of a safe name for this art is not hard to explain. In part it is due to the enigmatic status of meanings; they were felt to be such dubious entities that few could be sure what was being done when they were discussed. In part it is due to people giving the art names much used for other things: RHETORIC, for example, EXEGESIS and, worst of all SEMANTICS, including Korzybsky's General Semantics. Two good names exist covering parts of this study. LEXICOLOGY: the knowledge and skill and judgment required for good work in preparing articles in a Dictionary. But the art of comparing meanings requires ability to see what the setting of a meaning is as well as discernment as to which parts of a Dictionary article may be relevant. Study of SYNONYMY suffers from similar drawbacks.

Some principles

Indication of a few principles of this fundamental art, strangely neglected in schools eminently useful though it is, will help to show what it should try to do.

1. Cooperation and Interference. One has just been mentioned: the dependence of meanings on the meanings of other words surrounding them in the setting as well as upon other factors in the ambience. What should be brought out is how what a word does is changed by a change made elsewhere in a passage. In this, words behave very like people engaged in what should be a cooperative undertaking.

This principle emerges from comparisons between alternative phrases. To risk overstating it: any change in the phrasing entails some change in the meaning of a sentence. Sometimes it is a change that matters, sometimes not. To question WHY is continually a penetrating thrust of inquiry.

2. Tenor and Vehicle. A long while, some forty or more years ago, I tried to further inquire into metaphor by introducing two new terms (to be technicalized, if possible) to replace the appalling welter of highly ambiguous phrasings that laboured to distinguish (1) what was being said (offered, presented) from (2) the way in which it was being said (offered, presented). They were: (1) TENOR, (2) VEHICLE, to stand respectively for the what (the Tenor) and the way (the Vehicle). I did not then, I think, so generalize, being too close to the problems of metaphor.

Nor did I write the distinction down depictively as $\frac{T}{V}$, making V into SIGNANS and T into SIGNATUM. I did however realize, then as much earlier, that what T, the Tenor, would represent could not normally be unaffected by changes in V.

Notations have strange powers (as has been frequently shown in the history of mathematics). They can simplify and make routine what otherwise might call for an effort of thought, a recalling of principles. Korzybsky (the Apostle of General Semantics, mentioned above; he was not averse to being introduced to gatherings as Count Korzybsky, the Time Binder) tried, in his *Science and Sanity*, in its day a gospel for a cult, to introduce various useful notations to serve as reminders of what we all know but frequently forget. Typical was the sign *etc.* – to remind us of the rest that should be in our awareness more often than it is. He proposed to abbreviate it to ., or .. as it was placed in the midst or at the end of a sentence. This doubtless, would be a salutary procedure, though so inconspicuous a sign would be likely to be overlooked or treated as a misprint. I have tried out, myself, a set of specialized inverted commas with various intents. One of these is concerned with the Tenor-Vehicle terminological innovation mentioned above. It is the affixing, as superscripts, of ^{sw}————^{sw} in place of ^{sw}quotation marks^{sw}, to distinguish words and phrases which the writer knows may very possibly be taken by the addressee in senses seriously different from that in which he hopes to have them understood. ^{sw}————^{sw} is short for SAID WITH, which is again an abbreviation of ^{sw}something that may be said with^{sw}. The implication is that language at that point, as it can be used for the particular purpose being pursued is deficient (at least, as the writer can use it). And that, failing a perfectly fit term, something known to be less than fully efficient is being used. The indulgence of the reader is being begged for and his guessing capacity being alerted by the little alphabetic fleas perched so round the word or phrase.

This notational device, neither complex nor exacting, can serve, I believe, several compatible purposes. It can warn the reader to ^{sw}step warily^{sw} and to ^{sw}select wisely^{sw}. It can, furthermore, help to defend us from an error into which we far too frequently fall: the mistake of supposing that our statements are doing more than they possibly can, that they are indeed putting the very truth down on the paper. One of Korzybsky's most famous metaphoric slogans is useful here: "The map is not the territory." In a cool moment we may perhaps suppose we couldn't think it is. And a moment later we find ourselves so doing, and realize once more how great is the power of signs and at the same time how strict their limits.

3. Object and meta-languages. A third principle of this art of comparing meanings will seem from one point of view to be the same thing said in another way. It can be put as an injunction: Don't confuse statements about things with statements about the language used in the statements. In other words: Distinguish between object-language and meta-language. Object language is talk about 'the context referred to'; meta-language is about the code being used in the communication. But, here again, we must distinguish without separating and remember that a sentence can very well be both referential: tell us about something, and metalingual: tell us about the code. If I say: "That is quail", I may be telling someone something about a bird. How much I tell him will obviously depend upon how much he knows about quails already. Or I may be telling him something about the word *quail*: That it is the name for a certain sort of bird. What is referential for one addressee may be metalingual for another. Into all comparisons of meanings, all attempts to assess and describe the powers and limits of signs in their actual operation, the inevitable differences enter. Occasions differ, speakers differ, recipients differ. In spite of which human communication can somehow be maintained.

3. LINGUISTICS INTO POETICS

What may very likely prove a landmark in the long-awaited approach of descriptive linguistics to the account of poetry is now appearing in the studies of many kinds of poems in many different languages that Roman Jakobson is issuing and about to issue. For the general reader of English the most decisive of these will probably be the analysis of Shakespeare's sonnet 129 "Th' expence of Spirit . . ." (recently published as a pamphlet: *Shakespeare's Verbal Art in Th' expence of Spirit,* The Hague: Mouton). This candidate for topmost rank among sonnets is now shown to have a degree of exactly describable structural order which — could it have been pointed out to them in such precise unchallengeable detail — would certainly have thrown Shakespeare himself along with his most intent and admiring readers into deeply wondering astonishment. Just what the consequences of these demonstrations — for readers, critics and poets — will be (or should be) is a topic deserving of as much concern as outcomes of, say, recent discoveries in genetics (with which there may be traceable linkages) or those of space exploration or those of man's ever-mounting capacity to destroy himself. Those who take poetry, and what it might do for man, seriously may think, indeed, of these new revelations of order as a powerful helping hand offered to us in this time of frightened and bewildered disaffection. Throughout history, and long before it, poetry has been among man's chief sustainers. A big general increase in his understanding of how it works may well be a practical aid toward saner policies.

Before presenting detail let us look at some of the key ideas, instruments of the demonstration. Most of these are familiar and all are highly intelligible. What is new is that Jakobson and his co-worker Lawrence Jones have applied them in a manner as impressive in its scope as in its scale.

Below is the sonnet with its four strophes and the binary oppositions of its rimes and some other structural features indicated.

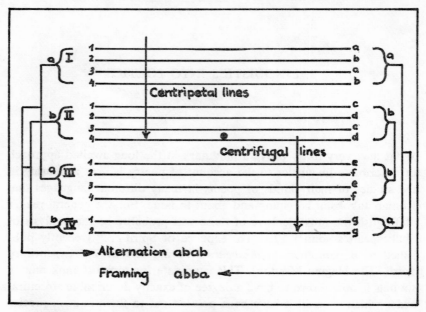

The first key ideas are of ODD and EVEN. In each quatrain the odd lines rime. So do the even, and so do the two lines of the couplet. Now apply odd and even to the strophes: I, III odd; II, IV even. The next key idea is that of BINARY CORRESPONDENCE: presence or absence, at a place, of a character, e.g., being a noun, as opposed to not being a noun.

In terms of binary correspondences we can now, with the distinctions developed in linguistics, display precisely for a four-strophe poem:

(1) how far the odd pair (I and III), how far the even pair (II and IV), and how far the two pairs correspond;

(2) how far the outer strophes (I and IV), how far the inner strophes (II and III), and how far inner and outer correspond;

(3) how far the first pair I and II, how far the last pair III and IV, and how far the two pairs correspond.

We will be concerned with correspondences (agreements and oppositions in specific respects) at all levels: from sound-character up, through grammatic and sentence form to utterance aim — between the four strophes taken in these groupings and not omitting relations between the couplet and the rest.

The next key idea is that of CENTER of the poem. In this sonnet the central distich (II 3, 4) is this center and more narrowly the point marked ●.

Now we are ready to consider Jakobson's indications of the breaks in its lines, the binary oppositions of its rime pattern and the repetitions of its rime words.

I 1 Th' expence of Spirit | in a waste of shame [gram.
  2 Is *lust* in action, | and till action, *lust* [n-gr. noun
  3 Is perjurd, murdrous, | blouddy full of blame, [gram.
  4 Savage, *extreame*, rude, | cruel, not to trust, [non-noun

II 1 Injoyd no sooner | but dispised straight, [not-noun
  2 Past reason hunted, | and no sooner *had*
  3 Past reason hated | as a swollowed bayt, [noun

●

  4 On purpose layd | to make | the taker *mad*.
III 1 *Mad*(e) In pursut | and in possession so, [not-noun
  2 *Had*, having, and in quest, | to have *extreame*, [not-noun
  3 A blisse in proofe | and provd | a(nd) very wo, [noun
  4 Before a joy proposd | behind | a dreame, [noun

IV 1 All this the world | *well* knowes | yet none knowes *well*
                                                    [not-noun
  2 To shun the heaven | that leads | men to this hell. [noun

---

Note first that the position of the breaks and, with that, the movement of the poem, changes at the center after the word *layd*. Until that point the break in each line comes in the middle of the middle foot. After it, the breaks come either at the beginning or at the end of the third foot or at both points. With the centrifugal lines the placing of the breaks and the degree of dominance allotted them are more optional than with the centripetal lines.

Take now the repetitions of rime words. The second rime word of each quatrain is repeated and so is the rime word of the couplet. In the first and last instances the repetition occurs in the same line: I, 2 *lust*, IV, 1 *well*. Moreover, around and framing the central distich —

Past reason hated as a swollowed bayt, On purpose layd to make the taker mad

— *had* (II, 2) is repeated in III, 2 as an initial rime to *Mad(e)* (III, 1), which is itself an instance of Puttenham's figure: REDOUBLE (last word of one line = first word of next). Note further the accord between *On purpose* and *In pursut:* the nasals of *On* and *In,* the common prefixes of *purpose* and *Pursut.* A very remarkable frame is thus built up around *make the taker mad/Mad(e).*

This will be the moment to consider these two-bracketed ( ) ?m prints?: *a(nd),* we will grant, should be *a*; but *Made(e) In?* Is that as certain? It is with an agreeable sense of relaxation that one realizes that he need not always agree with Jakobson, who points out (citing Kökeritz) that the plays can spell *mad, made* and *made, mad* and that Shakespeare could pun on these two words, yet concludes, "the adjective *mad* and not the participle *made* is evidently meant". Why not *Made* with a supplied *mad* and a merely auditory full stop following it? The added emphasis by double echo of *make* and *mad* to the key line of the poem –

On purpose layd to make the taker mad

– is worth weighing; and the capital *I* of *In pursut* could be so explained. It is one thing to become mad; it is another to have been deliberately *made mad,* with the preceding line so driving the point home.

As Jakobson remarks, Puttenham's figure, TRANSLACER (repetition of the same root with different affixes), is very evident throughout the inner strophes: *Injoyd* (II, 1 – *joy* (III, 4), *had – having – to have* (III, 2), *in proofe – provd* (III, 3), as well as *On purpose* (II, 4) – *In pursut (III, 1) – proposd* (III, 4), are the instances. And a complementary figure (repetition of the same qualifiers with different root), is as evident: *Past reason hunted – Past reason hated* (II, 2, 3). Reflections, all these, perhaps, of what happens when a taker is made mad and undergoes those pervasive changes.

Look now at the conduct of the rimes. The first rime, but none of the others, is grammatical. That is, *of shame* and *of blame* can be put into the same grammatical pigeonhole. The second rime is non-grammatical, the riming words *lust* and *trust* belong to different word-classes; the first is a noun, the second is not. In II, *straight, bayt* invert this noun – non-noun order, as do all the remaining pairs except the crucial central rimes, *had-mad,* final and initial, commented upon above.

Is the reader by this time beginning to think that such a degree of order and design in a poem is somewhat preternatural? Jakobson is in a position to reply that it is the reader's notions as to what is natural that need to be extended.

SALIENCE OF THE CENTRAL THEME

What do all these evidences of order (and many more) amount to? To an immense concentration and convergence on giving clarity and salience to the central theme of the poem embodied in the central distich (II, 3-4). As Jakobson brings out, these two lines are different in vital respects from the six lines preceding and from the six lines following them. In these other lines there are striking grammatical parallelisms between features of their hemistiches:

I,	1	of Spirit — of shame;
I,	2	in action — till action;
I,	3	murdrous — blouddy;
I,	4	Savage — cruel;
II,	1	injoyd — dispised;
II,	2	hunted — had;
III,	1	In pursut — in possession;
III,	2	having — to have;
III,	3	A blisse — a . . . wo;
III,	4	a joy — a dreame;
IV,	1	well knowes — knowes well;
IV,	2	heaven — hell.

In the middle two lines there is none of this. But there is a simile, the only simile in the poem: II, 3 *as a swollowed bayt.* And more: there is a construction with subordinates dependent step by step: A) *hated,* B) *as a swollowed bayt.* C) *on purpose layd,* D) *to make,* E) *the taker,* F) *mad.* Significantly, an analogous construction appears in the other even strophe, the couplet: A) *none knowes well,* B) *to shun,* C) *the heaven,* D) *that leads,* E) *men,* F) *to this hell.* Between these there is another sort of parallelism: C) *on purpose layd = heaven,* D) *to make = that leads,* E) *the taker = men* (the only two animates in the poem), and F) *mad = to this hell.* And through this parallelism the only simile: *as a . . . bayt,* prepares for the only metaphor: *the heaven . . . this hell.*

Not a few deeply challenging questions arise if we try now to explore the implications – for the reader, the critic and the poet – of the presence of so much relatively unnoticed order in a poem. Jakobson, in his "Subliminal Verbal Patterning in Poetry" (*Studies in General and Oriental Linguistics,* Tokyo, 1970, which he and Shigeo Kawamoto have edited), after enshrining the central problem in the first word of his title alludes pertinently to the widespread occurrence, in highly diverse fields, of orderings which "cannot be viewed as negligible acci-

dentals governed by the rule of chance". Leaves and shells show a-
mazingly systematic structure which the plants and molluscs cannot be
supposed to know anything of. We do not with these appeal to any
subliminal awareness though recent advances in genetics – as acutely
discussed by Jakobson in his Rapport: *Actes du Xe Congrès International des Linguistes, Bucarest*, 28 Août – 2 Septembre, 1967 – seem
almost ready to suggest effective substitutes. But with the poet the
variations both in his knowledge of what he is doing and of how he
does it, do suggest that Herbart's notion of a variable threshold, a LI-
MEN below which he is not aware and above which he may to some
degree be aware, has its services to offer. Most readers, perhaps, after
some immersion in Jakobson's demonstrations, may agree that their
thresholds as regards noting what lines of verse are doing have been
somewhat lowered. Our knowledge of how we put our sentences together can be highly variable. Sometimes we speak with much conscious
control and insight; sometimes with so little that we may be deeply surprised by what we have been doing. This last has been a good joke
against poets since Socrates, who remarks in the *Apology:* "They are
like oracles in that."

But Socrates took oracles seriously too. That a poet may know hardly
anything about his compositions entails nothing as to their value or as
to his knowing how to compose. Plainly we have two senses of *know* at
work here: almost the two that Shakespeare has opposed in the last line
but one of his sonnet:

All this the world well knowes yet none knowes well.

Just as "the adverb *well* when preposed and postposed displays two
distinct semantic nuances: 'widely knows' in the former case and 'knows
enough' in the final position" (p. 23), so the two *knowes* do distinct
work; the first = 'is cognizant of'; the second = 'is able to'. KNOW-
LEDGE ABOUT and KNOW HOW are being contrasted.

OUTCOMES OF JAKOBSON'S ANALYTICS

For reader, critic, and poet it seems highly important that these two
sorts of ?knowing? be not confused. Both have their variable thresholds.
We fluctuate in our knowledge about anything (with degree of fatigue,
for example) and also in our ability to perform. But the two do not
necessarily vary together. Raising 'knowledge about' need not raise

ability to perform. Unfortunately, there are obdurate institutionalized pedagogic prepossessions which cling to beliefs that it will. In practice and general opinion these two sorts of knowing are misleadingly entwined. The typical instance arises with Grammar as a school subject. Being able to pass a hard paper in Grammar and being able to write effectively need not go together. The abilities required are different. Which brings us back to the possible outcomes of Jakobsonian analytics in the teaching and discussion of poetry.

There are bound to be dangers; all new powers bring them. One is that teachers and discussants will substitute busy-work with the descriptions for concern with the poetry. They may become too pre-occupied with marking the items for the items to take other effect. There is little profit in noting that strophes I and II here present nine diphthongs /ai/ (with only the nearby doubtful *Mad(e)* in the rest) if the words in which they occur don't transfix the reader.

Another risk is that critics may develop a presupposition that poetry which doesn't lend itself so well to such investigations, or reward them so richly, MUST somehow be inferior. Critics are fond of doing that. They pick on something as a merit: say, metaphor or sensory imagery. Then any poem not crowded with tropes or vivid with presentations they look down on. We have to recall Coleridge: "Let us not pass an act of Uniformity against poets." The business of any good poem is to be itself, not anything else.

As to the poet, writing is not the only pursuit in which means can get in the way of ends. Consciously crafty composition may distract from and quite occult poetic aim and outcome. But that is hardly a new hazard.

There are subtler considerations than these which more need exploration. Let us assume that many at least of the structural relations Jakobson displays so perspicuously are among the necessary means by which the poem works. Then any good reader (any in whom the poem has worked) will have been worked on by them. In THAT sense he will have noticed them, i.e., RESPONDED TO THEM. On the other hand most readers, I believe, will admit that they had not themselves noticed all or much of what has now been pointed to conclusively, in sonnet 129. None the less they may have responded to it. Thus we have, here, too, two senses of *notice* corresponding to 'be conscious of' (= 'be able to give an account of') and 'respond to' (= 'know how to take').

Keeping these as clearly distinct as we can, we may observe:

1. That probably only some, not all, of the features consciously dis-

cerned and included in the ACCOUNT will be actually operative in shaping the RESPONSE. The machinery of distinctions used in the account has developed to meet general linguistic needs and purposes. It has only in part been devised primarily and expressly for the description of poetic structure. It may therefore distort, may invite attention to features not essential to the poetic process.

2. That the separation of essential features from others (for which conscious notice may be distractive or obstructive) is inevitably a very tricky undertaking. It is not easily paralleled in simpler tasks of analysis. Changing the consciously noted features, adding or removing features, opening up or shutting down what is consciously attended to, may very likely not leave the other features unchanged – as regards their participation in the work of the poem (in chemistry it may be otherwise). So how can we EXPERIMENT and compare in the matter?

3. And yet we do. Any writer weighing one word as against another, any reader wondering which of two interpretations to prefer, is experimenting. But neither (ordinarily) is, in his comparings, recognizing the phonological or grammatical characters of selected items in the Jakobsonian way. He is only trying out one RESPONSE as against another. What sways and guides him then (ordinarily) as he chooses between them is something in many respects OTHER THAN (and working through different compromises from) the phono-grammatic-semantic interplay that Jakobson so adroitly and discerningly puts on exhibit. That fine, multi-dimensional network of distinctions and relations traces, catches, and places – more and more justly every year – what it has been painstakingly and resourcefully devised to display: essential aspect of the characters and relations of words, the conditions of their cooperations toward what they jointly are doing. But there is still MUCH MORE to be in some way taken account of before a fully satisfying description of how a poem works can be given.

We may recall that rather similar reflections to these have accompanied many stages of the attempt throughout history to say a little more about how the human being works. And poems are but specific examples of the working of human beings.

That MUCH MORE, of course, is what we label as the semantic, thematic structure, whose exact and systematic description still must (and for long will) elude linguistics. It is, however, that for which the phonologic and grammatical achievements (mostly of recent decades and many due to Jakobson) are indispensable preparation. What they have prepared us to expect is that – in due time and after prodigious labour – it will be possible to present distinctions and relations between components of meanings of utterances (in all their dimensions) much on the model of the ancillary studies: phonology and grammar. The semantic-thematic network needed for describing at all exactly how words, sentences, utterances, discourse . . . build up meanings may well be more complex still; but, as an intellectual instrument, it is likely to rely on analogous combinations of opposition and requirement. There is much indeed here waiting to be done, in remedy of current muddle. As Jakobson has remarked with his characteristic candour and sense of reality: "We stand before a nearly unexplored question of inter-relation between message and context." (*Parts and Wholes,* edited by Daniel Lerner, New York, 1963, p. 159.)

TOWARDS THE DEEP STRUCTURE

Meanwhile, though no SYSTEMATIC technique for the analysis and description of meanings is as yet available, there is no lack of paraphrastic LITERARY means of indicating them. The technical and the literary means cooperate, while they contrast most interestingly. Here in Jakobson's treatment is an example of technical description:

All this the world well knowes yet none knowes well,
To shun the heaven that leads men to this hell.

The sound texture of the couplet is particularly dense: in initial position we observe five instances of /th/ three of /w/ (against two /th/ and two /w/ throughout the twelve lines of the quatrains). In stressed words initial and final /n/ occur seven times and /l/ five times (whereas the twelve lines of the first three strophes show no /n/ and a mere total of three /l/ in the same position). Among the vowels the six / ε / of the couplet (3+3) are the most apparent. The sequence of three monosyllables with an internal / ε /, heaven/h ε vn/—men/m ε n/—hell/h ε l/, follows the vertical iconographic disposition and developmental order of the story; the affinity of the first noun with the second is underlined by the final / n/ and with the third one by the initial /h/. [pp. 27-8]

With this technical account we may compare:

If the first centrifugal line of the sonnet introduces the hero, *the taker,* however, still not as an agent but as a victim, the final centrifugal line brings the exposure of the malevolent culprit, *the heaven that leads men to this hell,* and thus discloses by what perjurer the joy was proposed and the lure laid. [p. 18]

Both personal nouns of the poem (II *taker* and IV *men*) characterize human beings as passive goals of extrinsic non-human and inhuman actions. [p. 20]

and

The final line seems to refer to the ultimate persona, the celestial condemner of mankind. [p. 27]

In a much used and often misleading term of current linguistics, these explications seem indeed to be reaching toward the 'deep structure' of the poem. The interpreter seems to be placing Shakespeare at a viewpoint not too far removed from that of the author of *Milton's God*.

Many readers, many minds. These elucidations can perhaps prepare us for what will be, I suspect, for more than a few of today's readers an overriding and truly a revolutionary question: What about the position which sonnet 129 is so intricately, so miraculously, designed to define, to display and to sanction? If, in Shelley's phrasing, poets are indeed "the hierophants of an unapprehended inspiration . . . the trumpets that sing to battle . . . the influence that is moved not, but moves . . . the unacknowledged legislators of the world", what poem more than this could better confront such terms? To put 'today's question' in appropriately frank and simplicist fashion: "Is not Shakespeare's view of lust now out of date? Does not a re-spelling of that old four-letter word with three letters instead, as *sex,* make all the difference in the world?" This way of putting it may suggest that today's questioners seem to be mistaking a poem – radically dramatic in genre as it may be – for a preachment, a hortatory discourse. This would be a mistake which linguistic analysis as impressive as this might conceivably encourage. Guardedly taken it will not.

With due caution, however, the reply that other readers may be inclined to offer – basing it, they will believe, on a more comprehensive experience and a sharper awareness of human behaviour, not omitting today's figures for crimes of violence – could be something like this: "Much though we might like to think so, we doubt whether that would be wise." Obviously an immensely complex profit and loss budget has here to be heeded. And what alert reflective mind, able to look into and attempt to weigh more than one position for living, more than one view of what matters more than what, will lightly decide? May it not be wiser to compare a variety of positions – including, say, that of Donne who, in Shakespeare's time, was the first man, they say, to use the word *sex* in its presently dominant sense.

We see by this, it was not sexe;
We see, we saw not what did move.

(Both Donne and Shelley above are echoing Aristotle on the "unmoved mover" and Aristotle was echoing Plato.) It is mutually illumining to put a stanza of *The Extasie* beside sonnet 129:

So must pure lovers' soules descend
T'affections, and to faculties,
That sense may reach and apprehend;
Else a great Prince in prison lies.

The affections and faculties are here those sentiments and loyalties (structures of feelings and will) which can mediate between reason and lust and restore the deposed rule of order. And beside *The Exstasie* we might put that strangest of poems *The Phoenix and the Turtle* which so resembles *The Exstasie,* being in its central theme another "dialogue of one":

Property was thus appalled,
That the self was not the same:
Single nature's double name
Neither two nor one was called.

Those venturing such a reply would not perhaps suppose that it would be of effect. They might as readily wonder whether they will not see Shakespeare, and this sonnet 129 in particular, put on tomorrow's Index as especially corrupting to the innocent mind. This controversy is as much a matter of choice as of evidence; the eye of the soul, as *Republic* (518C) has it, is not so readily turned round. I find I wrote (forty-six years ago) at the end of the preface to my first book: "The controversies which the world has known in the past are as nothing to those that are ahead." I wish I could now feel that I was mistaken or that Man's incredibly increasing powers were about to yield greater protection than peril. The ability to read better, more discerningly and justly, which Jakobson's demonstrations could promote, may, we should hope, be a help.

4. "THE PHOENIX AND THE TURTLE"

Is it not fitting that the greatest English poet should have written the most mysterious poem in English? "The Phoenix and the Turtle" is so strange a poem – even so unlike anything else in Shakespeare, as to have caused doubts that he wrote it. And yet, no one else seems in the least likely as author.

One of the odd things about the poem is that it has engendered curiosity and praise only in relatively recent times. Emerson was among the first: "To unassisted readers", he says, "it would appear to be a lament on the death of a poet, and of his poetic mistress." "This poem", he adds, "if published for the first time, and without a known author's name, would find no general reception. Only the poets would save it."
Since then many notable efforts have been made to assist "unassisted readers" without taking us perhaps very much further than Emerson himself went: "a lament on the death of a poet" -or is it the poetic endeavor?- "and his poetic mistress" -or could it be that whereto the poetic endeavor devotes itself: poetry?

Let us see. Let us read the poem through twice, once for detail and structure and pondering, and then again for life and motion.

THE PHOENIX AND THE TURTLE

Let the bird of lowdest lay,
On the sole *Arabian* tree,
Herauld sad and trumpet be:
To whose sound chaste wings obay.

But thou shriking harbinger,
Foule precurrer of the fiend,
Augour of the feuers end,
To this troupe come thou not neere.

From this Session interdict
Euery foule of tyrant wing,
Saue the Eagle feath'red King,
Keepe the obsequie so strict.

Let the Priest in Surples white,
That defunctive Musicke can,
Be the death-deuining Swan,
Lest the *Requiem* lacke his right.

And thou treble dated Crow,
That thy sable gender mak'st,
With the breath thou giu'st and tak'st,
'Mongst our mourners shalt thou go.

Here the Antheme doth commence,
Loue and Constancie is dead,
Phoenix and the *Turtle* fled,
In a mutuall flame from hence.

So they loued as loue in twaine,
Had the essence but in one,
Two distincts, Diuision none,
Number there in loue was slaine.

Hearts remote, yet not asunder;
Distance and no space was seene,
Twixt this *Turtle* and his *Queene*;
But in them it were a wonder.

So betweene them loue did shine,
That the *Turtle* saw his right,
Flaming in the *Phoenix* sight;
Either was the others mine.

Propertie was thus appalled,
That the selfe was not the same:
Single Natures double name,
Neither two nor one was called.

Reason in it selfe confounded,
Saw Diuision grow together,
To themselves yet either neither,
Simple were so well compounded.

That it cried, how true a twaine,
Seemeth this concordant one,
Loue hath Reason, Reason none,
If what parts, can so remaine.

Whereupon it made this *Threne*
To the *Phoenix* and the *Doue*,
Co-supremes and starres of Loue,
As *Chorus* to their Tragique Scene.

THRENOS

Beautie, Truth, and Raritie,
Grace in all simplicitie,
Here enclosde, in cinders lie.

Death is now the *Phoenix* nest,
And the *Turtles* loyall brest,
To eternitie doth rest,

Leauing no posteritie,
Twas not their infirmitie,
It was married Chastitie.

Truth may seeme, but cannot be,
Beautie bragge, but tis not she,
Truth and Beautie buried be.

To this vrne let those repaire,
That are either true or faire,
For these dead Birds, sigh a prayer.

The Phoenix here is a unique bird, singular indeed – there can be
but the one Phoenix. And the Turtle Dove is so devoted a lover of his
Queen – so entirely hers, as she is his – that, like an Indian suttee, he
is consumed, burnt up on the pyre, in the flames of her regeneration.

Let the bird of lowdest lay,
On the sole *Arabian* tree,
Herauld sad and trumpet be:
To whose sound chaste wings obay.

Who is speaking? Who is this "bird of lowdest lay" who summons
this company of birds and has this authority over "chaste wings"? (You
will note, near the end, a very strong use indeed of the word "Chastitie".)

I like best the suggestion that the reborn Phoenix herself is here sum-
moning the birds to the celebration of her own (and the Turtle's) obse-
quies. If so, this Phoenix, this Queen, is perched on her own throne. In
The Tempest (III, iii, 22-24) Sebastian cries:

> Now I will believe that . . . in Arabia
> There is one tree, the phoenix' throne; one phoenix
> At this hour reigning there.
> [On the sole *Arabian* tree]

If so, she herself is *Herauld sad and trumpet;* and the sadness is for the Turtle–lost in the fiery rite required for the Phoenix' rebirth.

Various birds are excluded: the ill-omened, the screech-owl, say, because this is a beginning anew, another cycle of the Phoenix' life.

> But thou shriking harbinger,
> Foule precurrer of the fiend,
> Augour of the feuers end,
> To this troupe come thou not neere.

Birds of prey are to be kept out too – except the symbol of authority, the Kingly Eagle, which can overawe violence as Henry VII put an end to the Wars of the Roses. Nothing arbitrary or unjust has a place here:

> From this Session interdict
> Euery foule of tyrant wing,
> Saue the Eagle feath'red King,
> Keepe the obsequie so strict.

Obsequie is a deep word here: a following after and a due compliance. These birds are to take part in a commemorative procession, chanting the anthem, a song with the power of a spell.

> Let the Priest in Surplus white,
> That defunctive Musicke can,
> Be the death-deuining Swan,
> Lest the *Requiem* lacke his right.

Defunctive Musicke: music which has to do with death; the Swan knows how to sing its swan song before its death and knows beforehand when it is to die.

Lacke his right: lack a rightness his participation can give. Some dictionaries say *right* is just Shakespeare's misspelling of *rite* (ritual). More modern critics will call it a pun. It is better perhaps to reflect and recognize how closely interwoven the meanings of the two words can be. A rite may be the observance it is right to give, to accord.

This choral service contains an anthem, a song of praise and gladness; a requiem, a solemn dirge for the repose of the dead; and a *threne* or *threnos,* a lamentation or dirge of honor. Note, too, a curious thing about the structure of the poem: the mourning birds, when assembled and ordered, chant an anthem in which Reason (something being described, talked about, conjured up, released, in the anthem) after going through a strange change, cries out suddenly and then composes the threne, sung at the close, and this threne, so composed

> To the *Phoenix* and the *Doue*,
> Co-supremes and starres of Loue,
> As *Chorus* to their Tragique Scene

ends with directions for a pilgrimage and a prayer.

This singular involvement – each part of the poem being included in and produced by, put into a mouth created in the part before it – has a lot to do with the power and spring of this most concentered and compacted poem.

The next bird, the last of the birds, the only one to be mentioned after the Swan-Priest, may have an importance suited to this special position. The *treble dated* Crow lives, so the legend says, three times, any number of times, longer than man. A "lived happily ever after" flavor hangs about him. Moreover, he engenders his offspring by breathing: a very ethereal mode of propagation, the mode by which poems and poetic ideas interinanimate and beget their successors. He is as black as ink, dressed in proper funeral attire, and yet is directed, somewhat as though he did not belong and could not expect to be invited, to join the mourners. Perhaps, being a carrion crow, he is a kind of contaminated character. Here he is:

> And thou treble dated Crow,
> That thy sable gender mak'st,
> With the breath thou giu'st and tak'st,
> 'Mongst our mourners shalt thou go.
>
> Here the Antheme doth commence,
> Loue and Constancie is dead,
> *Phoenix* and the *Turtle* fled,
> In a mutuall flame from hence.

Loue and Constancie: the attraction to beauty and the attachment in truth.

Notice *is dead:* the two are so much one that even from the first mention the verb used is singular: "is" dead, not "are" dead. This confounds grammar, as Reason, itself, is going to be confounded in what follows.

> So they loued as loue in twaine,
> Had the essence but in one,
> Two distincts, Diuision none,
> Number there in loue was slaine.

They loved as do two people who love one another, and yet they were not two but one, and one is not a number. For this duality the same questions arise as in the Doctrine of the Trinity.

> Hearts remote, yet not asunder;
> Distance and no space was seene,
> Twixt this *Turtle* and his *Queene*:
> But in them it were a wonder.

But in them it were a wonder: in any others than "this concordant one" all this would be "a wonder"; not so here.

> So betweene them loue did shine,
> That the *Turtle* saw his right,
> Flaming in the *Phoenix* sight;
> Either was the others mine.

The Phoenix' eyes are traditionally of fire; they flame like the sun. But, more than that, the Turtle sees *his right* flaming in them.

His right: all he can ask or be entitled to; all that is due and just; all that he truly is, his true being.

Let me quote a few lines here from *The Birds Parliament* by Attar, the twelfth century Persian saint and mystic, also about the Phoenix, which in Attar's poem is the leader in the soul's return to God. The poem is translated by Edward Fitzgerald, who translated Omar Khayyám.

> Once more they ventured from the Dust to raise
> Their eyes up to the Throne, into the Blaze;
> And in the Centre of the Glory there
> Beheld the Figure of THEMSELVES, as 'twere
> Transfigured — looking to Themselves, beheld
> The Figure on the Throne enmiracled,
> Until their Eyes themselves and that between
> Did hesitate which SEER was, which SEEN.

Or as in Shelley's lines from his "Hymn of Apollo":

> I am the Eye with the universe
> Beholds itself and knows itself divine.

Either was the others mìne: diamond mine, ruby mine, yes, perhaps; but, more important, each entirely possessed and was possessed by the other.

> Propertie was thus appalled,
> That the selfe was not the same:
> Single Natures double name,
> Neither two nor one was called.
>
> Reason in it selfe confounded,
> Saw Diuision grow together,
> To themselves yet either neither,
> Simple were so well compounded.
>
> That it cried, how true a twaine,
> Seemeth this concordant one,
> Loue hath Reason, Reason none,
> If what parts, can so remaine.

Any other poem, I sometimes think, would have made Reason cry

> How true a one
> Seemeth this concordant twain.

But the poem goes the further step, makes *Reason in it selfe confounded* speak in character and show itself to be confounded. Very Shakespearean, this dramatic actuality!

> Whereupon it made this *Threne*
> To the *Phoenix* and the *Doue*,
> Co-supremes and starres of Loue,
> As *Chorus* to their Tragique Scene.

Note that Reason is the singer

THRENOS

> Beauty, Truth, and Raritie,
> Grace in all simplicitie,
> Here enclosde, in cinders lie.
>
> Death is now the *Phoenix* nest,
> And the *Turtles* loyall brest,
> To eternitie doth rest,

To the Phoenix, death is now a nest, a symbol of rebirth, but to

> the *Turtles* loyall brest,

it is a place of final repose.

> Leauing no posteritie,
> Twas not their infirmitie,
> It was married Chastitie.

What these

> Co-supremes and starres of Loue

have been concerned with has not been offspring. Besides, there can be but the one Phoenix, although in this poem, we may imagine, the sacrifice, the devotion of a Dove is needed for each new regeneration or reincarnation.

> The intellect of man is forced to choose
> Perfection of the life or of the work,

wrote W. B. Yeats. Must poets give up their lives so that poetry may be renewed?

> Truth may seeme, but cannot be,
> Beautie bragge, but tis not she,
> Truth and Beautie buried be.

As a poem may be something beyond anyone's reading or apprehension of it?

> To this vrne let those repaire,
> That are either true or faire,
> For these dead Birds, sigh a prayer.

This prayer is wordless; it is sighed only, not spoken. What it might have said is what the whole poem has been conveying, an endeavor to apprehend a mystery. And it is no good asking what this mystery is apart from this endeavor itself.

We may say if we like that this mystery is the mystery of being, which is forever dying into cinders and arising to flame and die anew; and always, perhaps, demanding a sacrifice of constancy for the sake of that to which it is loyal and true. But no remarks on this poem can be more than snapshots of something someone has thought he saw in it: helpful maybe to some but merely curiosities of opinion to others.

There are two remarks I would like, however, to make before inviting the reader to read the poem again straight through.

> Beautie, Truth, and Raritie.

The truth celebrated in the poem is chiefly loyalty, faithfulness, and constancy, which, as with Troilus, the true knight, the true lover, is truth spelled *Troth*. At first sight troth may not seem to have very much to do with the ways in which a statement in a science may be true (or false), or evidence offered in a law court may be true (or false), or philosophical or critical or historical or literary views may be true (or false). And yet, for all of these, if we search and imagine faithfully enough, we will find that the statement or opinion, whatever it is, hangs in the midst of and is dependent upon a vast network of loyalties toward everything that may be relevant. Its truth is a matter of inter-in-animations and co-operations among loyalties, among troths.

And very significant parallels to all this hold for beauty.

This poem, one may well think, is not about any such high and remote abstractions but about two people; two people, who may be thought to have been "the very personifications, the very embodiments", as we lightly say, of beauty and truth, though they are spoken of in the poem as two birds. That is how the poem feels, no doubt about it. But, as certainly, there is a religious quality in its movement, a feeling in it as though we were being related through it to something far beyond any individuals. This Phoenix and this Turtle have a mythic scale to them, as though through them we were to become participants in something ultimate. All this, however, is so handled that it seems as easy and as natural and as necessary as breathing.

Let us read the poem again with a wider and more relaxed attention. Was it Mr. Eliot who remarked: "There is such a thing as page fright as well as stage fright"? The very greatness of a poem can stupefy the reader.

. . . .

To this vrne let those repaire . . .

No one who repairs to this urn will think there can be any end to wondering about it.

5. REVERSALS IN POETRY

The late Ellery Sedgwick, editor in its great days of *The Atlantic Monthly,* used to recall, as among his earliest memories, being sung to sleep nightly by his mother with a lullaby of markedly unusual character. He was then a very small poetry-lover indeed. He recalled its lines too – as he remembered most other verses he liked – though not how they came to be known to his mother. It is improbable that she made them up. They never ceased to haunt him and with his characteristic eagerness he inquired throughout his life of all who might be expected to have come across them. But in vain; they were unknown to everyone. Since these consultants began with his uncle Professor Child of the Ballads and included any number of eminent 'library cormorants' from Kittredge and Lowes on to Edwin Muir and T.S. Eliot, this is itself interesting. Many admired the lines very much, but none had heard them before. They are not lines which anyone who has met them will easily forget. Here they are:

> White was the sheet
> That she spread for her lover,
> White was the sheet;
> And embroidered the cover.
>
> But whiter the sheet
> And the canopy grander
> When he lay down to sleep
> Where the hill-foxes wander.

Let us try out their movements again.

> White was the sheet that she spread for her lover.
> White was the sheet and embroidered the cover.
>
> But whiter the sheet
> And the Canopy grander
> When he lay down to sleep
> Where the hill foxes wander.

It has a powerful plot – hasn't it? The pull and tension are pretty strong between the expectations generated by the opening:

> White was the sheet that she spread for her lover.

and the grimness of the last five words

> Where the hill foxes wander.

Strange verses, someone may think, for a mother to sing to her little boy as he dozes off. At any rate you'll agree that these verses are NOT namby-pamby. I'll hope you agree too that they are a very high quality of infants' food indeed – packed with poetic vitamins.

Look at some of the phrases: *hill foxes wander* – When there is any snow on the ground you see their tracks everywhere in the border-ballad country between Scotland and England (or for that matter on the White Mountains of New Hampshire too). Do you hear a perhaps Scottish sound about *grander* and *wander*?

But look now, with this violent grim reversal, how the words *White* and *sheet* and *canopy* suddenly take on meanings almost the very opposites of those you give them at first:

1. 'Safety, comfort, rest, security, ease, joy . . . life at its highest';

2. 'Mortal danger, the struggle, the defeat . . . exhaustion and death'.

And add to that something else which in the *Iliad,* for example, or in the First Book of Kings, (at the very roots, that is, of our tradition) is thought of with the utmost abhorrence as more to be dreaded than death.

> . . . and sent down into Hades many
> strong souls of heroes, and gave
> their bodies to be food for dogs and birds.
>
> *Iliad,* 1 : 4

> Him that dieth of Ahab in the city
> shall the dogs eat; and him that
> dieth in the field shall the fowls
> of the air eat.
>
> *I Kings,* 21 : 24

This is an extreme reversal – sprung upon us as suddenly and unpreparedly as possible.

Look at *canopy:* all the 'sheltering, protective, easeful, comfortable, reassuring, snug' suggestions of the 'enclosing, cossetting, top to a four-poster bed' turned, – without warning – into nothing less than the night-sky itself (in which the planets wander), the night-sky over the snows.

And it's all done with just the one word *grander* which gets its take-up and confirmation in *hill foxes wander*.

How the echo, here, of the rime, as so often, reinforces, parallels, confirms the sense. Those hill foxes are at home and secure, there where the sleeper is lost.

One can feel pretty sure about some of these 'inter-verbal interinani-mations' without feeling at all certain that talking about them helps to bring them out. Other examples of the same sort of thing, I think, help better.

Have any of you, I wonder, formed any conjectures yet as to what these verses may be? My own guess is that they are a bit of Sir Walter Scott that he never happened to write down.

Anyhow, the nearest parallels I can think of are in Scott: Here is "Proud Maisie":

> Proud Maisie is in the wood
> Walking so early;
> Sweet Robin sits on the bush
> Singing so rarely.
>
> 'Tell me, thou bonny bird,
> When shall I marry me?'
> — 'When six braw gentlemen
> Kirkward shall carry ye.'
>
> 'Who makes the bridal bed,
> Birdie, say truly?'
> — 'The grey headed sexton
> That delves the grave duly.'
>
> 'The glow-worn o'er grave and stone
> Shall light thee steady;
> The owl from the steeple sing
> Welcome, proud lady.'

Here are the same grim surprises: the same sudden reversals and the same polarities of *Love* and *Death*. And, even as *canopy* in our lullaby turns into its very opposite – the roofless sky – so here with *steady*.

> The glow-worn o'er grave and stone
> Shall light thee steady;

How steady is a glow-worm and what sort of light does it give?

As swiftly as the cold green light of the glow-worm wanes, so swiftly
will Proud Maisie's morning freshness cease.

The reversal, prepared, as in the lullaby, by the very phrase (here,
six braw gentlemen) at first promising, but, as it sinks in, turning into
the undoing – as with the bridal bed = canopy – is as clear. In
each instance what at first seems comforting grows daunting. We may
note the three steps of the confirmation: *sexton, glowworm, owl* and
the triumphs in *steady* and *welcome,* which seem to me to have affinity
with what is done by *grander* and *wander.*

Here is a slighter instance of same movement to be compared
with the lullaby. Scott used to put mottoes in verse at the heads of
his chapters. After a time he stopped digging suitable mottoes up out
of memory or out books of verse and plays. It was quicker and much
less trouble just to make them up. "Hang it, Johnnie", he said one
day to his publisher Ballantyne, "I believe I can make a motto sooner
than you will find one." Here's one he made up so.

> Dark on their journey frowned the gloomy day.
> Wild were the hills, and doubtful grew the way.
> More dark, more gloomy and more doubtful showed
> The mansion which received them from the road.

There are, at the least, curious thematic parallels to be explored here.
In both, what the first two lines may seem to promise, is grimly with-
drawn by the rest. On a miniature scale there is a tragic reversal in the
action. In both, the very thing which seems to offer safety, comfort,
succour and rest, becomes suddenly deadly: the whiteness of the sheet
that turns, through *whiter,* the comparative, to snow; and the mansion
showing more dark, more gloomy and more doubtful than that from
which it might have offered protection. The three-fold repetition may
also be remarked. Compare further this change in the mansion with
what happens through the word *canopy:* the snugness of the four-poster
so smoothly turning into the bleak infinity of the night sky.

The very thing which should have been the remedy: this should-be
hospitable mansion – becomes only the ills made worse.

None of these you'll agree, whatever else you may call them, can be
said to be namby-pamby.

"Namby-pamby". The name commemorates the brief success – in its
day, which was early 18th Century – and the long neglect of the verse
of Ambrose Philips.

Would you like to see the verses which earned this disparaging label?

Dimply Damsel, sweetly smiling,
All caressing, none beguiling,
Bud of beauty fairly blowing
Ev'ry charm to Nature owing.
This and that new thing admiring
Much of this and that inquiring
Knowledge by degrees attaining
Day by day some virtue gaining.

This sounds a bit too much perhaps like a super-testimonial as to her scholastic aptitude for a young lady on her way to Radcliffe ... but still I offer you these verses as by no means – What do you think? – entirely devoid of Poetry.

We may have been unjust to Ambrose Philips. After all the poor man did nothing more criminal than write verses which pleased many good judges (Goldsmith, for example, thought things Ambrose Philips wrote "incomparably fine"). Whether he deserved Pope's scoff

Lo: Ambrose Philips is preferr'd for wit!

and Carey's ridicule, matter little enough; the derisive term has been useful. We have no name so handy for its opposite. Anyhow there he is stuck in posterity's ear for ever as namby-pamby. What a dangerous thing it is to be the fashion!

Sir Walter Scott, of course, is very much OUT of fashion – in part no doubt, because he was once so very much in it; in part, perhaps, because people don't know his best things, though they would be interested in what, at his best, he writes about. They just don't know!

However, one of his last mottoes for chapter headings illustrates very well something which often seems fundamental in poetic composition and really important: the way verses can be ABOUT a many-stepped hierarchy of situations simultaneously: up, up, up or, if you like, down, down, down, deeper deeper.

Things with Scott had been going from bad to worse. He had got involved with his publishers in a failure for £ 170,000 (a terrific sum in those days). He had managed within five years by his writing to reduce the debt by £ 63,000. But he had begun to have a series of shocks, or strokes, leaving behind increasing paralysis, attacks of aphasia and recurrent mental blank-outs. Worst of all, the novel in hand, *Count Robert of Paris,* wasn't up to standard. His advisers – publisher and bookseller – were complaining and Scott himself agreed:

I have lost, it is plain, the power of interesting the country and ought, in justice to all parties, to retire while I still have some credit.

That's from a letter. What follows is from his diary:

There is just another die to turn up against me in this run of ill luck. i.e. if I should break my magic wand in the fall from this elephant, and lose my popularity with my fortune.

Here's a precious job. I have a formal remonstrance from those critical people, Ballantyne and Cadell (publisher-bookseller) against the last volume of *Count Robert* which is within a sheet of being finished.

I suspect their opinion will be found to coincide with that of the public; at least it is not very different from my own. The blow is a stunning one, I suppose for I scarcely feel it.

I cannot conceive that I have tied a knot with my tongue which my teeth cannot untie. We shall see.

A day came when Scott was held up in Edinburgh by a great snow-storm – days and days of it. While the snow was still falling heavily Ballantyne reminded him that a motto was wanting for one of the chapters of *Count Robert*. Scott went to the window, looked out for a moment, and then wrote:

> The storm increases:
> 'tis no sunny shower,
> Foster'd in the moist breast
> of March or April,
> Or such as parching summer
> cools his lips with.
>
> Heaven's windows are flung wide;
> the inmost deeps
> Call, in hoarse greeting
> one upon another;
> On comes the flood
> in all its foaming horrors;
> And where's the dike shall stop it?

The Deluge: a Poem

What is that about? Is it about the story in the chapter it is to be a motto to? Is it about the storm raging outside? Is it about Scott's own intelligence and sanity being swept away? Is it about any and every threat of final disaster? What anyone might think he was facing any morning when apprehensively reading his newspaper?

the inmost deeps / Call in hoarse greeting / one upon another: what are these inmost deeps of Heaven which have such appetite for ruin?

The title of the original talk was *Ballads*. I have not, so far, touched on any authentic traditional ballad. I thought I could approach the queer relish of disaster, the fascinated harping on a grief to cut the heartstrings, the taste for the daunting and horrific that is characteristic of so many ballads more easily with less familiar material. But here is "The Unquiet Grave":

> "Cold blows the wind to my
> true love
> And gently drops the rain.
> I never had but one sweetheart
> And in greenwood she lies slain.
>
> I'll do as much for my sweetheart
> As any young man may:
> I'll sit down by her grave
> and weep
> For twelve month and a day."
>
> The twelve month and the day
>   were past,
>   The ghost began to speak,
> "What make you sitting
>   along my grave
>   And will not let me sleep?"
>
> "What is it that you want of me
>   And will not let me sleep?
> Your salty tears, they trickle down
>   And wet my winding sheet."
>
> "What is it that you want of me
>   Of me what dost thou crave?"
> "One only kiss from your
>   lily-white lips.
>   Then I'll go from your grave."
>
> "My lips are cold as clay,
>   sweetheart,
>   My breath is earthy and strong;
> And if you kiss my lily-white lips,
>   Your time will not be long."

"My time be short; my time be long:
   Tomorrow or today!
May Christ in Heaven have all
      my soul
But I'll kiss your lips of clay."

"When shall we meet again,
      sweetheart,
   When shall we meet again?"
"When the oaken leaves that fall
      from the trees
   Are green as spring again."

Whoever made up "White was the sheet...", though saturated with feelings frequent in ballad, uses poetic devices that are not, I think, in the style of true ballads. One of these is that sudden immense change in the meaning of a word: *White* or *sheet* or *canopy*. It is so big a change that the word almost feels as if it became another word. But it doesn't. If it were another word, we would have a frank pun.

Now, to think of puns and ballads together is to think of Thomas Hood. "Faithless Nelly Gray", which I am going on to read now, came out in 1826, the year of Scott's failure. It is very unlike Scott, very unlike "The Unquiet Grave". And yet... he calls it *A Pathetic Ballad*. It is that. But it has about the queerest sort of pathos ever.

You'll soon wonder where you are with Hood. The use he makes of his puns is as atrocious as the puns themselves. It is all excruciatingly heartless and heartbreaking. There will be those who will want to complain, I know: "Why call that Poetry?"

There is never any answer to that, is there? But it may be apposite (a word exquisitely related to opposite) to quote from Jakobson again and from *On Translation,* p. 238, "Phonemic similarity is sensed as semantic relationship. The pun, or to use a more erudite, and perhaps more precise term – paronomasia, reigns over poetic art" *(On Translation,* p. 238). It is clear enough, though, that the poet of those two highly original poems: "The Song of the Shirt" and "The Bridge of Sighs" is here eyeing man's inhumanity even more sternly though he cloaks his rage in such a dazzling display of uproarious jocosity and verbal wit. This is another mode of reversal, where the frivolity of the treatment conflicts with the various grimnesses of the content. (I have found in my readings that the poem gains by the repetition of the fourth line of each verse – to allow more time for the TOUR DE FORCE to sink in.)

Here is:

FAITHLESS NELLIE GRAY
A Pathetic Ballad

Ben Battle was a soldier bold
    And used to war's alarms:
But a cannon-ball took off his legs,
    So he laid down his arms!

Now as they bore him off the field
    Said he 'Let others shoot
For here I leave my second leg,
    And the Forty-second Foot!'

The army-surgeons made him limbs:
    Said he, "They're only pegs:
But there's as wooden members quite
    As represent my legs!"

Now Ben he loved a pretty maid
    Her name was Nelly Gray;
So he went to pay her his devours
    When he'd devoured his pay!

But when he called on Nelly Gray,
    She made him quite a scoff;
And when she saw his wooden legs,
    Began to take them off!

'O Nelly Gray! O, Nelly Gray!
    Is this your love so warm?
The love that loves a scarlet coat
    Should be more uniform!'

Said she, 'I loved a soldier once,
    For he was blythe and brave;
But never will I have a man
    With both legs in the grave!'

'Before you had those timber toes,
    Your love I did allow
But then, you know, you stand upon
    Another footing now!'

'O Nelly Gray! O, Nelly Gray!
    For all your jeering speeches,
At duty's call, I left my legs
    In Badajos's breaches!'

'Why then,' said she, 'you've lost
  the feet
 Of legs in war's alarms
And now you cannot wear your shoes
 Upon your feats of arms!'

'O false and fickle Nelly Gray;
 I know why you refuse:
Though I've no feet, some other man
 Is standing in my shoes!'

'I wish I ne'er had seen your face;
 But now, a long farewell
For you will be my death; — alas!
 You will not be my Nell!'

Now when he went from Nelly Gray,
 His heart so heavy got —
And life was such a burden grown,
 It made him take a knot!

So round his melancholy neck,
 A rope he did entwine
And, for the second time in life
 Enlisted in the Line.

One end he tied around a beam,
 And then removed his pegs,
And, as his legs were off, of course
 He soon was off his legs!

And there he hung till he was dead
 As any nail in town,
For though distress had cut him up,
 It could not cut him down!

A dozen men sat on his corpse,
 To find out why he died —
And they buried Ben in four cross-
  roads
With a *stake* in his inside.

In their very different ways, all these poems have been presenting the human condition without offer of comfort.

ADDITIONAL NOTES

Linebreaks

The practical problem: how best accommodate longish lines to the re-
strictions of the T.V. valve, gives rise to reflections on the visual aspects
of printed verse and on the cooperations of ear and eye in reading them.
Some of these may be worth noting.

I have printed *White was the sheet . . . The storm increases . . .* and
"The Unquiet Grave" as I would, on the whole, advise that they be
displayed on the screen. There are obviously other arrangements that
may recommend themselves. The interesting questions are: What are
we weighing in making such choices? and which, from case to case, is
predominant – the eye or the ear?

Print gives an individuality and distinctness of being to words that
by no means actually belongs to them in ordinary speech – and perhaps
still less in verse which is being spoken with full regard for the poetic
function (see pp 23 and 30 above). Print, among other things, brings
out the grammatical character of words, especially of the shorter words,
as speech does not. Moreover, print displays alliterative and assonance
patternings in fashions that vocal utterance may treat otherwise. By
these means (and probably by many further means that a closer examination would reveal) the printed poem has powerful quasi-independent
contributions to make towards the poem's overall being. Some of these
are well recognized: punctuation, for example, and insettings, which
reflect the metrical and rime schemes, alerting the reader, preparing
him to expect and accept the rime; but there are other influences which
the placing of the printed word can exert and it is these which line-break
decisions can bring out.

White was the sheet is in the interesting position of having been – so
far as I know – still oral poetry until I put it on the T.V. screen. It
might be printed as a four line poem. But to my eye-and-ear, reading
in accord, it seems more entirely itself: all its parts testifying that – to
quote Coleridge again – it "contains in itself the reason why it is so and
not otherwise", in the arrangement I print here. For this some of the
grounds may be:

1.   The three *sheet's* gain a peculiar salience, optically, that matches
with their thematic moment.

2.   The repetition, from the final word *sheet* of the first line, of the
second word *she* dramatizes, optically, what she is doing. In a sense, she
is being that sheet.

3. A slight space (not too much or . . .) between this four-line verse and the second will hint at the drear reversal.

4. In the sixth line *And,* as initial word, prepares for the terrific key word: *grander.*

5. The two opening words of the following lines: in their initial *(Wh),* that superlatively questioning form and sound; – echoing *White* as they do and closing with *wander*; English is fortunate in having this motion of the speech organs coincide with the outlet of breath after surprise – round up the poem in a way that print should do all it can to support and confirm.

More problematic decisions attend *Dark on their journey.* Scott, I believe wisely printed it as four lines, each too long for me to put them legibly within the confines of T.V. I had to break them up for my purposes, and how that could be done with minimal damage to the poem is our problem. I print here two proposals: one, relatively mechanical, for comparison with that on the right, which may have been the one I actually used.

> Dark on their journey frowned the gloomy day.
> Wild were the hills, and doubtful grew the way.
> More dark, more gloomy and more doubtful showed
> The mansion which received them from the road.

Compare these arrangements:

> Dark on their journey
>   frowned the gloomy day,
> Wild were the hills
>   and doubtful grew the way.
>
> More dark, more gloomy
>   and more doubtful showed
> The mansion which received them
>   from the road.

> Dark on their journey frowned
>   the gloomy day,
> Wild were the hills and
>   doubtful grew the way.
>
> More dark, more gloomy and
>   more doubtful showed
> The mansion which
>   received them from the road.

I have some doubt whether the grounds for decisions between these (and the other alternatives) are as yet clear enough – to any but the original poet as he composes – to warrant any certainties.

The storm increases: The arrangement offered is, as evidently as I can make it, an invitation to others to compare, question, re-dispose and assess variant placings of the words.

The printing of long lines in "The Unquiet Grave" will, I hope, draw further attention to what is still, I think, a neglected question.

6. THE INTERINANIMATIONS OF WORDS

There should be an ancient saying, "If you talk too much about words, your tongue will become a stone." More than once in this lecture you will see why. I have been minded again and again to change my title or dodge the topic. "Whereof we cannot speak, thereof we must be silent", remarked Ludwig Wittgenstein some twenty years ago, but men have gone on inventing languages in which to talk about that silence.

What are these words we talk with and talk so much about? Taking poetry to be an affair of the interinanimation of words, how far will we get in a discussion of poetry if we are in real doubt about what words are and do?

This essay threatens thus to become an attempt to define 'a word'. I am extremely loath to inflict that upon you. The definition of 'a word' has been a task from which the best authorities have rightly shrunk, an obligation which had made even psychologists into mystics and left the adepts in linguistics at a loss. But when the subject has been tactlessly raised, how are we to avoid it? How are we to conceive the interinanimations of words without forming as clear a conception as we can of the words themselves?

"As clear a conception as we can"! But what are "conceptions" and how can they be "clear"? The implications of this word CONCEP-TION, if we take it literally and thereby awaken it to full metaphoric liveliness, are a philosophy of poetic language – as Plato pointed out, in the *Phaedrus (277)*. It is true he calls them "scientific words" there, but he was concerned with "the dialectic art" which I arbitrarily take here to have been the practice of a supreme sort of poetry – the sort which was to replace the poetry he banished from the Republic. Here is the passage.

Noble it may be to tell stories about justice and virtue; but far nobler is a man's work, when finding a congenial soul he avails himself of the dialectic art to sow and plant therein scientific words, which are competent to defend themselves, and him who planted them, and are not unfruitful, but bear seed in their turn, from which other words springing up in other minds are capable of preserving this precious seed ever undecaying, and making their possessor ever happy, so far as happiness is possible to man.

Plato is fond of this sort of language. If you look for it you will find it everywhere in the *Republic*, used with a frankness which embarrassed his Victorian translators.

What are these conceptions through which words, by uniting, bring new beings into the world, or new worlds into being? A truly philosophic definition of "a word" would be, I suppose, an all-purposes definition. I am hoping for no such thing – only for a definition useful for our purpose: the study of the language of poetry. But limits to that are not easily set. However, I can escape some of the most dreadful parts of the undertaking by assuming frankly that our purposes are not those of psychology or of linguistics. Their troubles come in part from the uses for which they require their definitions of "a word". Poetics has a different set of purposes and needs a different sort of definition. If so, I can work at it without the tedious attempt to relate it to the other definitions that other studies need. Philosophically speaking, this leaves Poetics 'up in the air'; but that is perhaps where, in the present state of philosophy, it will be safest.

But very likely someone will already be saying: "Wait a moment. Are these troubles real or only philosophic? Do we really need any definition poetic or otherwise? Are not most of us in fact clear enough about what poetry and words in general are and do? This marvellous, this miraculous thing we call our language works somehow for us and within us; the better, it may well be, for our not knowing too much about it. Our digestions, to take a humble parallel, do not depend, fortunately, on our knowledge of physiology. Don't our poetic difficulties also arise with particular instances only? Isn't this pretence that we never understand what we are saying or how we say it rather like witchcraft – an epidemic invented to give employment to specialists in its treatment?"

I would meet you upon this honestly. Such questionings can be barren. To ask "What is a word and how does it work?" may do us no good. On the other hand, there is a sense in which this question is the very foundation, the source, the origin, the ἀρχή (to use Plato's word), the starting point and final cause of the intellectual life. But I do not know how, IN WORDS, to distinguish the idle from the vital question here.

In the philosophy of poetry this vital question is not a question of fact but one of choice or decision. In that, it is like the fundamental definitions of mathematics. Facts, by themselves, do not, in any simple direct way, settle what we should define "a word" to be. Facts, which we are aware of and can compare only through words, come later. None the less our definition must let the facts be facts. We do well to be humble here; this "What is a word?" is one of the founding questions – along with "What am I?" "What is a fact?" and "What is God?" – on which all other questions balance and turn. The art of entertaining such questions, and of distinguishing them from other questions which we might ask with the same sounds, is the dialectic study of poetry. And the founding questions – those that establish and maintain our state as men – are themselves poetic. But that might mean so many false things that I tremble as I say it.

Still, the other ways of saying it, and ways of guarding it, suffer equal danger. If I add, for example, that this poetic basis of ours is no matter of MERE MAKE-BELIEVE, well, we have the varying possible ways of understanding that richly mysterious phrase, "make-believe", before us. "Mere make-believe". Here is a notable example of the interinanimation of words. Just where do its disparaging or mocking implications come from? Are beliefs NOT to be made (i.e. forced)? Is THAT the point? Or is it the poor quality of the belief so made? Are beliefs which WE make not genuine? Must the world, something not ourselves, make them for us? And if so, WHICH world will we trust to do that? The world of tradition, of theology, of current public opinion, of science, or one of the worlds of poetry? Which will give us the beliefs we need? Is that the question, or is it the inferior quality of such beliefs which is being mocked, the immature craftsmanship, the inexperience which knows too little about either the materials or the purpose of the belief?

All this and more is to be considered in asking seriously if the poetic basis of our world is make-believe. This phrase, MAKE-BELIEVE, like a good watch dog, warns us off sternly – if we have no proper business with these premises. But if we were their master, it would be silent. There is another possibility of course. In the Chinese story the stone-deaf visitor remarked, "Why do you keep your dog up so late? He did nothing but yawn at me as I came through the gate."

However, if we know what we are doing, and what the phrase "make-believe" is doing – and it has several senses which should alarm us for one which is supporting – we may say that our world rests on make-belief or – to use a more venerable word – on faith. But it is OUR world, mind you, which so rests, our world in which we live as men, so different from the bullet's world, in which IT travels. And yet our world includes the bullet.

I have been trying with all this to revive for you the sense of the word "maker", in which a poet may be seriously said to be a maker. This is the sense in which poetry matters because it is creative – not the sense in which we say it is "creative" because we feel it matters. The poet is a maker of beliefs – but do not give here to "belief" the first meaning that comes to mind, for it is as true that for other senses of "belief" poetry has nothing to do with them. What does the poet MAKE and what does his work CREATE? Himself and his world first, and thereby other worlds and other men. He makes through shaping and molding, through giving form. But if we ask what he shapes or molds or gives form to, we must answer with Aristotle that we can say nothing about that which has no form. There are always prior forms upon which the poet works, and how he takes these forms is part of his making. He apprehends them by taking them into forms of more comprehensive order. To the poet as poet, his world is the world, and the world is his world. But the poet is not always poet. All but the greatest poets in the most favorable societies seem to have to pay for being poets. Of recent poets, Yeats has put this best:

> The intellect of man is forced to choose
> Perfection of the life or of the work,
> And if it take the second must refuse
> A heavenly mansion, raging in the dark.
> When all that story's finished, what's the news?
> In luck or out, the toil has left its mark:
> That old perplexity, an empty purse
> Or the day's vanity, the night's remorse.

The work of the poet is the maintenance and enlargement of the human spirit through remaking it under changing circumstances; through molding and remolding the ever-varying flux. The molds are sets of words, interacting in manifold ways within a language. At first sight this old Platonic image of the mold looks crude. What could be less like a mold than a word – which endlessly changes its work with its company as we all may note if we care to look? But the mold metaphor – the dominant metaphor of the Greek invention of education – is there to shock us into thought. The poetic problem is precisely the mainte-

nance of stability WITHIN minds and correspondence BETWEEN them.
It is NOT how to get the flux into molds supposed somehow to be fixed
already; but how to recreate perpetually those constancies (as of sets of
molds) upon which depend any order, any growth, any development
– any changes, in fact, other than the chance-ridden changes of chaos.

It is through the interinanimations of words within a language that a
poet works. In a sense all literary men are inquiring concretely into the
detail of this in all their work, but let us try to take a more general and
comprehensive view before going on to contrast two types of verbal
interinanimations. If I can show you how I conceive words, the rest
will be easier. First I spoke of the QUESTION, "What is a word?", not of
any answer to it, as one of the founding forces, and as thereby poetic.
Answers to it of many sorts can be contrived and offered. Linguistics
and psychology in their different divisions have many very different
answers and the debate between them, as studies aspiring to become
sciences (in various senses of "science") must be a long one. But these
answers would answer different questions from my poetic "What is a
word?" That question is nourished by awareness of them, but it is not
reducible to them. It is not answered by an exhaustive dictionary or
encyclopedia article on the word WORD. That would answer only the
set of historical, factual, linguistic, psychological, religious, metaphysical, and other questions which I am trying – by these very odd means
– to distinguish from the poetic question. With any of these questions,
and the same with itself. But the poetic question has to be its own ans-
it would be shocking – would it not? – to suggest that its answer is one
wer – as virtue in its own reward, to cite the wider rule of which this
is an example. As an answer it is aware that it is a bundle of possibilities dependent on other possibilities which in turn it in part determines;
as a question it is attempting through its influence on them to become
more completely itself. It is growing as a cell grows with other cells. It
is a conception. It is being "divided at the joints" and recombined.
Phaedrus' "attempting" and "growing" are not metaphors here. A word,
a question or its answer, does all that we do, since we do all that in the
word. Words are alive as our other acts are alive – though apart from
the minds which use them they are nothing but agitations of the air
or stains on paper.

A word then by this sort of definition is a permanent set of possibilities of understanding, much as John Stuart Mill's table was a permanent
possibility of sensation. And as the sensations the table yields depend
on the angle you look from, the other things you see it with, the air,

your glasses, your eyes and the light ... so how a word is understood depends on the other words you hear it with, and the other frames you have heard it in, on the whole setting present and past in which it has developed as a part of your mind. But the interinanimations of words with one another and with other things are far more complex than can be paralleled from the case of the table – complex enough as those are. Indeed they are not paralleled anywhere except by such things as pictures, music or the expressions of faces which are other modes of language. Language, as understood, is the mind itself at work and these interinanimations of words are interdependencies of our own being.

I conceive then a word, as poetry is concerned with it, and as separated from the mere physical or sensory occasion, to be a component of an act of the mind so subtly dependent on the other components of this act and of other acts that it can be distinguished from these interinanimations only as a convenience of discourse. It sounds nonsense to say that a word is its interinanimations with other words; but that is a short way of saying the thing which Poetics is in most danger always of overlooking. Words only work together. We understand no word except in and through its interinanimations with other words.

Let me now come down to detail. I invite you to compare two very different types of the interinanimations of words in poetry: I will read the first twelve lines of Donne's *First Anniversary*.

AN ANATOMY OF THE WORLD

The first anniversary
Wherein

By occasion of the untimely death of Mistress
Elizabeth Drury, the frailty and the decay
of this whole world is represented.

When that rich Soule which to her heaven is gone,
Whom all do celebrate, who know they have one,
(For who is sure he hath a Soule, unlesse
It see, and judge, and follow worthinesse,
And by Deedes praise it? hee who doth not this,
May lodge an In-mate soule, but 'tis not his.)
When that Queene ended here her progresse time,
And, as t'her standing house to heaven did climbe,
Where loath to make the Saints attend her long,
She's now a part both of the Quire, and Song,
This world, in that great earthquake languished;
For in a common bath of teares it bl~d.

Let us compare with that the first stanza of Dryden's

Ode: To the Pious Memory of the accomplished
young lady, Mrs. Anne Killigrew, excellent
in the two sister arts of Poesy and Painting

Thou youngest virgin-daughter of the skies,
Made in the last promotion of the blest;
Whose palms, new pluck'd from Paradise,
In spreading branches more sublimely rise,
Rich with immortal green above the rest:
Whether, adopted to some neighboring star,
Thou roll'st above us, in thy wandering race,
Or, in procession fixt and regular,
Mov'd with the heaven's majestic pace;
Or, call'd to more superior bliss,
Thou tread'st with seraphims the vast abyss:
Whatever happy region is thy place,
Cease thy celestial song a little space;
Thou wilt have time enough for hymns divine,
Since Heaven's eternal year is thine.
Hear, then, a mortal Muse thy praise rehearse,
    In no ignoble verse;
But such as thy own voice did practice here,
When thy first-fruits of Poesy were given,
To make thyself a welcome inmate there;
    While yet a young probationer,
        And candidate of Heaven.

In the Donne, I suggest, there is a prodigious activity between the words as we read them. Following, exploring, realizing, BECOMING that activity is, I suggest, the essential thing in reading the poem. Understanding it is not a preparation for reading the poem. It is itself the poem. And it is a constructive, hazardous, free creative process, a process of conception through which a new being is growing in the mind. The Dryden, I suggest, is quite otherwise. No doubt there are interinanimations between the words but they are on a different level. The words are in routine conventional relations like peaceful diplomatic communications between nations. They do not induce revolutions in one another and are not thereby attempting to form a new order. Any mutual adjustments they have to make are preparatory, and they are no important part of the poetic activity. In brief Dryden's poem comes before our minds as a mature creation. But we seem to create Donne's poem.

Donne's poem is called *The First Anniversary* because he wrote it a year after the death of Elizabeth Drury. He was going to write a similar poem every year but only wrote one other. The editor of the Nonesuch Edition says this "concluded the series of preposterous eulogies". Whether Mr. Hayward thinks them preposterous, whether they are eulogies, and whether, if we took them as such, they would be preposterous – are questions I leave till later.

Opinion about them has always been mixed. Ben Jonson is reported to have said that "they were prophane and full of blasphemies; that he told Mr. Donne if it had been written of the Virgin Marie it had been something; to which he answered that he described the Idea of a Woman, and not as she was". That is a helpful hint. It points to the Platonism in the poem. But the Nonesuch comment is: "However this may be, the subject of the two poems was a real woman, a child rather, who died in 1610 at the age of fifteen." Two things are worth a word here. Doubtless, in one sense, Elizabeth Drury is the subject; but in a more important sense, the subject of the poem, what it is about, is something which only a good reading will discover. That discovery here is the poetic process. Secondly if we say "a child rather", we are being twentieth century, not seventeenth century. A fifteen year old girl was a woman for the seventeenth century. In Donne's poem *Upon the Annunciation and the Passion* he writes of the Virgin Mary:

> Sad and rejoyc'd shee's seen at once, and seen
> At almost fiftie and at scarce fifteene.

For Donne the Annunciation came to Mary when she was "scarce fifteene". Elizabeth's youth is of course no bar – rather the reverse – to Donne's taking her very seriously as a symbol. We may recall that Beatrice, when she first transfigured Dante, was "at the beginning of her ninth year almost" *(La Vita Nuova, II)*.

Dryden's *Ode* has long been an anthology piece. Dr. Johnson called it "the noblest Ode that our Language produced" and "the richest complex of sounds in our language". A modern critic has called this "a judgment then bold but now scarcely intelligible". There are seventy-five years between the poems.

Now let us consider the lines in detail and especially this question, "How closely should we be examining them in our reading?" I will take Dryden first. You may guess perhaps that even in taking him first here I am expressing a judgment between them.

How near should we come to the *Ode*? The only way to find out is by experimenting. Public declamation – the style of reading which the *Ode* suggests as right – does not invite close attention to the meaning.

The façade of a public building is not to be studied with a handglass. Gulliver, you remember, thought nothing of the complexions of the Brobdingnagian ladies. Let us try looking a little closer.

> *Thou youngest virgin-daughter of the skies*

Why "youngest virgin-daughter"? "Youngest" may here mean "new-born"; but then, why *virgin*? New-borns are necessarily virgins. And why, then, "daughter of the skies"? Do we need especially to be reminded that daughters of the skies – in Christian mythology – as denizens of Paradise, are virgins? On earth she was a virgin, it is true. In Heaven, there is neither marriage nor giving in marriage. And there is no special relation to the Virgin. We gain nothing by such ponderings here.

Again:

> *Whose palms, new plucked from Paradise*
> *In spreading branches more sublimely rise*
> *Rich with immortal green above the rest.*

Why *from* Paradise? Has she left it? Why not *in* Paradise? The answer might be in terms of resonance of the line.

But why should these palms of hers *more sublimely* rise? or be "rich with immortal green *above the rest*"? Do Paradisaic palms wilt and fade like florist's goods here on earth? Or does the row of palms get greener and greener, richer and richer, loftier and loftier, as we get further along the line from the first saints?

Clearly these questions and all others of the sort are quite irrelevant and out of place. We are looking too close, looking for a kind of poetic structure, an interinanimation of the words which is not there and is not needed for the proper purpose of the poem.

The same thing would appear if we questioned similarly Dryden's suggestions about what she is doing and where she is: on a planet, "in thy wandering race" or on a fixed star "in procession fixt and regular". Or if we wondered whether "the vast abyss" so described seems a *happy* region. Or again if we ask whether she need really stop singing to listen to Dryden. Or again whether Dryden really, for a moment, considers her earthly verses to have been such as his own voice is practising here? Of course, he doesn't. Or again, if we ask whether her *verses* could possibly make her welcome *in Paradise?* Or if they would advance her as a "candidate for heaven"? Or lastly if we asked why she is called an "inmate"? We shall see later that the same word in the Donne is packed with implications.

The outcome of all such close questioning is the same. Dryden's words have no such implications and we shall be misreading him if we hunt for them. In brief, this is not a poetry of Wit – in the technical. sense of the word in which Donne's verses are, as Coleridge called them,

> Wit's fire and fireblast, meaning's press and screw.

On this question of wit, let us listen to Dr. Johnson a moment. He is talking about conversation and has been comparing styles of conversation with beverages. He says,

Spirit alone is too powerful to use. It will produce madness rather than merriment; and instead of quenching thirst, will inflame the blood. Thus wit, too copiously poured out, agitates the hearer with emotions rather violent than pleasing; everyone shrinks from the force of its oppression, the company sits entranced and overpowered; all are astonished, but nobody is pleased.

One might retort, "Please, why should we please?" Or, when he says, "It will produce madness rather than merriment", we might recall the link between poetry and madness that has been noted from Plato's time to Shakespeare's. Dr. Johnson had deep personal reasons for distrusting this connection. He would have replied that he was talking about conversation, social intercourse. "Instead of quenching thirst", he says, "wit will inflame the blood." Quenching thirst? "Do you converse, Sir, in order to have had enough of it?" But Dr. Johnson's prose here no more requires us to pursue such implications and interinanimations than Dryden's verses.

Turn now to the Donne. Let us see what minute reading brings out of that.

> When that rich Soule which to her heaven is gone,

rich: in two senses – possessing much (a rich man); giving much (a rich mine). Compare Coleridge:

> Oh lady, we receive but what we give
> And in our life alone does Nature live.

or Croce: "Intuition is Expression": we HAVE only that which we can give out.

her heaven: again the double force; she possesses it and it possesses her, as with "her country", or "her place".

> Whom all do celebrate, who know they have one;

celebrate: a new word then in the sense of "praise, extol, or publish the fame of". This may be its first occurrence in that sense. Prior to 1611 it means 'commemorate or perform publicly and in due form (with a ritual – as in a celebration of the Eucharist) or solemnize'. There is a very serious suggestion of participation or partaking or ritual imitation. Thus, all who know they have a soul partake of that rich Soule, in knowing that (i.e. in having a soul). Then follows Donne's gloss:

> For who is sure he hath a Soule, unlesse
> It see, and judge, and follow worthiness;

sure is more than 'confident, without doubts about it'; it means 'safe, firm, immovable', because seeing, judging and following worthiness are themselves the very possession of a soul, not merely signs of having one. To see and judge and follow worthiness is to have a soul.
worthiness: excellence in the highest of all senses. That use was going out in Donne's time (1617).
And by Deedes praise it: no verbal praise, but imitation of or participation in actual works;

> he who doth not this,
> May lodge an In-mate soule, but 'tis not his.

in-mate: a word of very ill suggestions. We keep some of them in "an inmate of a penitentiary or an asylum". For Donne it suggests a lodger or a foreigner. Compare Milton:

> So spake the Enemie of Mankind, enclos'd
> In Serpent, Inmate bad, (P.L. ix, 495)

Who does not see and follow worthiness hasn't a soul but is possessed by something not truly him.

As so often with Donne, what seems a most farfetched conceit is no more than the result of taking a commonplace of language seriously. We say daily that a man is 'not himself' or 'beside himself' or 'not his true self', and we do the same thing when we say he is 'alienated' or call a psychopathologist an 'alienist'. Donne is just expanding such expressions, making their implications explicit, increasing their interinanimation, as heat increases chemical interaction. That is the technique of most 'metaphysical poetry'.

> When that Queene ended here her progresse time
> And, as t'her standing house to heaven did climb,

Here Donne's metaphor takes seriously the doctrine of the Divinity of Kings. The Ruler is to the body politic as the soul is to the body. Sickness or departure of the Ruler is sickness or death to the state. He is reversing the metaphor which created the doctrine of Divine Right. He adds a pun. A Queen made royal progresses through her dominions so that her subjects might come together and realize themselves as a State in her. But the soul, as in Bunyan, also makes a pilgrim's progress. Her "standing house" is where she RESTS at the end of her progress. Compare Augustine: "Thou has made us for Thyself and our souls are restless until they find their rest in Thee."

> Where loath to make the Saints attend her long,
> She's now a part both of the Quire, and Song,

A soul so conceived need not delay in joining the company of the Saints. *Quire:* How deep we could take this word you can see from Ruskin's note in *Munera Pulveris*. But the main point of the line is that the Soul becomes both a singer and the song. That goes to the heart of Aristotelianism – where the Divine thinking is one with the object of its thought. (Metaphysics 1075 a). It is itself that thought (or intellect) thinks, on account of its participation in the object of thought: for it becomes its own object in the act of apprehending it: so that thought (intellect) and what is thought of are one and the same. We come back here to our founding questions where the distinction between matter and activity vanishes – as it does for the modern physicist when his ultimate particles become merely what they do.

But to elucidate Donne's line it is better perhaps just to quote another poet: from the last verse of W. B. Yeats's "Among School Children" in *The Tower*:

> O Chestnut tree, great rooted blossomer,
> Are you the leaf, the blossom or the bole?
> O body swayed to music, O brightening glance,
> How can we know the dancer from the dance?

or this from T. S. Eliot's *Burnt Norton*:

> At the still point of the turning world . . .
>   at the still point, there the dance is,
> But neither arrest nor movement. And do not call
>   it fixity . . .
>   Except for the point, the still point,
> There would be no dance, and there is only the dance.

Donne's next line contains the word upon which, with the word Soule
– as on two poles – the entire interpretation of this poem turns, as for
that matter all philosophy must, the word *world*.

> This world, in that great earthquake languished;

world: not of course this planet, the earth, but this present life as
opposed to the other, the realm of departed spirits. Or more narrowly
"the pursuits and interests of the earthly life", as the *Oxford Dictionary*
puts it, with the note, "especially in religious use, the least worthy of
these". Donne was extremely fond of playing with the word "world".
It is one of the chief of his wonder workers. Compare *A Valediction of
Weeping*:

> On a round ball
> A workman that hath copies by, can lay
> An Europe, Afrique, and an Asia,
> And quickly make that which was nothing, *All*,
> So doth each teare,
> Which thee doth weare,
> A globe, yea world by that impression grow,
> Till thy tears mixt with mine doe overflow
> This world, by waters sent from thee, my heaven dissolved so.

That is metaphysical metaphor at its height. Donne, of course, plays
throughout his poem on shifts between the private solipsistic world and
the general public world of mundane interests. It is his general theme
that both these worlds die, corrupt, and disintegrate in the absence of
the Soule – as defined in the parenthesis of lines 3 to 6.

Is this extravagance? Is the poem a "preposterous eulogy"? Is it not
rather that Donne is saying something which if said in our everyday
style would seem so commonplace that we would not notice what we
were saying? If so, what was he saying? To put it with our usual crude
and unilluminating briefness, he was saying that Elizabeth Drury was
an example, an inspiration, and would have been to all who knew her.
That looks little enough to say, IF SO SAID. It took a Donne to expand
the implications of those two words "example" and "inspiration" into
the poem. But the more we look into the poem, the more we will discover that the understanding of those two words is an understanding
of the whole Platonic Aristotelian account of the fabric of things. These
words take their meaning, by participation, directly from the founding
questions. The best witness will be the closing lines of *The Second
Anniversary*:

nor would'st thou be content,
To take this, for my second yeares true Rent,
Did this Coine beare any other stampe, than his,
That gave thee power to doe, me, to say this.
Since his will is, that to posteritie,
Thou should'st for life, and death, a patterne bee,
And that the world should notice have of this:
The purpose, and th'authoritie is his;
Thou art the Proclamation; and I am
The Trumpet, at whose voyce the people came.

To read the poem rightly would be to hear and come.

7. "THE EXSTASIE"

I am taking a poem now which has been understood in very different ways and praised and blamed for surprisingly different reasons. It is John Donne's "The Exstasie", first printed in 1633, probably written in 1611.

In my TV talks I treated it in two installments. In the first I read it verse by verse supplying as much commentary on the puzzling words and phrases as they seem to need if one is to be able to take the poem as a whole and ask oneself: What is it? What is it saying? How should I understand it?

In the second installment I presented a few of the more sharply opposed opinions on it formed by equally able readers (as far as any academic qualifications and standing can vouch for that.)

Here, I omit this exhibit feeling that it would unnecessarily expose readers whose other opinions I much respect.

(*Stanza* 1)   Where, like a pillow on a bed,
        A Pregnant banke swel'd up, to rest
    The violets reclining head,
        Sat we two, one anothers best;

To a newcomer to the poem the first puzzling thing is the scenery, isn't it? This mixture of bedroom and out of doors. And many people feel a discomfort over this *violet* and its *reclining head*. How small a bank would do that?

However, violets are mentioned again: the lovers are in some way like violets and they are to rest their own reclining heads through most of the rest of the poem.

The fourth line is the one to ponder. Note that at this stage they are sitting

        Sat we two, one another's best;

Not only: each the one the other likes best, but: each the one who is best for the other. The poem is going to be about what this being *best* is, and in the deepest possible sense of *best*.

(*Stanza* 2)   Our hands were firmely cimented
             With a fast balme, which thence did spring,
         Our eye-beames twisted, and did thred
             Our eyes, upon one double string;

They are hand in hand. *cimented*: secured together, *fast balme*: balm of Gilead, warmth and comfort; a place of shelter and protection in the Alps is often a *balme*.

It's the next two lines which make people blink. These eyes which are gazing into one another so are close together here: so close that each pair of eyes sees and is seen as only one eye ... over near ... almost unseen and unseeing. Notice how the strain is conveyed. You can verify if you like – with a mirror.

(*Stanza* 3)   So to'entergraft our hands, as yet
             Was all our meanes to make us one,
         And pictures on our eyes to get
             Was all our propagation.

Pictures on our eyes to get: The lovers separating their faces a little become able to see now – each on the gleaming surface of the other's eyes (or within the pupil's inkwell) miniature images of their own heads. It's not just "We can see reflections of one another" but "Within one another's eyes images of ourselves seem already to be living".

Let me quote you Shakespeare on this. Here is Achilles in *Troilus and Cressida* Act III, Scene iii, 103-110.

> The beauty that is borne here in the face
> The bearer knows not, but commends itself
> To other's eyes: nor doth the eye itself —
> That most pure spirit of sense — behold itself,
> Not going from itself; but eye to eye oppos'd
> Salutes each other with each other's form;
> For speculation turns not to itself
> Till it hath travell'd and is mirror'd there
> Where it may see itself.

Note the six-fold repetitions of "itself": this is deep reflection on the self – just as Donne's poem is going to be. One other thing: some very good judges think Shakespeare really wrote *married there* – not *mirror'd there* and that *mirror'd there* is just an editorial effort to make Shakespeare more obvious.

To go back to Donne: *as yet* is fair warning – isn't it? – that far deeper *meanes to make us one* are to follow.

(Stanza 4)   As 'twixt two equal Armies, Fate
        Suspends uncertaine victorie,
    Our soules, (which to advance their state,
        Were gone out,) hung 'twixt her, and mee.

What is this sudden and surprising military metaphor doing here? We are suddenly swept off into the atmosphere of high politics or of *The Iliad:* Achilles chasing Hector round Troy and Zeus hanging up his golden balance.

gone out: to battle, that is; "gone out" has been a way of saying 'fought a duel'.

to advance their state: in a spirit of self-aggrandisement, each the would-be out-doer, conquerer, subjugator, of the other. But they are *two equal Armies*. It won't do. There can be no military outcome. Nor can it be a sort of cold-war situation. They are *one anothers best* – as they are now coming to know.

(Stanza 5)   And whil'st our soules negotiate there,
        Wee like sepulchrall statues lay;
    All day, the same our postures were,
        And wee said nothing, all the day.

What a change from the eye to eye posture of stanza 2. Here, in this grim tombstone image, they lie like effigies of the dead: *sepulchrall statues*. Why? Is it because that *victorie* business had threatened a sort of death to their love? Or is it rather a reminder that the going forth of the soul in ecstasy leaves the body as though it were dead?

(Stanzas   If any, so by love refin'd
6 and 7)   That he soules language understood,
    And by good love were grown all minde,
        Within convenient distance stood,

    He (though he knew not which soule spake,
        Because both meant, both spake the same)
    Might thence a new concoction take,
        And part farre purer then he came.

Poems do often, and rightly, stop off to tell the reader what they are doing. Here for 2 verses *The Exstasie* does this.

so by love refin'd: this poem is, I take it, a description of how this refining, this purifying is done. The root meaning of *fine,* here, is 'end, aim': made again as it should be. Refining is especially the process of separating metal from ore and the poem is going to talk of dross and alloy later.

soules language: as distinguished from what tongues can say. They *said nothing, all the day.* But the souls in their negotiation talk on and on. What they agree upon is reported in the rest of the poem which is simply this report. *And by good love were grown all minde:* the report is going to explain, very exactly, that *grown all minde* doesn't mean the exclusion or disregard of the body but its development to become one with mind.

concoction: a sort of ripening or remaking by heat, as in cooking; *farre purer:* the poem is going to explain what it means by that. Perhaps, though, an excerpt from the Book of Wisdom may be helpful:

For wisdom, which is the worker of all things, taught me; for in her is an understanding spirit, holy, one only, manifold, subtil, lively, clear, having all power, overseeing all things, and going through all understanding, pure and most subtil spirits. For wisdom is more moving than any motion: she passeth and goeth through all things by reason of her pureness. (*Wisdom,* vii)

In what follows through the rest of the poem these two souls become one joint and abler soul – *both meant, both spake the same:* the outcome in any qualified hearer (reader) is a *new concoction* in him, the new truth that "the worker of all things" has enabled them, *who are this new soule,* to learn.

Here is the account of ecstasy which Grierson quotes from Plotinus:

Even the word, 'vision', does not seem appropriate here. It is rather an ecstasy, a simplification, an abandonment of self, a desire of contact, a perfect quietude, in short, a wish to merge oneself in that which one contemplates in the Sanctuary.

(Sixth Ennead ix, ii.)

(*Stanza* 8)   This Exstasie doth unperplex
                 (We said) and tell us what we love,
             Wee see by this, it was not sexe,
             Wee see, we saw not what did move:

doth unperplex: what has been perplexed, tangled, ravelled becomes simpler.

and tell us what we love: the greatest of all our quests is to learn what it is we love.

it was not sexe: according to the Oxford Dictionary this is the first appearance of the word *sex* – in this its distinctively modern use. It looks as if Donne introduced this meaning for it. What a career it has had!

Wee see, we saw not what did move: both (1) We see now, and did not see before, what did move; and (2) We see that we did not see then, what did move. Now *what did move?* What does this mean? – especially if we take it together with *what we love?*

Let me show you a passage from Plato's *Republic* and one from Aristotle's *Metaphysics* which, I think, can help a lot.

Socrates: Isn't it clear that there are plenty of people who are ready enough to *seem* just, or to have what *seems* beautiful, without its being at all so in fact; but when it comes to the good, everyone wants the thing itself and what only *seems* good isn't good enough for anyone.
Adeimantus: That's so.
Socrates: This, then, is what every soul is looking for, and for this every soul does all that it does, feeling in some way what it is, but troubled and uncertain and unable to see clearly enough.

Republic, Book VI (50 6E)

It is the Idea of the Good that is really, in and behind all we do, what everyone, all the time, is seeking.

And here is what Aristotle did with this hint:

There is a mover which moves without being moved, being eternal . . .
And the object of thought and the object of desire move in this way; they move without being moved.

(*Metaphysics,* 1072a)

Since the Ecstasy can *tell us what we love* it thereby makes us *see . . . what did move.*

(*Stanza* 9)   But as all severall soules containe
                    Mixture of things, they know not what,
            Love, these mixt soules, doth mixe againe,
            And makes both one, each this and that.

several soules: separate souls.

they know not what they have in them: When they become one soul they do know just that.

each this and that: each is both. 'Each is both': here is Coomaraswamy on the Indian concept of love:

In India ... sexual love has a deep and spiritual significance. There is nothing with which we can better compare the 'mystic union' of the finite with its infinite ambient ... than the selfoblivion of earthly lovers locked in each other's arms, where 'each is both'.

(Ananda Coomaraswamy, *The Dance of Shiva*, p. 124)

(Stanza 10)   A single violet transplant,
      The strength, the colour, and the size,
  (All which before was poore, and scant,)
      Redoubles still, and multiplies.

Helen Gardner comments: "I believe Donne is referring to the fact that transplantation will produce double from single flowers" and gives contemporary references (*The Elegies and the Song and Sonnets*, p. 185)

(Stanza 11)   When love, with one another so
      Interinanimates two soules,
  That abler soule, which thence doth flow,
      Defects of lonelinesse controules.

interinanimates: like two logs each of which makes the other flame the better.
Defects of lonelinesse: the chief of which is ignorance, ignorance of what we are.
When *that abler soule* comes into being

(Stanza 12)   Wee then, who are this new soule, know,
      Of what we are compos'd, and made,
  For, th'Atomies of which we grow,
      Are soules, whom no change can invade.

Now comes a turning point of the poem and the place from which the greatest differences of opinion as to what the poem is doing chiefly start out. We should remember that the two are still using *soules language* together.

(Stanza 13)   But O alas, so long, so farre
      Our bodies why doe wee forbeare?
  They'are ours, though they'are not wee, Wee are
      Th'intelligences, they the spheare.

forbeare: some want to take this in the sense 'endure, put up with'. Push that far enough and you would get "Why don't we commit suicide?" Others take *forbeare* as 'control, refrain, desist and abstain, keep from using and enjoying'. You have to choose here according to how you understand the rest.

Th'intelligences . . . the spheare: This is Ptolemaic astronomy: each of the nine concentric spheres has its angelic intelligence which governs it. Here the two souls who have become this abler soul have a joint sphere: their bodies.

(*Stanza* 14)   We owe them thankes, because they thus,
        Did us, to us, at first convay,
     Yeelded their forces, sense, to us,
        Nor are drosse to us, but allay.

Did us, to us, at first convay: For example, it was their bodies which first enabled them to see and talk to one another.

Yeelded their forces, sense, to us: their forces, that is to say their sensory powers, appetites etc. And they are not *drosse* – worthless remainder to be thrown away – but *alloy* – like the nickel, etc. which can make steel so much stronger, sharper etc. than iron.

(*Stanza* 15)   On man heavens influence workes not so,
        But that it first imprints the ayre,
     Soe soule into the soule may flow,
        Though it to body first repaire.

Medieval physics. They did not think that planets and stars could influence people except through doing something to the air. Action at a distance did not seem reasonable.

(*Stanza* 16)   As our blood labours to beget
        Spirits, as like soules as it can,
     Because such fingers need to knit
        That subtile knot, which makes us man:

Medieval physiology: The animal spirits produced by the blood were thought necessary to tie soul and body together. But, beyond this, and well within the probable influences from Plato impinging upon Donne (via whatever Leone Ebreo or other channels) is what may reasonably be regarded as the central thought of the theory of Government taught in *The Republic*: the role of Spirit in the governance of the individual, and equally, of the executive and police in the ruling of the state. This may most simply and directly be conveyed by a diagram. It is NOT Plato's but a recent derivative:

The head: Seat of the Government: the Guardians, Organ of knowledge, the *psyche,* the Guardians.

The thorax: Seat of Spirit, organ of courage and control, breathing
and heart, the Guards.

The abdomen Source of energies, nutriment, desires, the productive
component: the workers.

The Poem may be telling us that, correspondent to the physiological
Spirits needed *to knit*

> That subtile knot, which makes us man:

there are, as Socrates so elaborately insists in *The Republic,* an order
of agencies needed to intermediate BETWEEN the Guardians and the
energy suppliers, the Workers, and equally between the soul and the
senses. These intermediaries (the affections, feelings, and attitudes:
'the sentiments' we might call them: tenderness, pity, regard . . . and
the faculties, the volitional system: resolution, courage, the impulse
to help, to sustain . . .) are what the next, the key stanza, is about.

(*Stanza* 17)   So must pure lovers soules descend
         T'affections, and to faculties,
    Which sense may reach and apprehend
    Else a great Prince in prison lies.

Not altogether surprisingly it is these climactic lines which, textually
as well as semiotically, have been less uniformly interpreted than any
others. Donne's latest editor, Helen Gardner, has felt a difficulty so
strongly that "against the consensus of 1633 and all manuscripts" she
has "amended 'Which' to 'that' . . . assuming that 'Which' was sub-
stituted under the mistaken notion that 'That' was the relative and not
the conjunction". (p. 187) She adds "If we read 'That' (in order that)
the action of the souls parallels the action of the blood". But this can
equally be secured if we retain 'Which' provided we give the poem
credit for knowing and using here its *Republic*. The doubts Gardner
mentions (p. 259) "over the genuineness of the poem's 'Platonism'"
may have been the doubters' rather than the poem's fault. She reports
– out of her unequalled acquaintance with and deep study of what
has been written hitherto on "The Exstasie" – some questioning by the
most qualified – typically, and most notably, by Grierson, himself –
as to its complete success. My own feeling is that the poem, as Dame
Helen suggests, set itself initially as its problem the exploration of
ecstasy. I find that it succeeded, but by asking of its readers an under-

standing of Plato's prime theme in the *Republic* that they have not, all
of them, been able to bring. In the *Republic* just as the philosopher
kings, Lovers of Knowledge whose virtue is Wisdom, require their
executives, Lovers of Honor whose virtue is Courage, in order to rule
over the rest of the citizens, Lovers of Pleasure (or profit) whose virtue
should be Sophrosyne, so in the man who is the small letter analogue
to the great letters of the State, Knowledge and the senses (and their
desires) are too far apart. They need recourse, both of them, to the
intermediaries

> T'affections, and to faculties,
> Which sense may reach and apprehend,
> Else a great Prince in prison lies.

The grammatical possibilities are extraordinarily flexible here:

Which sense may reach and apprehend: Which way do you take
that? Is it the affections and faculties which reach and apprehend sense
– as a policeman can apprehend a disturber of the peace? Or is it sense
which manages to understand and take in what the affections and the
faculties would teach it? It makes curiously little difference provided
we realize that only through this *descent* of the soul to *affections* and
to *faculties* can this *great Prince* be free'd from prison.

And what is this great Prince? Some say it is Love; some say it is
the Soul; some that it is Sense; and some that it is none of these sep-
arately but the whole Man which includes Soul, the affections and
faculties AND sense. We should remember that it is the business of a
Prince to rule.

Whatever it is, there is a conclusive sort of ring in *Else a great Prince
in prison lies* which seems to warn us that here is the point, the end,
the summit of the poem.

In the last two stanzas the lovers' souls returning from their ecstasy
proceed exactly thus to *descend,* to put into effect their rule, via the
sentiments, over the senses, and their appetites.

(Stanza 18) To'our bodies turne wee then, that so
          Weake men on love reveal'd may looke;
        Loves mysteries in soules doe grow,
          But yet the body is his booke.

The poem continues to divide its readers into groups with extremely
different positions for living.

To our bodies turne wee then: we have to choose a meaning for *To
our bodies* which will join up with

But O alas, so long, so farre
Our bodies why doe wee forbeare?

And again in

(*Stanza* 19)   And if some lover, such as wee,
                    Have heard this dialogue of one,
                Let him still marke us, he shall see
                    Small change, when we'are to bodies gone.

for *to bodies gone.*

There are those – as we shall see – who put a very simple meaning
into these phrases: physical intercourse. And of these, some profess
to be shocked, as others are gleefully excited at what they take to be a
startling exhibitionism. We have to remember, however, that this *lover,*
such as wee, who has, throughout *this dialogue of one soules language*
understood, as before he had to listen to what the lovers, who *said*
nothing, all the day, did not utter, so now he is invited to *marke* what
is invisible. The more closely we read the poem, I believe, the less we
will be tempted to any simple meaning. We, like this witness, *shall see*
Small change. Out of their ecstasy, as within it, order will rule. Their
Spirits[1] will continue *to knit*

That subtile knot, which makes us man.

---

[1]   (Plato's 'spirited part', parallelled so curiously by 'the thin and active part of
the blood', 'the instrument of the soule, to perform all his actions' 'able to ... apply
the faculties of the soul to the organs of the body'. See Burton and Donne cited
in Gardner, pp. 186-187.)

8. "THE GARDEN"

Marvell's *The Garden* is four lines shorter than Donne's *The Exstasie*, and there is quite as much to be found behind and in it. Newcomers to it often take a little while getting used to its peculiar mixture of tones and their interplay. So let us read it in a leisurely, sauntering fashion appropriate to a garden. It is a highly compressed, whimsical, reflective, contemplative poem; and it would be most unseemly to hurry.

Let me read it all through, slowly, first, – it is in nine eight-line stanzas. Then we will look at the general structure and come down to detail.

THE GARDEN

How vainly men themselves amaze
To win the Palm, the Oke, or Bayes;
And their uncessant Labours see
Crown'd from some single Herb or Tree.
Whose short and narrow verged Shade
Does prudently their Toyles upbraid;
While all Flow'rs and all Trees do close
To weave the Garlands of repose.

Fair quiet, have I found thee here,
And Innocence thy Sister dear!
Mistaken long, I sought you then
In busie Companies of Men.
Your sacred Plants, if here below,
Only among the Plants will grow.
Society is all but rude,
To this delicious Solitude.

No white nor red was ever seen
So am'rous as this lovely green.
Fond Lovers cruel as their Flame
Cut in these Trees their Mistress name.

Little, Alas, they know, or heed,
How far these Beauties Hers exceed!
Fair Trees! where s'eer your barkes I wound,
No Name shall but your own be found.

When we have run our Passions heat,
Love hither makes his best retreat.
The *Gods*, that mortal Beauty chase,
Still in a Tree did end their race.
Apollo hunted *Daphne* so,
Only that She might Laurel grow.
And *Pan* did after *Syrinx* speed,
Not as a Nymph, but for a Reed.

What wond'rous Life in this I lead!
Ripe Apples drop about my head;
The Luscious Clusters of the Vine
Upon my Mouth do crush their Wine;
The Nectaren, and curious Peach,
Into my hands themselves do reach;
Stumbling on Melons, as I pass,
Insnar'd with Flow'rs, I fall on Grass.

Mean while the Mind, from pleasure less,
Withdraws into its happiness:
The Mind, that Ocean where each kind
Does streight its own resemblance find;
Yet it creates, transcending these,
Far other Worlds, and other Seas;
Annihilating all that's made
To a green Thought in a green Shade.

Here at the Fountains sliding foot,
Or at some Fruit-trees mossy root,
Casting the Bodies Vest aside,
My Soul into the boughs does glide:
There like a Bird it sits, and sings,
Then whets, and combs its silver Wings;
And, till prepar'd for longer flight,
Waves in its Plumes the various Light.

Such was that happy Garden-state,
While Man there walk'd without a Mate:
After a Place so pure, and sweet,
What other Help could yet be meet!
But 'twas beyond a Mortal's share
To wander solitary there:
Two Paradises 'twere in one
To live in Paradise alone.

How well the skilful Gardner drew
Of flow'rs and herbes this Dial new;
Where from above the milder Sun
Does through a fragrant Zodiack run;
And, as it works, th' industrious Bee
Computes its time as well as we.
How could such sweet and wholsome Hours
Be reckon'd but with herbs and flow'rs!

Now for a kind of diagram of the over-all motion of the poem. We can use the same sort of division from The *Republic* that we used in discussing *The Extasie*:

    I. The love of Honor
   II. Quiet and Solitude
III-V. The love of Pleasure
VI-VII. The love of Wisdom
 VIII. Paradise Regained
   IX. Coda

In the first stanza the ambitious, of all sorts, are mocked at.

In the second, the Garden is praised by contrast with the scenes where men strive to win Honor.

In the third, it is praised in comparison with the objects Fond Lovers pursue.

In the fourth, Poetry and Music make fun of these Fond Lovers and prepare for the sixth.

In the fifth, the Garden woos the Poet.

In the sixth, Philosophy affirms its supremacy.

In the seventh, the Mind prepares for Heaven.

In the eighth and ninth, the poem climbs wittily and delicately down from this altitude.

That is, as I see it, the motion, very roughly sketched. But its steps weave in and out through a Ballet of Thoughts with all sorts of advances and retreats, leaps and turns: tantalizing the reader, leaving him guessing and guessing again as to:

1. Whether and how far the poem takes itself seriously.

2. Whether there isn't a sort of semi-private game going on of teasing somebody who isn't openly addressed or mentioned.

3. Whether the garden is just a garden or something more august than even a Garden, cultivate it how we will, can stand for.

4. And whether part of the shimmer of the poem – "the various light" of it – isn't given by its being sometimes just an actual garden, sometimes much, much more.

I am trying with this to suggest reasons why we can't expect to agree easily on all its points – as we will see when we get down to the details. The whole poem from title to close is an invitation to plant things in it; and it is only too easy to lose it in quarrels between gardeners.

However, let's see!

> How vainly men themselves amaze
> To win the Palm, the Oke, or Bayes;
> And their uncessant Labours see
> Crown'd from some single Herb or Tree.

amaze: greatly astonish? Yes, but like people who are lost in a maze too; they become less and less able to find their way out. In *Paradise Lost,* Book IX, when Satan – the most ambitious character in literature and the greatest of all Lovers of Honor[1]: – is tempting Eve to be equally ambitious with him, this word *amaze* comes back and back as he talks on.

Line 551 *Not unamazed, she thus in answer spake –*

Line 613   *and Eve*
         Yet more amazed, unwary thus replied.

and in

Line 640 the "dire snake" is compared to the will o' the wisp which
         Misleads th' amazed night wanderer from his way.

Milton, composing these lines perhaps very few years later, might have known *The Garden.*

How vainly: both 'Through what vanity' and 'With what futility'.

To win the Palm, the Oke, or Bayes: emblems and tokens of success, triumph, fame. And do not let us trouble ourselves about which of them honors what. Together, these awards make up not a bad symbol of a maze.

> Whose short and narrow verged Shade
> Does prudently their Toyles upbraid;
> While all Flow'rs and all Trees do close
> To weave the Garlands of repose.

---

[1] *Wolsey:* By that sin fell the angels. (*Henry VIII*, III, ii, 442.)

narrow verged Shade: We need a thermal and visual image here, say, of a Roman consul, preferably bald, riding through Rome in his Triumph – with only a thin circlet of leaves to shield him from the scorching rays of the sun.

Toyles: 'labours' of course, but also, 'nets and snares'. There are two especially grand quotations which back up this meaning: the first is Octavius Caesar at the end of *Antony and Cleopatra* when he sees Cleopatra, dead:

> she looks like sleep
> As she would catch another Antony
> In her strong toil of grace.

The other is from Milton :

> Extol not Riches then, the toyl of Fools.

The suggestion here is that the rich are fools because they have caught themselves in their own contrivances. The same suggestion comes in the ironic *prudently* and in *upbraid* with its background pun *(upbraid*: 'censure, scold' AND 'interweave, plait'

do close: as opposed to all that the first six lines have been about, *close* has a very strong suggestion of rest and shelter; Cathedral closes, the cloister feeling. Compare Thomas Tusser's

> In the pleasant orchard closes
> God bless all our gains say we
> But may God bless all our losses
> Better suits with our degree.

These two lines are closing the first stanza as the last stanza will close the poem.

> Fair quiet, have I found thee here,
> And Innocence thy Sister dear!
> Mistaken long, I sought you then
> In busie Companies of Men.

What sort of Quiet and Innocence would a man seek *In busie Companies of Men?* Something more than mere absence of noise and din. We have to put into *Fair quiet* and *Innocence* something like those *first affections* which in Wordworth's *Intimations Ode*

> have power to make
> Our noisy years seem moments in the being
> Of the eternal Silence.

> Your sacred Plants, if here below,
> Only among the Plants will grow.
> Society is all but rude,
> To this delicious Solitude.

These mysterious plants may not grow at all on Earth, but, if they do, it will be in this Garden.

Society: supposed to set standards of civility and politeness, is almost

rude: 'crude, uncultivated' compared with this delicious Solitude.

Aristotle (and after him Lord Bacon) observed "A man who would live to himself alone must be either a Beast or a God.

Now comes the transition from Lovers of Honor to Fond Lovers, lovers of mortal beauty. After repudiating the *busie Companies of Men* the poem now seems gaily willing to decline even the company of an Eve in this *Paradise Regained.*

This is the beginning of a vein of teasing. It is almost as though the poem had in part been written to say to some girl in the most acceptable possible fashion: "Look here! I see a lot of you in other places. I want this garden for my meditations."

> No white nor red was ever seen
> So am'rous as this lovely green.
> Fond Lovers, cruel as their Flame,
> Cut in these Trees their Mistress name.

white nor red: conventional poetic shorthand of the period for pretty faces: white for brow and neck and teeth, red for cheeks and lips. But what about this *green* which is so much more *am'rous* than white or red?

am'rous: in love and of love, giving love and receiving love. We hear more of this lovely green in stanza six. But it is worth, I think, noting here that *green* is the color of HOPE. When Beatrice – who is Theology – receives Dante in the Earthly Paradise at the top of Mount Purgatory she is wearing GREEN in addition to the WHITE and RED she wore on earth.

There is a risk of a misapprehension here. This poem isn't a cryptogram, a secret message we have somehow to decode! None should suppose that references such as this are actually IN the poem (only under cover) and that a reader has to know them before or guess them correctly in order to read it aright. If that were true there wouldn't be much hope for Poetry, would there?

It is more like this: These meanings are in the poem because they are in the language, as servant and supporter of the tradition. Any poem which is using language with a lively sense of how words have been variously used before it, invites a certain sort of academic to think of instances which may help to suggest and bring out the latent powers of the words. But that needn't (and shouldn't, I think) imply that anyone would have to know any of these sorts of things in order to enjoy the poem.

I remember being extraordinarily happy reading *The Garden* long before I ever had to talk about it to anyone. It was only when I found myself preparing a lecture on it that many of these background things occurred to me. I am pretty sure I never thought of them before. All this sort of commentary is only a way of trying to bring out the flavours in the words.

Fond Lovers: a mocking phrase: they are fond, yes, but they are foolish; they are as foolish as their fond hopes.

cruel as their Flame: Why do they put themselves and their 'dear objects' to such pains? Why do their 'dear objects' give THEM such a time!

Flame: The poem is enjoying this word particularly. Let me fan it a little with a small story:

An Old Lady was giving a hand-out at her door to a Tramp and the Tramp was telling her in return his life-story.
  "Yes, my lady, time was when I had money to burn. And where I made my mistake was — I did burn it!"
  "And what did you burn it with, my good man?"
  "With an Old Flame of mine, my lady!"

It is a ranging word, *flame:* in an especially poignant use Shakespeare's *Phoenix* and his *Turtle are fled / In a mutual flame from hence.*

> Little, Alas, they know, or heed
> How far these Beauties Hers exceed!
> Fair Trees! where s'eer your barkes I wound,
> No Name shall but your own be found.

How seriously are you going to take that?

Little, Alas, they know: If you took it quite literally: "Really, you know, these beeches and so on are much more beautiful than girls" where would you be? Why stalking around with Reginald Bunthorne in Gilbert and Sullivan's *Patience*:

> If he's content with a vegetable love,
> Which would certainly *not* suit me,
> Why, what a particularly pure young man
> This pure young man must be!

It seems likely that Gilbert borrowed *vegetable love* from Marvell's "To his Coy Mistress".

If these are somehow not literally trees, what are they? Let us not overdo it, but – once you have Paradise and Greek myths being mentioned in a poem – trees can become very remarkable: Trees of Knowledge, of Eternal Life, and more too, as we see in the next verse.

> When we have run our Passions heat,
> Love hither makes his best retreat.
> The Gods, that mortal Beauty chase,
> Still in a Tree did end their race.

This stanza is one of the most elaborate nests of puns in all poetry.

heat: as heat in a race, was a new word just coming in round 1650 – the sporting-lingo smack to it is hardly exalting, is it? Moreover there is the suggestion that the Runners haven't even got into the semi-final. The point of running heats is to eliminate entrants. The other meanings for *heat* here aren't any more dignifying. To cool down

> Love hither makes his best retreat.

An army *retreats* after defeat, or to avoid defeat. But it is just like Marvell that, at the same time, there is a still bigger and better meaning of the word – the religious sense of *retreat* coming in, as the rest of the poem shows. And there is *Genesis,* 6:1,2, "And it came to pass, that the sons of God saw the daughters of men that they were fair; and they took them wives of all that they chose." Also to be thought of is Blake's Proverb of Hell: "Eternity is in love with the productions of Time." Neither of these is in the poem but between them they light up things the stanza is playing with.

Again, it is Marvell all over that together with religious RETREAT from the WORLD two delicious metamorphoses come skipping in with another reverberating pun

> Still in a Tree did end their race.

race: their chasing and racing, yes, AND their progeny, their family line too. Baffled, frustrated in these escapades? Not at all: these outcomes were just what was intended. These Gods are not so silly after all, as the verse goes on to explain.

> Apollo hunted Daphne so,
> Only that She might Laurel grow.
> And Pan did after *Syrinx* speed,
> Not as a Nymph, but for a Reed.

Daphne, you recall, was turned into a Laurel bush to escape Apollo and Syrinx into a reed to baffle Pan.

Laurel: as in Poet Laureate, the laurel crown of poetry. (How well the second line of the poem avoids the word Laurel!)

Reed: the panpipes made from the reeds Syrinx turned into.

As Miss Bradbrook and Miss Lloyd Thomas justly remark in their admirable book on Marvell:

> He finds, as the gods found, that the only lasting satisfaction for the instincts is an activity which does not employ them for their original purpose.
> (*Andrew Marvell* by M. C. Bradbrook and M. G. Lloyd Thomas, p. 60.)

Marvell keeps this theory of the origin of Poetry and Music in sublimated passion from becoming stodgy partly by extraordinary compression – partly by a tone of tender mockery: "You may have thought otherwise, my dear; but . . ."

We are far from invited to sympathize with poor Apollo or poor Pan or poor Daphne or poor Syrinx. Compare Keats' "Hymn to Pan" in *Endymion*

> Bethinking thee how melancholy loth
> Thou wast to lose fair Syrinx

Marvell's Pan here is just the opposite. Not *melancholy loth*, not at all! Cheerfully eager!

But, to avoid putting Keats and Marvell into any misconceived and false antithesis, let us recall some further lines from this "Hymn to Pan". Besides being

> Hearkener to the loud-clapping shears,

the Hoof-heel'd One is there,

> Dread opener of the doors
> Of universal knowledge.

Next time we will go on to the philosophic, the contemplative, the Neo-Platonic parts of the poem. It too describes an ecstasy.

II

There has been controversy as to how relevant biography can be to the interpretation of a poem. But this is a question we could only decide from case to case and by trying. As Mao Tse Tung puts it: "No investigation, no opinion."

How about this as a general recommendation? That we should read a poem as carefully as we can FIRST and turn to the biographical information AFTERWARDS – to see how it goes along with or goes against what we have felt already about the poem?

With Marvell's *The Garden* there is a certain amount of useful information. It is very probable indeed that he wrote it in 1650 while he was living at Nunappleton House in Yorkshire, acting as tutor to Mary Fairfax, the daughter of Lord Fairfax. Marvell was a highly accomplished linguist and was teaching Mary "the tongues". She would be 12 or 13 when he went there. There is a good deal about the poem which belongs probably to the Nunappleton atmosphere. Lord Fairfax – one of the greater soldiers of the time – had somewhat surprisingly retired, given up his high position and gone to live in the country.

The opening stanzas on the renunciation of ambition and the search for the *sacred plants* of *Fair quiet* and *Innocence* fit the setting well. Marvell wrote a long poem of 97 stanzas in the same measure called *Upon Appleton House, to My Lord Fairfax*, full of astonishingly vivid pictures of the scene and ending up with a grand mock-celebration of *the young Maria* and her *judicious eyes*

> She that already is the Law
> Of all her sex, her Ages Aw.

You can see very well what these hyperboles are up to.

Some of the stanzas are strong and straight didactic poetry. How do you like this one:

> Go now fond Sex that on your Face
> Do all your useless Study place
> Nor once at Vice your Brows dare knit
> Lest the smooth Forehead wrinkled sit.
> Yet your own Face shall at you grin,
> Thorough the Black-bag of your Skin;
> When *Knowledge* only could have fill'd
> And *Virtue* all those Furrows till'd.

You'll see, as I go on, why I have quoted this. *Fond sex* here incidentally points up *Fond lovers* in *The Garden*. One stanza sums up the main theme of *The Garden*.

> For *She*, to higher Beauties rais'd,
> Disdains to be for lesser prais'd.
> *She* counts her Beauty to converse
> In all the Languages as *hers*;

That is clearly written – isn't it? – for his pupil's benefit. But, *to higher Beauties rais'd*, can help us with Stanza VI of *The Garden*

> Meanwhile the Mind, from pleasures less,
> Withdraws into its happiness.

Note how it goes on:

> Nor yet in those *her self* imployes
> But for the *Wisdome*, not the *Noyse*;
> Nor yet that *Wisdome* would affect,
> But as 'tis Heavens Dialect.

Noyse: not the pronunciation only, acquiring ability to scream away in the various tongues, but all the distractions. The communications engineer today defines NOISE as 'additions to the signal not proceeding from the source' and Marvell here (as in *The Garden*) is concerned as deeply as anyone ever could be – with the SOURCE, the ultimate source – that from which all comes.

> Nor yet that *Wisdome* would affect

affect: pretend to have – all the affectations, pretensions (as we would say) of scholarship.

> But as 'tis Heavens Dialect.

Dialect: What is talked in Heaven, yes. (I am reminded of the New England worthy who began the study of Greek in his 80th year. When someone asked him why, he replied: "O, I expect to find it so useful in the next world.") But there could be much more in the word *Dialect* than this. There could be the Platonic Dialectic and here are two pieces of Plato's account of that:

The ability to render and exact an account of the true being of things.
(Republic 534B)
Taking the arts and sciences together into a synoptic view of their connections with one another and with what truly is.
(537 C)

Where are we now?

Ready to go on through *The Garden* to the place where Contemplation of WHAT TRULY IS supervenes on the sensual pleasures: Here is the Orchard Scene Stanza 5 – halfway through the Poem:

> What wond'rous Life is this I lead!
> Ripe Apples drop about my head;
> The Luscious Clusters of the Vine
> Upon my Mouth do crush their Wine;

Note how the fruits here woo the poet. As Miss Bradbrook and Miss Lloyd Thomas wittily observe, they "do not behave in the least like Daphne and Syrinx". There is no running away: on the contrary.

> The Nectaren, and curious Peach,
> Into my hands themselves do reach;
> Stumbling on Melons, as I pass,
> Insnar'd with Flow'rs, I fall on Grass.

It is all gay and joyous don't you think? Would you choose anything but such grass to fall on? It is true that there are apples here as well as a Fall and that this is a Paradise – but it is all perfectly harmless surely? Nothing portentous whatever, that I can hear, or of Eve's trespass. There will be, however, a smiling glance at that in Stanza 8, line 4.

You may have noticed a rather special lilt or swing or canter I have been, perhaps, forcing on certain lines here.

> The Nectaren, and curious Peach
> Into my hands themselves do reach

Let me show you where I am taking this from:*Cherry Ripe* by Thomas Campion c. 1617.

> There is a garden in her face
> Where roses and white lilies grow,
>   A Heavenly paradise is that place
> Wherein all pleasant fruits do flow
>   There cherries grow which none may buy
>   Till "cherry ripe" themselves do cry

> Those cherries fairly do enclose
> Of orient pearl a double row,
>   Which when her lovely laughter shows
> They look like rosebuds filled with snow.
>   Yet them nor peer nor prince can buy
>   Till "cherry ripe" themselves do cry

Her eyes like angels watch them still;
Her brows like bended bows do stand,
Threatening with piercing frowns to kill
All that attempt with eye or hand
These sacred cherries to come nigh:
Till "cherry-ripe" themselves do cry.

There may be reasons why this shouldn't have any actual connection with Marvell's lines. But I think it can be helpful for *The Garden,* and the *no white nor red* story and the Heavenly Paradise and *all pleasant fruits* and the guardian *eyes* and *brows* and *frowns,* and most of all, for the *"Cherry Ripe" themselves do cry.*

It is useful to have something by comparison with which we can ask ourselves: How much ASCETICISM there really is in Marvell's poem. How much renunciation and serenity? Not very much I am inclined to think.

Mean while the Mind, from pleasure less,
Withdraws into its happiness:

Mean while here is important perhaps. These orchard delights don't – in this poem do they? – preclude the withdrawal into ecstasy that is preparing.

Not every form of care for the inferior need wrest the providing
Soul from its own sure standing in the highest.
(Plotinus, *Ennead* IV, Viii, 2)

from pleasure less: some ingenious readers have tried to make out that this means 'from the lessening of pleasure' (satiation) or 'made less by this pleasure'. But that won't do. Here is a place where the passage in Plato from which Marvell's poetry is stemming really is decisive. It is the famous conclusion, near the end of Book Nine of the *Republic* (583), that the pleasures of the Lover of Knowledge are greater than those of the lovers of Honor and of Gain.

its happiness: its own peculiar delights

Here is a description of the lower levels of these delights from Dr. Johnson:

"When I had once found the delight of knowledge and felt the pleasure of intelligence and the pride of invention", said Imlac, "every hour taught me something new. I lived in a continual course of gratifications."
(Johnson, *Rasselas*)

But there is more than this to it for Marvell: *Happiness* is a very strong word indeed, because it is the word through which Aristotle's elaborations of Plato have operated in English. Let us look at one or two of the sentences the pupils wrote down from his lectures:

It is a man's activities in accordance with virtue that constitute his happiness ... it is for the sake of happiness that we all do everything else ... Happiness does not consist in amusement ... the activity of contemplation is the highest activity ...

A man should seek immortality and live in accordance with the highest in him. It would seem that this is the true self of each. It would then be strange that a man should choose not to live the life which is properly his own.

(Aristotle, *Nicomachean Ethics*)

It is truly very odd – isn't it? – that men ARE like that!
So much for what these first two lines of the stanza are saying.

> The Mind, that Ocean where each kind
> Does streight its own resemblance find;

The Mind, that Ocean: that boundlessness
where each kind: where every different sort of thing
Does streight its own resemblance find: not only 'does IMMEDIATELY, DIRECTLY, WITHOUT INTERMEDIARY, find its likeness' but also 'finds what shows it what to be' for this Ocean is the Order of the Platonic IDEAS and FORMS; and things (*each kind*) are what they are only by participating, each, in its appropriate FORM.

"The Mind", said Aristotle, "is the place of FORMS."

There is a Mind which like some huge living organism contains potentially all the other forms.

(Plotinus, *Ennead* IV, vii, 3)

From Sir John Davies' *Nosce Teipsum*, that treasury of Platonism:

> Then what vast body must we make the mind,
> Wherein are men, beasts, trees, townes, seas, and lands,
> And yet each thing a proper place doth find,
> And each thing in the true proportion stands?

But I mustn't start lecturing here on the Ideas and their friends, any more than Marvell does in his poem. He just affirms that he is a Friend of the Ideas and goes on into Depth after Depth of Contemplation:

> Yet it creates, transcending these,
> Far other Worlds, and other Seas;
> Annihilating all that's made
> To a green Thought in a green Shade.

Back to, Creation? I have never found any comment on them which is at all as clear as these lines can become at times if you can listen to them in sufficient quietude – in *Fair quiet*! This is for meditation not for exposition. As Plotinus says:

The main difficulty is that awareness of this . . . comes not by knowing but by a presence passing knowledge.

> > *(Ennead VI, ix, 4)*

and as Plato says:

There is no way of putting it in words . . . but it is brought to birth in the soul on a sudden as light is kindled by a leaping spark and thence forward feeds itself.

> > (Plato, *Epistle VII*, 341 D)

Here let me quote Keats again from the same "Hymn to Pan" I quoted from above.

> Be thou still the unimaginable lodge
> For solitary thinkings such as dodge
> Conception to the very bourne of heaven,
> Then leave the naked brain.

But back to *The Garden* –

> Here at the Fountains sliding foot,
> Or at some Fruit-trees mossy root,
> Casting the Bodies Vest aside,
> My soul into the boughs does glide:
> There like a Bird it sits, and sings,
> Then whets, and combs its silver Wings;
> And, till prepar'd for longer flight,
> Waves in its Plumes the various Light.

whets: gets ready for? Hark back to Donne's lines:

> Here th'admyring her my soule did whett
> To seeke thee God. So streames do show their head.
> > *(Holy Sonnet XVII)*

till prepared for longer flight: Compare Shakespeare:

> Tarry, dear cousin Suffolk!
> My soul shall thine keep company to heaven;
> Tarry, sweet soul, for mine: then fly abreast.
>
> (*Henry V*, **IV**, vi, 15-7)

And here are some lines Marvell may well have recalled:

> Beginning then below, with th'easie vew,
> Of this base world, subject to fleshly eye,
> From thence to mount aloft by order due
> To contemplation of th'immortal sky,
> Of the soare falcon so I learn to fly,
> That flags awhile her fluttering wings beneath.
> Till she her selfe for stronger flight can breathe.
>
> (Edmund Spenser, *An Hymn of Heavenly Beauty*)

Waves in its plumes: spiritual exercises, trial flights.

the various Light: part of the strength of the Platonic tradition is that so many different kinds of poetry can illustrate one another. The light of eternity is single, that of time multiple and diverse.

> The One remains, the many change and pass . . .
> Life like a dome of many-coloured glass
> Stains the white radiance of Eternity
>
> (Shelley, *Adonais*, lines 460-2)

I used to try asking people how they saw this dome. You would be surprised how many said they saw a sort of Saint Peter's or Saint Paul's or a Santa Sophia, like an iridescent bubble at a distance. But of course the point is that WE ARE INSIDE the dome, inside the bubble, and can only see the white radiance through it and as coloured by

> Time's vast . . .
> skeined stained veined variety

(to quote Gerard Manley Hopkins).

How to get the poem down from such an Elevation? By return to this gentle mocking praise of Adam's state before he was accorded Eve.

> Such was that happy Garden-state,
> While Man there walk'd without a Mate:
> After a Place so pure, and sweet,
> What other Help could yet be meet!
> But 'twas beyond a Mortal's share
> To wander solitary there:
> Two Paradises 'twere in one
> To live in Paradise alone.

Disastrous Eve has to be here both Help-meet ("help meet for him", Genesis, II, 18.) and Helpmate. Mary Fairfax might retort that Adam only became Mortal with the Fall.

After that we come right out into the actual garden with its ingenious and novel sundial composed in formal patterns.

> How well the skilful Gardner drew
> Of flow'rs and herbes this Dial new;
> Where from above the milder Sun
> Does through a fragrant Zodiack run;
> And, as it works, th' industrious Bee
> Computes its time as well as we.
> How could such sweet and wholsome Hours
> Be reckon'd but with herbs and flow'rs!

milder sun: milder than that of Paradise? According to Milton,

> the Sun there shot down . . . more warmth than Adam needs.
> *(Paradise Lost, V, 301-2)*

th' industrious Bee looks back to the *busie Companies of Men* of the second stanza.

Computes its time as well as we: Both man and bee have to take care to spend their time aright and watch the hours. Both have their proper work to do: the Bee its honey-gathering and Man? – "the activity of contemplation is the highest activity".

> How could such sweet and wholsome Hours
> Be reckon'd but with herbs and flow'rs!

Compare

> Your sacred Plants, if here below,
> Only among the Plants will grow.

We have been seeing what these *sacred Plants* of *Fair quiet* and *Innocence* are in this poem.

9. COLERIDGE'S OTHER POEMS

This lecture will be, in several ways, an experiment. I had better say a
TRIAL, perhaps: EXPERIMENT suggests something scientific with a verifi-
able outcome, Yes or No. We are not yet ready in Poetics for any such
decisive procedure. So a TRIAL let it be, a sort of field-test – not only of
your patience – but of how a pretty drastic re-design of current practice
and mode of approach will work out. There will be three novelties.
(1) I am going to throw the poems and passages on the screen while I
read and discuss them – so that you can look at them with your own
eyes, read them for yourselves, while listening to my readings and to
what I have to say. (2) I am going to annex to them no biographical
detail or setting. I have put in the dates, known or conjectural, because,
if you look them up – and I will be disappointed if you don't – you will
see the dates. Coleridge having said that "the chronological order is
best", in connection with Wordsworth's departure from it, editors are
more than usualy concerned, in his case, with just when was it written
and so forth. (3) I am going to try to assume – in my reading and in my
commentary – no theories at all about what sort of a man Coleridge
might be. I am inviting you to come to the poetry direct – with only
your knowledge of the language to help you and forgetting as much as
we can of what we are supposed to know about him.

There is a rather rich set of reasons behind each of these novelties
that I ought to indicate.

(1) *The screen projection.* The poem, as we are concerned with it, isn't,
of course, either the marks I throw on the screen or the sounds you
hear me making as I read them. It is SOMETHING ELSE. The shadows on
the screen, the sounds I make and you hear, are only the physical
VEHICLE. The 'something else' we care about isn't physical in any such
simple sense. What the vehicle conveys – the IMPORT, let me call it,
has a different order of complexity from that of anything physics can

handle. It has quite another sort of status in the cosmos. Patterns on paper (or on screens: made with photographs of typescript) and sounds (as they may be recorded on tape or disk) are public, marketable, highly identifiable things. Their imports, on the contrary, are private, are not marketable, are indeed most extraordinarily hard to identify. How do we ever know whether we are reading a poem aright: whether what we take to be 'in it' is 'in it' or not; whether anyone else reads it as we do or not?

What I have just uttered sounds like a rhetorical question; and in part it is. It was uttered to voice and invoke a doubt. But my question is also a genuine and very important inquiry. How do we, in fact, attempt to find out what this 'something else' is or should be: this IMPORT which isn't the marks on a page or any sounds we make and hear. And the answer, of course, is: "Through the marks and sounds – the verbal vehicle – PLUS such further marks and sounds, further verbal vehicles, as we can find or make up that may seem to help us."

No two people – having different voices and different habits of mind – can read anything quite alike merely as vocal utterance, merely as verbal vehicle. Nonetheless language works (more or less). There are invariants somehow despite all the variety; the letter A is the same letter however it is printed or written: the sound OO may differ vastly from voice to voice but works as the same sound. Nonetheless, for all who recognize, through it, that some one is, for example, saying the word "fool": talking not of a wise or full man but of a fool. Of course, as I have just illustrated, it is reciprocal: we guess what sound it is because we know what sound it must be: and we know what sound it must be from other sounds in other verbal vehicles around it, and we know what the sounds must be IN THEM because they are connected, VIA IM-PORT, with the word "fool". And this holds all the way up from the vowel-consonant level to the intonation patterns that tell us with what sorts of attitudes or implications some one is reading a line of verse: what sorts of confidences or doubts or prayers, what sorts of accep-tances, suspensions or rejections are being supposed to be in and ani-mating the utterance.

So – to study a poem for itself: as such and such lines before us: as the English language exerting its powers at this point – we need both print: to show us WHICH THE WORDS ARE, and sound: to show us HOW SOMEONE THINKS THEY MAY BE READ.

(2) *Absence of biographical setting.* We are all, I suggest, more or less

under the sway of an opinion that if we knew enough about how a poem came to be written we would thereby be helped towards knowing what sort of a poem it is, what is in it and what is not in it and how it should be read. That looks obvious, doesn't it –as obvious as the pre-Copernican cosmos looked to most people in its day? But there are many questionable assumptions behind it. One is that poems are like other uses of language. You meet somebody: he says "Hello!" or makes a remark or two about the weather. Fine, you know all about why he says it and what he is saying: the situation and what he says in it belong together. Or the man is red in the face and shouting "Fire!" Fine again: no mystery about the situation or the utterance or about their relations one to another. Or the man is making an inventory in a hardware store. All clear still – if you are not certain what his technical labels mean, you can just watch what he is doing: the biographical detail, his history through those minutes, settles for you what his utterance imports. Jump up higher: Mr. Khrushchev makes a speech. Here you might (but almost certainly you won't) know enough about his situation to infer something precise and reliable as to the import of his utterance: but anyhow, in theory: IF you knew enough, what you knew WOULD be highly relevant. Now, by what sort of analogy do you conclude that such a series of examples will lead you to a similar dependence of a poem upon a situation in the poet?

I suggest that very much which we do know – in various ways, but with high certainty – about poems indicates that, with very many poems and among them many of the greatest, the analogy just stops dead and it stops dead because of something very central and constitutive about much poetry: I mean what we hint at by calling it CREATIVE – what the etymology of the word POETRY hints at with POIEIN: to make. If the poet, as Coleridge declared at the end of Chapter XIV of *Biographia Literaria*, and as many, rethinking his thoughts as best they can, come ever more fully to agree, if the poet, "in ideal perfection, brings the whole soul into activity" then the poet is no longer speaking from within, and under the control of, a situation. Instead, he is creating through the poem the situation within which the poem is to live. I am echoing Coleridge – here and almost in all I say – "nothing can permanently please which does not contain in itself the reason why it is so and not otherwise" or, as Shelley put it, echoing Coleridge also: "contain . . . within itself the principle of its own integrity". If you take that seriously, then the inference from an alleged situation the poet is in to the interpretation of the poem just lapses.

In the case of Coleridge's poems – to which I am coming in a moment or two now – there is an accidental circumstance which ought, I think, to keep the biographer out of the poetry. There are some poets who haven't any biographies, happy immortals: the author of the Book of Job, and Homer, and Shakespeare among them. There are others, though, who have too much biography: Coleridge among them. They are hidden from us in a cloud of witnesses: it is the documentation on Hitler, shall I say, compared with the documentation on Tamberlane. And the documentation is growing. Kathleen Coburn's superb work on the *Notebooks* will in time come to the period of the poems I'll be mostly presenting; the completion of the *Collected Letters* will march along; the *Marginalia* will catch up; the huge piles of still unedited *Talk* will swarm out. In, say, ten years the extent of our opportunities to be misled will have much increased. If inferences from biographical detail to interpretation of the poems were valid, he would be a foolish man who committed himself just now.

(3) *Absence of theories or conjectures as to what sort of a man Coleridge was.* I am keeping out of that because thought about Coleridge has suffered so much, I think, from rather vulgar stereotypes. Too many almost insanely self-satisfied judges have pronounced on him. The picture has been changing in his favor. The more that is known about him, the less confident any would-be judge should be. And – to come now to the poems – there may more often be a legitimate inference from a poem to a mind than the other way about. Poems are very often a means by which a poet (and his readers after him) enquire into and re-order their positions for living.

Not out of perversity, but for a reason which, I hope, will appear, I begin with a short passage, not by Coleridge, but by Longfellow. It is from *To a Child*.

> By what astrology of fear or hope
> Dare I to cast thy horoscope!
> Like the new moon thy life appears;
> A little strip of silver light,
> And widening outward into night
> The shadowy disk of future years;
> And yet upon its outer rim,
> A luminous circle, faint and dim,
> And scarcely visible to us here,
> Rounds and completes the perfect sphere;
> A prophecy and intimation,

A pale and feeble adumbration,
Of the great world of light, that lies
Behind all human destinies.

These charming lines, I suggest, are highly Coleridgean: not only as expanding and expounding the opening description of Coleridge's *Dejection: an Ode* (I'll be reading it in a moment but as following him in his Platonism.

The great world of light that lies
Behind all human destinies,

is here that Sunlight up into which we prisoners in the Cave must – in Plato's parable – be led. It is the Sunlight which is the visible analog to that Idea of the Good (*Republic*, VI, 508) on which all the other Ideas and the Soul itself, the place of Ideas, depend. Notice the word *intimation*. Look now at the opening of *Dejection: an Ode*. (Those who would like to know the strange story of how it was written will find that in George Whalley's *Coleridge and Sara Hutchinson and the Asra Poems*, Routledge, 1955.)

DEJECTION: AN ODE

Well! If the Bard was weather-wise, who made
The grand old ballad of Sir Patrick Spence,
This night, so tranquil now, will not go hence
Unroused by winds, that ply a busier trade
Than those which mould yon cloud in lazy flakes,
Or the dull sobbing draft, that moans and rakes
Upon the strings of this Aeolian lute,
Which better far were mute.
For lo! the New-moon winter-bright!
And overspread with phantom light,
(With swimming phantom light o'erspread
But rimmed and circled by a silver thread)
I see the old Moon in her lap, foretelling
The coming-on of rain and squally blast.

The poem has a verse from "the grand old ballad of Sir Patrick Spence" as a motto. I'll recite it:

Late, late, yestreen I saw the new Moon,
With the old Moon in her arms:
And I fear, I fear, my Master dear!
We shall have a deadly storm.

That

> ... dull sobbing draught that moans and rakes
> Upon the strings of this Aeolian lute

is, of course, the mood of deep dejection, of deprivation, which is afflict-
ing the poem and *this Aeolian lute* is the *Eolian Harp* described with
such delight in the poem of that name, seven years before. Then, nothing
could be happier:

> its strings
> Boldlier swept, the long sequacious notes
> Over delicious surges sink and rise,
> Such a soft floating witchery of sound
> As twilight Elfins make, when they at eve
> Voyage on gentle gales from Fairy-Land,
> Where Melodies round honey-dropping flowers,
> Footless and wild, like Birds of Paradise,
> Nor pause, nor perch, hovering on untam'd wing.

But now, as you see, all is far otherwise with

> this Aeolian lute,
> Which better far were mute.

There is only one way in which the Eolian Harp can be truly silent. To
continue for a few lines with the earlier poem:

> O! the one Life within us and abroad,
> Which meets all motion and becomes its soul,
> A light in sound, a sound-like power in light,
> Rhythm in all thought and joyance everywhere —

Joyance: CREATIVE joy – though it be denied him – is celebrated in
this ode as much even as it is in Wordsworth's *Intimations Ode*, to
which *Dejection* is a sort of companion piece and rejoinder.

In Wordsworth's poem, you recall, Joy, the creative principle, its
coming and going, is as much the theme as even the *glory*:

> The earth and every common sight
> To me did seem
> Apparelled in celestial light
> The glory and the freshness of a dream.

and *the shadowy recollections* which are

> ... the fountain light of all our day,

these are the *truths that wake* . . ., the truths

> Which neither listlessness nor mad endeavor
> Nor Man nor Boy
> Nor all that is at enmity with joy
> Can utterly abolish or destroy.

Coleridge's poem too is about *all that is at enmity with joy.*

Before I put on the screen the stanza in which the poem describes that joy, let me remark here, in these opening lines, two things: the description of this light:

> For lo! the New-moon *winter bright!*
> And overspread with *phantom light.*

We are going to meet other phantoms in the following poems:

> (With swimming phantom-light o'er spread
> But rimmed and circled with a silver thread).

How closely Longfellow, closely and tenderly, has followed this with his:

> and yet upon its outer rim
> A luminous circle faint and dim
> And scarcely visible to us here
> Rounds and completes the perfect sphere;
> A prophecy and intimation.

Longfellow's poem, you see, is here conversing with the two Odes: *Intimations* and *Dejection.*

My other remark is about something which the rest of the poem does not take up (at least I think it doesn't) though it can be of immense significance, none greater. And I haven't ever met any notice of it – though no doubt many readers must have perceived it without commenting; as perhaps too evident to need comment. It is this: That *phantom light* which illuminates the old Moon in the young Moon's arms is, of course, Earthlight. We here are reflecting the light we receive from the Sun onto the Moon and that is how the Moon is

> With swimming phantom light o'er spread,
> But rimmed and circled by a silver thread.

When we perceive that light we are having returned to us what we have given.

Now let us move on to stanza **IV**.

> O Lady! we receive but what we give,
> And in our life alone does Nature live:
> Ours is her wedding garment, ours her shroud!
>   And would we aught behold, of higher worth,
> Than that inanimate cold world allowed
> To the poor loveless ever-anxious crowd,
>   Ah! from the soul itself must issue forth
> A light, a glory, a fair luminous cloud
>   Enveloping the Earth —
> And from the soul itself must there be sent
>   A sweet and potent voice, of its own birth,
> Of all sweet sounds the life and element!

Nature, when *apparelled in celestial light* in *the glory and the freshness of a dream* is – this Ode replies to Wordsworth's – receiving *but what we give.*

>   . . . in our life alone does Nature live:
>   Ours is her wedding garment, ours her shroud!

(It is in her shroud that this poem is having to apparel her.)

   Whence do we get all this that we can give: this light, this glory . . . this sweet and potent voice which can create: this Joy,

>   Which, wedding Nature to us, gives in dower
>   A new Earth and new Heaven?

Much of Coleridge's prose is his answer to this question. It is with this that the *abtsruse research* he blames in this poem was chiefly concerned. But somehow, no answer gets into this poem, probably rightly. At the end he prays that the Lady to whom the poem is addressed may ever, evermore rejoice.

>   Joy lift her spirit, joy attune her voice
>   To her may all things live from pole to pole
>   Their life the eddying of her living soul!

The eddying: an eddy is a type or example of that "balance or re-conciliation of opposite or discordant qualities" which *Biographia Literaria* (Chapter XIV) is to point to in the work of "the poet in ideal perfection".

   Five years later – in "To William Wordsworth, Composed on the

night after his reading of a poem on the growth of an individual mind"
(that is *The Prelude*) – we have this:

> Friend of the wise! and Teacher of the Good!
> Into my heart have I received that Lay
> More than historic, that prophetic Lay
> Wherein (high theme by thee first sung aright)
> Of the foundations and the building up
> Of a Human Spirit thou hast dared to tell
> What may be told, to the understanding mind
> Revealable; and what within the mind
> By vital breathings secret as the soul
> Of vernal growth, oft quickens in the heart
> Thoughts all too deep for words! —
>
> Theme hard as high!
> Of smiles spontaneous, and mysterious fears
> (The first-born they of Reason and twin-birth),
> Of tides obedient to external force,
> And current self-determined, as might seem,
> Or by some inner Power; of moments awful,
> Now in thy inner life, and now abroad,
> When power streamed from thee, and thy soul received
> The light reflected, as a light bestowed —
> Of fancies fair, and milder hours of youth,
> Hyblean murmurs of poetic thought
> Industrious in its joy, in vales and glens
> Native or outland, lakes and famous hills!
> Or on the lonely high-road, when the stars
> Were rising; or by secret mountain-streams,
> The guides and the companions of thy way.
>   1802

Now in thy inner life and now abroad: from *The Eolian Harp* – recall

> O! the one Life within us and abroad.

Reflected? Bestowed? What do we reflect or bestow? Is it the light
from the Sun that we reflect on to the Moon which in turn reflects it
back again to us?

Let us consider now a poem written much later – 25 years later and
near the end of the poet's life – the poem *Self-Knowledge*. I have little
doubt that into the genesis of this poem comes a commentary on a
famous passage, the opening of Epistle Two of Pope's *Essay on Man*.
So let us read that first.

Know then thyself, presume not God to scan;
The proper study of mankind is man.
Placed in this isthmus of a middle state,
A being darkly wise and rudely great;
With too much knowledge for the sceptic side,
With too much weakness for the stoic's pride,
He hangs between, in doubt to act or rest;
In doubt to deem himself a god or beast,
In doubt his mind or body to prefer;
Born but to die, and reasoning but to err;
Alike in ignorance, his reason such,
Whether he thinks too little or too much:
Chaos of thought and passion, all confused;
Still by himself abused and disabused;
Created half to rise and half to fall;
Great lord of all things, yet a prey to all;
Sole judge of truth, in endless error hurled,
The glory, jest, and riddle of the world.

Here is Coleridge:

SELF KNOWLEDGE

Gnothi seauton! – and is this the prime
And heaven-sprung adage of the olden time! –
Say, canst thou make theyself? – Learn first that trade; –
Haply thou mayst know what thyself had made.
What hast thou, Man, that thou dar'st call thine own? –
What is there in thee, Man, that can be known? –
Dark fluxion, all unfixable by thought,
A phantom dim of past and future wrought,
Vain sister of the worm, – life, death, soul, clod –
Ignore thyself, and strive to know thy God!
1832

Look now at another poem about a phantom.

PHANTOM

All look and likeness caught from earth
All accident of kin and birth,
Had pass'd away. There was no trace
Of aught on that illumined face,
Uprais'd beneath the rifted stone
But of one spirit all her own; –
She, she herself, and only she,
Shone through her body visibly.

While we have that before us, let me read you a Fragment – without a date – which might be a commentary:

> The body
> Eternal Shadow of the finite Soul,
> The Soul's self-symbol, its image of itself
> Its own yet not itself.

Shadow: as always in such connections, an echo, a reflection, of Plato's Cave. In Coleridge, as in Blake, as in Shelley, as in Yeats . . . shadows have that Source.

As a prelude to the most Platonic of Coleridge's poems: *Constancy to an Ideal Object*, let me read you a modern version of the opening of the parable of the Cave.

Let me offer you an analogy. Suppose a race of men who were born or brought up all their lives in a movie, who have never taken their eyes off the screen. All they have ever seen are the pictures, all they have ever heard, except each other, is their world . . . (*The Practical Cogitator* by Charles P. Curtis and Ferris Greenslet, p. 553 [Boston: Houghton Mifflin, 1953]).

Hear, after that, a distinguished poet of our day, William Empson:

> All those large dreams by which men long live well
> Are magic-lanterned on the smokes of hell.
> This then is real, I have implied,
> A painted small transparent slide.

Yes. And something else too: the lens system and the source of light, the lamp in the projector, and the energy there consumed.

CONSTANCY TO AN IDEAL OBJECT

> Since all that beat about in Nature's range,
> Or veer or vanish; why should'st thou remain
> The only constant in a world of change,
> O yearning Thought! that liv'st but in the brain?
> Call to the Hours, that in the distance play,
> The faery people of the future day –
> Fond Thought! not one of all that shining swarm
> Will breathe on thee with life-enkindling breath,
> Till when, like strangers shelt'ring from a storm,
> Hope and Despair meet in the porch of Death!
> Yet still thou haunt'st me; and though well I see,
> She is not thou, and only thou art she,
> Still, still as though some dear embodied Good,
> Some living Love before my eyes there stood
> With answering look a ready ear to lend,

I mourn to thee and say – "Ah! loveliest friend!
That this the meed of all my toils might be,
To have a home, an English home, and thee!"
Vain repetition! Home and Thou are one.
The peacefull'st cot, the moon shall shine upon,
Lulled by the thrush and wakened by the lark,
Without thee were but a becalmed bark,
Whose Helmsman on an ocean waste and wide
Sits mute and pale his mouldering helm beside.
And art thou nothing? Such thou art, as when
The woodman winding westward up the glen
At wintry dawn, where o'er the sheep-track's maze
The viewless snow-mist weaves a glist'ning haze,
Sees full before him, gliding without tread,
An image with a glory round its head;
The enamoured rustic worships its fair hues,
Nor knows he makes the shadow, he pursues!

A few words as glosses may be permitted. *The faery people of the future day*: these anticipations – these endless dreams of some future fulfilment – what is it that will in the end alone satisfy and quiet them? *Fond thought*: foolishness that yet is treasured,

> Till when, like strangers shelt'ring from a storm
> Hope and Despair meet in the porch of Death!

She is not thou; and only thou art she: the actual *she* is not the imagined Ideal and only that Ideal One lends any semblance of reality to the actual: It is Troilus confronted with his two Cressids in the opening of Calchas' tent. With that *Helmsman* we are back in one phase of *The Ancient Mariner*. But notice the capital to Helmsman, the mute Self-itself whose helm wouldn't answer if he tried to use it. There is something more terrible than any ordinary loneliness here. It is the Ideal itself – not the actual or the fancied embodiment – he is questioning. *Shadow* again: back in that cinema hall. *And art thou nothing?* Nothing, annihilation, 'blank Nought-at-all' has a peculiar place in Coleridge. It is the ultimate, the Antipodean Opposite of Being. In *Ne plus ultra*, the poem which follows *Limbo* in the *Notebook*, annihilation is

> Sole Positive of Night
> Antipathist of Light . . .
> The one permitted opposite of God . . .
> The Substance that still casts the Shadow, Death;
>   . . . sole despair
> Of both th'Eternities in Heaven.

The Eternity of Knowledge and the Eternity of Love. As such, NOTHING is the theme of Coleridge's queerest and direst poem: *Limbo*.

Recall how, in *Paradise Lost* (Book III, 420-500),

> Both all things vain and all who in vain things
> Built their fond hopes of glory or lasting fame . . .

(*Fond hopes, fond thought*) how that extraordinary catalogue of the foolish, mixed with Milton's pet aversions:

>   many more, too long
> Embyros and idiots, eremites and friars
> White, black and gray, with all their trumpery
> . . . all these up whirl'd aloft
> Fly o'er the backside of the World far off
> Into a Limbo large and broad, since called
> The Paradise of Fools; to few unknown
> Long after.

Coleridge's very strange, indeed almost incomprehensible, poem, *Limbo* begins – the *Notebook* shows – as a fantastic and facetious burst of punning and rhyming about the hero-subject of John Donne's poem, "The Flea". How it turned from a radically comic exercise into this poem, later named *Limbo*, is anyone's guess.

> The sole true Something this: in Limbo's Den
> It frightens Ghosts, as here Ghosts frighten men.
> Thence cross'd unseiz'd – and shall some fated hour
> Be pulveris'd by Demogorgon's power,
> And given as poison to annihilate souls –
> Even now it shrinks them — they shrink in as Moles
> (Nature's mute monks, live mandrakes of the ground)
> Creep back from Light – then lsten or ts sound –
> See but to dread, and dread they know not why –
> The natural Alien of their negative eye.

One guess is that *sole* in the opening phrase is a hang-over from the punning bout before it: "The Soul, true Something!" As to Demagorgon, if the date could slip a little, that might be an echo of *Prometheus Unbound*, and Shelley's Zeus (after the knock-down) dragged off to Limbo. But the quite peculiar feeling of this piece begins – does it not? – with the phrase *to annihilate souls* and grows stronger and stronger as the lines proceed. How to be negative; how to annihilate? Take away everything, all qualities and you are left with bare Time and Space. Your almost nothing is merely somewhere and somewhen . . . and can these two last determinants lapse too? The poem continues:

'Tis a strange place, this Limbo! – not a Place,
Yet name it so; – where Time and weary Space
Fettered from flight, with night-mare sense of fleeing,
Strive for their last crepuscular half-being; –
Lank Space, and scytheless Time with branny hands
Barren and soundless as the measuring sands,
Not mark'd by flit of Shades, – unmeaning they
As moonlight on the dial of the day!
But that is lovely – looks like Human Time,
An Old Man with a steady look sublime,
That stops his earthly task to watch the skies;
But he is blind – a Statue hath such eyes; –

How moonlight haunts this poetry!

Yet having moonward turn'd his face by chance,
Gazes the orb with moon-like countenance,
With scant white hairs, with foretop bald and high,
He gazes still, – his eyeless face all eye; –
As 'twere an organ full of silent sight,
His whole face seemeth to rejoice in light!
Lip touching lip, all moveless, bust and limb –
He seems to gaze at that which seems to gaze on him!
No such sweet sights doth Limbo den immure,
Wall'd round, and made a spirit-jail secure,
By the mere horror of blank Naught-at-all,
Whose circumambience doth these ghosts enthral.
A lurid thought is growthless, dull Privation,
Yet that is but a Purgatory curse;
Hell knows a fear far worse,
A fear – a future state; – 'tis positive Negation!
                    1817

From one species of dream poetry to another; from ghosts – "Pray,
Mr. Coleridge, do you believe in ghosts?" asked a lady. "No, ma'am, I
have seen too many!" – from ghosts to phantoms again, to a dream
as lucid as the *Limbo* nightmare is obscure.

PHANTOM OR FACT

A Dialogue in Verse

Author

A lovely form there sate beside my bed,
And such a feeding calm its presence shed,
A tender love so pure from earthly leaven,
That I unnethe the fancy might control,
'Twas my own spirit newly come from heaven,

Wooing its gentle way into my soul!
But ah! the change – It had not stirr'd, and yet –
Alas! that change how fain would I forget!
That shrinking back, like one that had mistook!
That weary, wandering, disavowing look!
'Twas all another, feature, look, and frame,
And still, methought, I knew, it was the same!

Friend

This riddling tale, to what does it belong?
Is't history? vision? or an idle song?
Or rather say at once, within what space
Of time this wild disastrous change took place?

Author

Call it a moment's work (and such it seems)
This tale's a fragment from the life of dreams;
But say, that years matur'd the silent strife,
And 'tis a record from the dream of life.
1832 (?)

Let me now draw toward an end with two epitaphs. The first needs as footnote a few sentences from the letter to Tom Wedgewood (September 16, 1803) in which it is found:

Night is my Hell, Sleep my tormenting Angel. Three nights out of four I fall asleep, struggling to lie awake – and my frequent Night-screams have almost made me a nuisance in my own House. Dreams with me are no Shadows, but the very Substances and foot-thick Calamities of my life . . . To diversify this dusky Letter I will write in a Post-script an Epitaph, which I composed in my Sleep for myself, while dreaming that I was dying. To the best of my recollection I have not altered a word.

EPITAPH

Here sleeps at length poor Col. and without screaming,
Who died, as he had always lived, a-dreaming:
Shot dead, while sleeping, by the Gout within,
Alone, and all unknown, at E'nbro' in an Inn.
1803

Thirty years later

Stop, Christian passer-by! – Stop, child of God,
And read with gentle breast. Beneath this sod
A poet lies, or that which once seem'd he.
O, lift one thought in prayer for S.T.C.;

That he who many a year with toil of breath
Found death in life, may here find life in death!
Mercy for praise – to be forgiven for fame
He ask'd, and hoped, through Christ. Do thou the same!

9th November, 1833

Not to end on so stern a note, here is a sunset piece to which Coleridge attached this note: "These lines I wrote as nonsense verses merely to try a metre; but they are by no means contemptible; at least in reading them I am surprised to find them so good." And we may think likewise.

A Sunset

Upon the mountain's edge with light touch resting,
There a brief while the globe of splendour sits
And seems a creature of the earth; but soon
More changeful than the Moon,
To wane fantastic his great orb submits,
Or cone or mow of fire: till sinking slowly
Even to a star at length he lessens wholly.
Abrupt, as Spirits vanish, he is sunk!
A soul-like breeze possesses all the wood.
    The boughs, the sprays have stood
As motionless as stands the ancient trunk!
But every leaf through all the forest flutters,
And deep the cavern of the fountain mutters.

10. THE VULNERABLE POET AND THE FRIEND

I. THE FRIEND

Those who have read oftenest in *The Friend* must feel the peculiar appropriateness of its title: the intimate, if occasionally mixed, responses it can summon. Coleridge had been somewhat exercised in his choice – omitting from his prospectus phrases which might make people suppose his periodical to be addressed chiefly to Quakers. What familiars find in it is a winning mind candidly, volubly, and penetratingly talking to itself and to all who will sustain the needed effort. It is talking about the things that matter most – not the less alluringly for so frequently skating along the brink of the incomprehensible. TALKING: Charles Lamb reaffirms the point: "Only now listen to his talk; it is as an angel's! . . . But, after all, his best talk is in *The Friend*."

As a periodical it was written in what may have been the worst of the sloughs of despond that Coleridge had to struggle through. To be bringing out a weekly paper of essays, to be distributed all over England through the post – with all the business entailed, his printer, paper supply, and securities (bonds for stamps, etc.) to be found, every detail of format to be settled and supervised, with the Kirkstone Pass between him and the press at Penrith ("O *Heaven*! What a Journey!"), and above all, the problem of collecting payments from subscribers of every category to be faced: it was a formidable venture. It frightened Wordsworth (with whom at Allan Bank, Grasmere, Coleridge was living) out of his wits and one can almost say, his humanity. He need not have written such hope-destroying letters – behind Coleridge's back – to S.T.C.'s other friends, advisers, and supporters. The whole tangled story is here told – as regards the publishing side of the launching and maintenance of *The Friend* – in precise detail and with admirable clarity. Professor Rooke also writes a most discerning introduction and her editing lives up to even the standards we have grown used to in the Coleridge studies of Kathleen Coburn.

Volume One gives us *The Friend* in its 1818 RIFACCIAMENTO, re-arranged and greatly expanded, with all the unbelievably various and often recondite sources, the variants, and the marginalia helpfully and ever-tactfully noted. It is hard to believe that so few of those sources, so often unindicated by S.T.C., have now still to be marked "untraced" or as possibly of Coleridge's own concoction. These are frequently in Latin. Volume Two adds, for overflowing measure, The Friend of 1809-10 as it first came out weekly, together with all the changes made in the 1812 reprinting – entrusted, alack, to a uniquely odious, fraudulent, clerical publisher. The further apparatus includes a revealing list of the subscribers to the periodical *Friend*. This presents notable evidence as to the range of Coleridge's influence already secured in 1809. In total, the outcome is a beautifully designed and produced reappearance – a Phoenix rebirth, with its S.T.C. sigil on its cover – of what has been, throughout a century and a half and will continue to be, a chief shaping force for those who seek (to quote its subtitle) "aid in the formation of fixed principles in politics, morals, and religion".

What of its relevance to our day – or should we call it our night? Newcomers – if they will bear with *The Friend* through a few pages – are likely to be startled by finding it embarrassingly timely and à propos. Here is a mind thinking, carefully though livelily, circuitously and directly, about THINKING: about the thinking that is required for any trustworthy judgment about anything. And what it offers is just what reflective readers of our own current weekly papers so often most miss: apprised views on central questions that too many current writers seem somehow not to have heard of. For example: "Literature is an *individual* matter and should be *valued*, not for its *moral* or *educational* influences but *simply for what it is*" (our italics). Think awhile about that "what it is" and about the conceptions of language it reveals. *The Friend* is able to turn the inquiring eye upon what those italicised words are doing here – to watch them show up, in such use, as mere NO TRESPASS boards, forbidding exploration, property claims belonging to the routines of journalistic wiseacredom. Nowhere better than in *The Friend* are such vacuities in discourse described and diagnosed.

Barbara Rooke quotes F. D. Maurice on the essential virtue of *The Friend*: "Its merit is, that it is an inquiry, that it shows us what we have to seek for, and that it puts us into a way of seeking." It was to youth that it was addressed and with youth it succeeded – in influence immensely. Oddly enough, it almost came off financially. Its aim was: "to prepare and discipline the student's moral and intellectual being – not to propound dogmas or theories for his adoption". It was this aim which won the sympathy of so many alert spirits heartwrung with disillusionment: such great hopes in ruin, such new possibilities being turned only into horrors. As Barbara Rooke well puts it, "to recall men to principles, to ask what human society is for, what the human individual is and what the organised community is: this was the steadying task of the creative imagination as Coleridge saw it". She helpfully notes Shelley's desire to "commune with Coleridge, as the one only being who could resolve or allay the doubts and anxieties that pressed upon his mind".

What in our current weeklies we are most likely to remark is something different: the reactions of a generation and a half 'emancipated from' (or starved of) the sorts of reflection which foster self-recognition. Philosophy visiting Boethius in prison soon diagnosed his malady. "Now I perceive", she says, "what aileth thee. Thou hast forgotten what thou art!" What *The Friend*, through whatever divagations, is attempting is the recovery of the strayed Soul. Not so different an attempt, perhaps, from what some shockers of their age are always trying to invent, though in far other terms. Naturally it can be annoying for such innovators to find the footprints, nay more, the model designs of vanished worthies all over their new territory. Dismaying to discover in our boldest thought just what Pindar said more succinctly.

That there are Coleridgeans and anti-Coleridgeans (by nature or nurture) is notorious. Few as yet can follow Mill and combine their admirations for S.T.C. and Bentham. The sad probability still is that whoever esteems the one will despise the other. For these outdated oppositions *The Friend* offers innumerable occasions and the remedy.

Thus: one of its prime concerns is to clear up the relative rank, work, and dignity of Reason and Understanding. *The Friend* repeatedly tells us, with an insistence which has the marks of release from doubts, that this distinction is the KEY, no less, to all that follows. Coleridgeans mostly find that it is so, while anti-Coleridgeans tend to shrug their shoulders.

I should have no objection to define Reason as an organ bearing the same relation to spiritual objects, the Universal, the Eternal, and the Necessary, as the eye bears to material and contingent phaenomena. But then it must be added, that it is an organ identical with its appropriate objects. Thus God, the Soul, the eternal Truth, etc, are the objects of Reason; but they are themselves *reason*.

After a page of elaboration he adds:

one other illustration to prevent any misconception. In this piece of *steel* I acknowledge the properties of hardness, brittleness, high polish, and the capability of forming a mirror. I find all these likewise in the plate glass of a friend's carriage; but in addition to all these, I find the quality of transparency, or the power of transmitting as well as of reflecting the rays of light. The application is obvious.

Coleridgeans and anti-Coleridgeans can find much to bicker about here. A Coleridgean may admit that maybe *The Friend* is leaving overmuch to the reader. Perhaps, however, Isabella on Angelo – that Representative Man,

> Man, proud man,
> Dressed in a little brief authority,
> Most ignorant of what he's most assured,
> His glassy essence –

will help in the exploration of Coleridge's frequent concern with transparency. Compare his poem:

> Where e'er the mist which hangs 'twixt God and Thee
> Defecates to a pure transparency
> That intercepts no ray and adds no stain:
> There Reason is and there begins her reign.

Coleridge has so often been accused of making over Shakespeare into his own mirror image that it is fair to note how Coleridge-like Isabella becomes in her principal line. Is it his *little brief authority* that makes *proud man Most ignorant*? The authority may be that of a vice regent or of a mere teacher. "Every teacher", Coleridge remarked, "has a mental odour". Is it his being *most assured* that gives this to him along with his ignorance? Or should we also take the line in another way, making it a far more profound observation? Is not *His glassy essence* (being his essence) something about which he must be *most ignorant* (except through its very activity of which he is the outcome)? *Most assured* of it he must be, since it is him, himself: that apart from which he would not be.

Reading Isabella so, then Coleridge's description of Reason can become man's *glassy essence*. Reason as "the organ of the Supersensuous", distinct from Understanding as "the faculty by which we generalise and arrange the phaenomena of perception" (including "its own acts and forms, that is, formal Logic"), can be reformulated as: Understanding (like steel) can receive order, disorder . . . reflections of God; but Reason (like glass) participates in the conduct of that operation.

"I earnestly entreat the reader not to be dissatisfied either with himself or with the author; if he should not at once understand . . . rather to consider it as a mere annunciation of a magnificent theme." All *The Friend* may be regarded as an exemplification, wide, diverse, and far-reaching, of presentations which the hitherto unpublished Coleridge materials to come in further volumes of *The Collected Works* seem likely to confirm and carry forward.

II. THE VULNERABLE POET

Well within the last hundred years, the energies of scholarship have organized themselves to investigate the details of the lives of literary figures with a thoroughness which even the day-by-day antics of monarchs and their mistresses in former times escaped. In part, this is due to the immense improvement in the techniques of scholarly work which the cumulative, competitive pressure of the university career has produced. In part it is due to the example of the sciences. New standards of comprehensiveness, self-criticism, and rectitude in the handling of evidence are being engendered. We often enough hear laments for the vanishing of ancient virtues; it is a pleasure therefore to celebrate the emergence of new. We may remind ourselves, however, that these meritorious advances in probity spring from a new certainty for the scholar that his sins will find him out: that is, his colleagues will.

We do not usually think of Dr. Johnson as an innovator. None the less his *Lives of the Poets* is a landmark. Before then, how poets lived or what they were like was not a matter of much interest. Today, with the increase of expenditures on literary research, the portentous growth of libraries, and the proportion of the available intellectual labor devoted to what is essentially the biographical study of the creative writer, it seems time to wonder what the true end of all this may be. First-class ability is the world's chief shortage. There should be some great cause which this sacrifice of talent serves. But what is it?

In the sciences we assume that increase of knowledge anywhere, if not immediately profitable, will sooner or later be found useful somewhere. In the humanities this is by no means so assumable. It is much easier there to waste all one's own and much of one's readers' time. No doubt a biologist, familiar with nature's wastefulness, will not let this worry him; but still these doubts do call for some answer. Can it be that this recent crescendo of concern with biography heralds a juncture of literary studies with biology?

Creativity is a first-order biological problem, not least as it occurs in man. Of late the creative artist – and most of all the writer, because he supplies more, and more manageable, evidence – has been receiving the attention that only founders of religions attracted in the past. Does all this point to a hidden hope that by studying the mortal journey of the author in sufficient detail we may in time learn how to obtain more and better poets? It may be added that – in comparison with the amount of classroom and other high-priced attention being paid him, as never before, and the facilities now provided for the would-be creator – the current output of work with any likelihood of lasting interest is laughably small.

To any such suggestion a due response must be at least a smile. Not the most confirmed believer in the importance of thorough biographical study will give it that sort of status. For the most part, no doubt, these studies of the days and nights of poets are chosen as opportunity offers and are performed as passages in the academic escalade. But occasionally an author – himself intently, troublingly, perhaps disastrously interested in the creative process, in others as in himself – may invite an editor to live with and learn from a mind so preoccupied what may or may not be learned. Among such minds none – it has been more and more recognized with each decade of study – is more truly instructive, more deeply 'seminal', more alive with promises of revelation than Coleridge's.

Recently there have been published the first large installments of both Coleridge's *Notebooks* (N) and *Collected Letters* (L). The first two volumes of the *Notebooks*, edited by Kathleen Coburn, cover the years 1794-1804 (Bollingen Series, Pantheon Books), and the first two volumes of the *Letters*, edited by Earl Leslie Griggs, cover the years 1785-1806 (Oxford University Press). These hundreds of pages are displaying Coleridge as one of the most fully and accessibly documented figures in the record. Our reflections, accordingly, as we make what way we may through them, must unavoidably be mixed. Without editorial labors whose thoroughness and quality are impressive witness to modern standards of scholarship, we would make uncertain progress with the *Letters* and little way at all, I think, with the *Notebooks*, though Miss Coburn is performing an astonishing feat of informed and inspired elucidation. None the less, the self-revelation in all this mass of writing is far indeed from being made to offer any clear and satisfying picture. No matter how carefully – under skilled and devoted guidance – we put the bits and pieces together, the thought recurs that the kinds of knowledge that Coleridge, beyond other sages, invites and urges us to pursue are probably not to be attained. This is not a consideration, however, likely to deter the suitable reader.

Writing of Spinoza's failure to reconcile God and nature, Coleridge commented: "the Wreck has become a Sea-mark for us and for all future Mariners" (N1500n). Wrecks appertain to philosophy with Coleridge; even Plato was "This plank from the wreck of Paradise thrown on the shores of idolatrous Greece" (*Aids to Reflection*, xxxii). His own philosophic enterprises had that boldness which invites ultimate disaster. But in his remark on Spinoza he is pointing, picturesquely, to the essential process of science. "It is the business of science to be wrong", as Oppenheimer observed. The best service to philosophy too is not in establishing some supposed unshakable, but in showing that an inviting path will not lead where we expect. There are many ways of showing such things; logical demonstration is but one of them and it is fully operable only in pure logic itself. More general and often more conclusive is that frustration − rich and fertile in its by-products though it may be − which Coleridge's life as a thinker may be taken to represent.

There is a deep irony here: that he who more perhaps than any other proposed *Gnothi seauton* 'Know thyself' − the "heaven sprung adage of the olden time" − as the prime directive in philosophy should, on such a prodigal and indeed prodigious scale, have furnished us with such varied reason to doubt. As a methodologist he is, in formal prose, as clear and as uncompromising as any writer can be: "The postulate of philosophy and at the same time the test of philosophical capacity, is no other than the heaven-descended KNOW THYSELF!" (*Biographia Literaria* xii). But as a poet, seventeen years wiser, we may think, he had something profounder to say:

> What hast thou, Man, that thou dar'st call thine own? −
> What is there in thee, Man, that can be known? −
> Dark fluxion, all unfixable by thought,
> A phantom dim of past and future wrought. . . .

"Failing powers!" some will say to this. "A recantation made near the end of an exhausted eloquence." Or, "A mere rejoinder to Pope's 'The proper study of mankind is Man.' " Or, "Only poetry!" − an accusation contemptuous of Coleridge's most famous and familiar position that in poetry "the whole soul of man" may be brought into activity, and that "Poetry is the completest mode of utterance". Whatever we may think, here in these volumes – provided with such facilities of reference as never – we have the wherewithal to judge what success in knowing himself this most reckless, tireless pioneer attained. They present the most intimate record, moreover, of the freshest, most formative period of his thinking: a record, in the *Letters*, for the eyes of friends to whom, if any man ever did, he opened wide his heart, in the *Notebooks*, a record often for his own eyes alone, as he hoped.

What kinds of knowledge of himself was he seeking? All kinds, with an increasing sense of the importance of discovering and distinguishing their "relative worth and dignity", however various the fields of his self-investigating curiosity were. It is a fair warning, however, that the extraordinary variety and liveliness of interests which make the *Letters* so fascinating – if sometimes most teasing – offer, in the *Notebooks*, perils of distraction not easily matched. Entry succeeds entry: extracts from his reading, comments only conjecturally attachable to text, cooking recipes, suggestions for possible poems, for figures of speech, for texts to sermons (his own or those he supplied to his brother) observations on the appearances of anything from a candle flame to the heavens, on his own sensations, scruples, indirections; political reflections, surmises as to the habitability of the moon, chronicles of symptoms, anecdotes, resolves, funny stories, philosophic germs, expense accounts, scenery . . . nothing can exceed the variety. With more of them than can be believed, SOMETHING about them whets our appetite. Swallowing the bait you turn to the admirably ordered companion volume of notes, wherein Miss Coburn takes over. There you find the probable setting, when conjecturable; pointers to phrases used elsewhere; relevant information about whatever may be being mentioned or alluded to: all and more than all that you might hope for, much less expect. Pursuing these through the admirable convenient cross-reference system, you wake up to realize that you have quite forgotten what you were originally hooked by. You have been learning a lot meanwhile – often much more than you were looking for.

But further, Miss Coburn has been reading; she gives one the impression of having become something of a "library cormorant" herself: "I am, ever have been, a great reader – & have read almost everything – a library cormorant" (L156). She has equipped herself, directly and through gifted helpers and consultants, uniquely well to follow her author and "trace him in the tedious ways of art" (but his are seldom tedious and art here is most often inseparable from nature). Taking as our instance the most momentous relationship in his life, let us see to what decisions in regard to self-knowledge we may be led.

Coleridge parted rather suddenly from William and Dorothy Words-worth in the middle of a jaunting car tour through Scotland. (Back to back is hardly helpful in seeing eye to eye). Coleridge writes to his wife: "W's Hypochondriacal Feelings keep him silent & self-centered . . . sit-ting in an open Carriage in the Rain is Death to me and somehow or other I had not been quite comfortable" (L514). His third entry after the parting was: "My words & actions imaged on his mind, distorted & snaky as the Boatman's Oar reflected in the Lake/–" (N1473). His editor points out the application to Wordsworth and then, via use of this image by Jeremy Taylor, is drawn on to later phrases in the sermon remarkably consonant with that gloss of glosses to *The Ancient Mariner*: "In his loneliness and fixedness he yearneth towards the journeying Moon, and the stars that still sojourn, yet still move onward. . . ." Thence to a series of indications of other entries on the Scottish tour united, as she observes, by the "breeze of feeling" that sustains that poem (N1473).

One of these is especially poignant. A few days before this parting: "What? tho' the World praise me, I have no dear Heart that loves my Verses – I never hear them in snatches from a beloved Voice, fitted to some sweet occasion of natural prospect, in Winds at Night" (N1468). Miss Coburn offers reason to think that Dorothy had been reciting Wordsworth's "Ruth". Coleridge himself was quoting from "Tintern Abbey" just before the separation.

Nine years later, in June 1812, after the great break with Words-worth was supposed to have been mended, Coleridge annotated some of these entries. To "Here I left W & D" he adds in Latin: "Would that I had never seen them!" (N1417). And a page earlier to "My Friend" (i.e. Wordsworth): "O me! what a word to give permanence to the mistake of a Life!" This is a bitterness that provokes reflection: is there more behind it than the spleen of a very sick man? What, if anything, had Wordsworth done to warrant such feelings? The answer, it now appears, may be "more than a little". He may, by behavior not easily excusable, have maimed the poet in his friend.

Coleridge's excessive worship of Wordsworth through these years (see L350) had early led to a warning from Poole, the best and truest of all his friends, against such "prostration" (L330) and a plaintive allusion by Lamb to "his god Wordsworth". There was also that prob-lematic thing: "T. Wedgewood's farewell Prophesy to me respecting W., which he made me write down, and which no human Eye ever saw – but mine" (see L350). What Coleridge was worshipping was the poet of

"The Brothers", "Ruth", and "Michael". He was very well aware, at times – as appears in the reasons he gives for the crack that opened on the Scottish Tour – of other sides. When the two met again, some six weeks later, we find Coleridge composing in his *Notebook* for transmission in letters a truly noble paean of praise that "he [Wordsworth] has bidden farewell to all small Poems . . . now he is at the Helm of a nobel Bark ["The Recluse"]; now he sails right onward . . ." and so on. These feelings about Wordsworth's "small poems" had not, however, prevented him from showing, three years before, what Mr. Griggs very truly describes as "a devotion as disinterested as it was remarkable" – devotion to the labor of preparing for the printers a re-issue of *Lyrical Ballads*, with a second volume under Wordsworth's sole name. Wordsworth seems to have left the transcribing to Coleridge and Dorothy, the instructions to the printers, an exacting and tedious task, to Coleridge, and even the composition of promotional letters to influential persons for Wordsworth to sign – much of this at a time when Coleridge was gravely ill: "the sense of Lassitude, if I only sate up in bed, was worst of all – I seem'd to fall in upon myself in ruin, like a column of sand, that had been informed and animated only by a whirlblast of the desert – such & so treacherous were my animal spirits to me" (L375). And this too when Coleridge desperately needed to fulfill the most pressing personal obligations. As Mr. Griggs well puts it,

Instead, however, of rescuing himself from a sea of embarrassments and paying heed to his own reputation, Coleridge gave his best efforts to Wordsworth's project. He made far-reaching revisions of *The Ancient Mariner*, probably at the instigation of Wordsworth, who was convinced that the poem had been 'an injury' to the *Lyrical Ballads* and that its 'strangeness' had 'deterred readers from going on.'

Furthermore, "after a tremendous expenditure of creative energy, he succeeded in composing Part II of *Christabel,* before Wordsworth decided not to include it."

One of the many points Miss Coburn admirably brings out is Coleridge's use – here and elsewhere – of Bartram's *Travels through North and South Carolina, Georgia, East and West Florida, etc.* Lowes, in *The Road to Xanadu*, pointed to passages there as suggesting much in *The Ancient Mariner* and in *Kubla Khan*, but Miss Coburn is able to show how influential was "Bartram's whole attitude towards, and relation to, the natural world, especially animal life" (N218n). Coleridge seems to have guessed this. In attempting to repeat the miracle of *The Ancient Mariner* with *Christabel*, he rereads Bartram, and reads him aloud to Sara Hutchinson, to whom he later gave his copy with the inscription: "This is not a Book of Travels, properly speaking; but a series of poems, chiefly descriptive, *occasioned* by the Objects which the Traveller observed. – It is a *delicious* Book; and like all *delicious* Things, you must take but a little of it at a Time" (N218n). No one who has sipped thus from this early American poet will, I think, fail to agree. It would certainly appear that Bartram is due for further study.

Whether he helped with *Christabel* again is an inviting question, but it seems likely that the struggle to continue *Christabel* was a turning point in Coleridge's life as well as in his poetry. What it had cost him he describes magnificently in a letter to Josiah Wedgewood of November 1, 1800 (L362). On September 17, he is writing of *Christabel*: "Every line has been produced by me with labor-pangs. I abandon Poetry altogether – I leave the higher and deeper kinds to Wordsworth, the delightful, popular & simply dignified to Southey; & reserve for myself the honorable attempt to make others feel and understand their writings. ... P.S. My wife was safely and speedily delivered of a fine boy last Sunday night" (L351). But ten days later: "alas! I fear he will not live." The *Notebook* entry is: "The child being very ill was baptized by the name of Derwent. The Child hour after hour made a noise exactly like the Creeking of a door which is being shut very slowly to prevent its creeking" (N813). In between, Coleridge has, he says, been writing for the *Morning Post* essays on "the War as respecting Agriculture, ... the Raising of Rents in consequence of the high Prices of Provisions, one on the Riots – and one on ... the King's Proclamation, and the probable views of the Minister" (L353). He had also found time to write, to William Godwin, the most suggestive speculations on language that even Coleridge ever entertained: "Are not words &c parts & germinations of the Plant? And what is the Law of their Growth? – In something of his order I would endeavor to destroy the old antithesis of *Words & Things*, elevating, as it were words into Things, & living *Things* too"; all this as well as some of the fiercest anti-baptism considerations conceivable (L352).

Derwent recovered and Coleridge dashed back to be with the Wordsworths and read them *Christabel*, which was to generate, we may recall, so much in William's poetry. Miss Coburn surmises that "Listening with untir'd eagerness while the un-snuffed Candle's Cone burnt with two points – " (N281) could record this reading, with which they were "exceedingly delighted" and "talked till 12 o'clock" as Dorothy noted in her *Journal*.

But what had Wordsworth been doing in Coleridge's absence? Writing for the edition of *Lyrical Ballads* a note on *The Ancient Mariner*, which Mr. Griggs doubts that Coleridge saw before it was in print. It contained such remarks as: "the Author was himself very desirous that it should be suppressed. This wish had arisen from a consciousness of the defects of the poem, & from a knowledge that many persons had been much displeased with it. The Poem of my Friend has indeed great defects; first ... secondly ... thirdly ... and lastly ..." (see L337). No wonder Lamb, when he read this, wrote Wordsworth very nearly what he thought of him.

Wordsworth's reason, as he stated it to the publisher, for not including *Christabel* was: "upon mature deliberation, I found that the Style of this Poem was so discordant from my own that it could not be printed along with my poems with any propriety" (unpublished letter; see L362). Coleridge accepted the decision very calmly, too calmly. Within a week he is writing to Davy: "The Christabel was so much admired by Wordsworth, that he thought it indelicate to print two Volumes with *his name* in which so much of another's man's was included." One would like to know why the addition of Coleridge's name would not have met this. Later, in the same letter: "I assure you, I think very differently of CHRISTABEL – I would rather have written Ruth, and Nature's Lady [presumably, "Three years she grew," Mr. Griggs notes] than a million such poems / but why do I calumniate my spirit by saying, *I* would rather – God knows – it is as delightful to me that they *are* written" (L356).

Is there not something a little over-resolute about this – as though his fortitude needed affirming? So too perhaps with the three chief statements of renunciation. To Thelwall, December 17, 1800: "As to Poetry, I have altogether abandoned it, being convinced that I never had the essentials of poetic Genius, & that I mistook a strong desire for original power." To Wrangham, December 19, 1800:

Wordsworth & I have never resided together – he lives at Grasmere, a place worthy of him, of which he is worthy – and neither to Man nor Place can higher praise be given ... As to our literary occupations they are still more distant than our residences – He is a great, a true Poet — I am only a kind of Metaphysician. – He has even now sent off the last sheet of a second Volume of his *Lyrical Ballads* (L371).

(I find it a relief here to turn back to an earlier passage in this same letter: "Wordsworth has received your letter, & meant to have answered it immediately. I'll write to him *to day*, quoth he. For you must understand, that *W*. has innovated very vilely the good old *Common-Law* of Procrastination – instead of Tomorrow, & Tomorrow, & Tomorrow it is To Day, To Day, and To Day.") To Godwin, March 25, 1801:

"The Poet is dead in me – my imagination (or rather the Somewhat that had been imaginative) lies, like a Cold Snuff on the circular Rim of a Brass Candle-stick, without even a stink of Tallow to remind you that it was once cloathed and mitred with Flame. That is past by! – I was once a Volume of Gold Leaf, rising and riding on every breath of Fancy – but I have beaten myself back into weight & density, & now I sink in quicksilver, yea, remain squat and square on the earth amid the hurricane, that makes Oaks and Straws join in one Dance, fifty yards high in the Element . . . If I die, and the Booksellers will give you anything for my Life, be sure to say – Wordsworth descended on him, like the *Gnothi seauton* from Heaven; by showing to him what true Poetry was, he made him know, that he himself was no Poet!" (L390).

Self-knowledge? Two nights later he is writing to Longman, in a hitherto unpublished letter: "My sickness has left me in a state of mind, which it is scarcely possible for me to explain to you – one feature of it is an extreme Disgust which I feel at every perusal of my own Productions, & which makes it exceedingly painful to me not only to revise them, but I may truly add, even to look on the Paper, on which they are written." This comes partly as excuse for delay over his never-written book of German travels, but also leads to an attempt to "send forth" *Christabel* – the terms to be left to Longman to diminish the risk, "if the success of this poem should not answer my *wishes*; for hopes & *expectations* I do not waste on things of such utter uncertainty" (L391).

What are we to make of all this from a poet whose greatest following poem, *Dejection*, is to be very largely about the loss of poetic power? Sickness? Yes, Coleridge's health really was variously and almost continuously bad from his arrival at Keswick (July 24, 1800) onwards. He suffered, certainly, from ailments which modern medicine would soon put an end to; but also, as he himself frequently suspects, from not less grave physical troubles stemming from spiritual frustrations. High among these were obstructions to his extreme outflowingness, his ardor of admiration, and his need to communicate with and devote himself to the admired one. Coleridge lacked that great protection: vanity. He was vulnerable as less ebullient and less self-critical natures are not. And though his generosity and humility could lead him to cover up the wound at first by overpraise of the offender and excessive acquiescence in the implied self-diminishment, that was no sort of cure; it could only drive the infection in the deeper.

We have, of course, in trying to do justice to Coleridge, to beware lest we do wrong to Wordsworth. Coleridge's remarks of eighteen years later about the Wordsworths, their "cold praise and effective discouragement of every attempt of mine to roll onward in a distinct current of my own – who *admitted* that the *Ancient Mariner* [and] the Christabel ... were not without merit, but were abundantly anxious to acquit their judgments of any blindness to the very numerous defects" (see L356) probably exaggerate. There had been much to brood over in the interval. But take a *Notebook* entry of October 1803, for which Miss Coburn suggests we may put A = Coleridge and B = Wordsworth:

I have had some *Lights* lately respecting Envy. A. thought himself unkindly used by B. – he had exerted himself for B. with what warmth! honoring, praising B. beyond himself. – &c &c – B. selfish – feeling all Fire respecting every Trifle of his own – quite backward to poor A. – The *up*, askance, pig look, in the Boat &c. Soon after this A. felt distinctly little ugly Touchlets of Pain & little Shrinkings Back at the Heart, at the report that B. had written a new Poem / an excellent one! – & he saw the faults of B & all that belonged to B. & detested himself dwelling upon them – & c ... Then, A. took himself to task respecting B ... But what is he on the whole? What compared with the mass of men? It is astonishing how powerfully this Medicine acted – how instantly it effected a cure ... (N1606).

Much in the rest of this long entry is relevant. So perhaps too is that it follows on an equally long entry applying to "my former Quarrel with Southey" the reflection "that the Almighty will judge us not by what we *do*, but by what we *are*". An exceedingly precarious distinction, especially for a Platonist: "The mark of being is its power to act and be acted upon" (*Sophist*, 247E). Coleridge's early submission to Southey is in many queer ways a try-out of his prostration to Wordsworth. Both hit him on his modest, un-self-recognizing side as would-be poet, as well as on the side which longed to find a perfection to revere: of Southey, "Not that he was Perfection; but because he was a far better man, than the vast majority of the young men, whom I knew" (N1605); of Wordsworth: "I feel myself a *little man by his side*; & yet I do not think myself the less man than I formerly did" (L190); "Wordsworth is a very great man – the only man, to whom *at all times* & in *all modes of excellence* I feel myself inferior" (L197); "I do not hesitate in saying, that since Milton no man has *manifested* himself equal to him" (L328); "the only one whom in *all* things I feel my Superior – & you will believe me, when I say, that I have few feelings more pleasurable than to find myself in intellectual Faculties an Inferior" (L277). This to Poole, his truest friend. Accordingly, Pantisocratically exalted, he let Southey push him into marriage with the sister of the girl Southey was to marry, knowing well enough, then, that he did not love her, thinking later he could, later still knowing he couldn't. And, following out the crazy pattern, knowing nothing of Wordsworth's intentions, he fell, desolately, incurably and hopelessly, in love with the sister of the girl Wordsworth was to marry. Coincidences abound here, and it may be inviting undue inferences to note that Coleridge's vast and crushing letter of dismissal reached Southey the day before his marriage to Edith Fricker and ends, "Sara would have you accept her Love & Blessing, accept it, as the future Husband of her best-loved Sister! Farewell" (L93); and that *Dejection*, originally a verse letter to Sara Hutchinson, after various changes of addressee for its key line: O Sara, O Wordsworth, O William, O Edmund, finally

> O Lady! we receive but what we give

was first printed, in the *Morning Post*, on October 4, 1802, Wordsworth's wedding day.

However such things may be, there is no shortage in these volumes of evidence of the dependence of Coleridge's ill-health and of the failings in his "genial spirits" upon domestic and other discords. What is strange and pathetic to notice is that even the "substantial Misery foot-thick, that makes me sit by my bedside of a morning, & *cry* – " does not prevent his letters from exhibiting abundance of "genial spirits" in a different sense. Creativity may be cut off; good humor and *energy* in communication are not. It is as though frustration in poetry and in the systematic prosecution of his many times too many literary projects led to epistolary overflow. If some of those who have depicted this man as an idler had, as a penalty, merely to transcribe a year of his letters and notebooks on the correspondent days they might learn a profitable lesson. We may perhaps speculate further, and suppose that the very liveliness, universality, and interconnection of his interests, his myriad-mindedness – to use the phrase he coined for Shakespeare – may itself have precluded their fulfilment. To use a sentence of his taken from a different context: "the whole Thinking of my Life will not bear me up against the accidental Press & Crowd of my mind, when it is elevated beyond its natural Pitch" (L325).

In letter-writing and in notebook scribbling (and, for that matter, in monologue), Coleridge's mind was so often elevated that "it becomes a matter of nicety in discrimination to know" what its natural Pitch could have been. Avoidable ill-health certainly lowered him. Here again his descriptive gift may sometimes make us wonder how ill he really was. How bad, for example, was the following:

a few straggling pains only remained: but *this morning* he returned in full force, & his Name is Legion! Giant-fiend of a hundred hands! with a shower of arrowry Death-pangs he transpierced me, & then he became a Wolf and lay gnawing my bones. – I am not mad, most noble Festus! – but in sober sadness I have suffered this day more bodily pain than I had before a conception of – My right cheek has certainly been placed with admirable exactness under focus of some invisible Burning-Glass, which concentrated all the Rays of a Tartarean Sun. – My medical attendant decides it to be altogether nervous . . . (L151, November 5, 1796 to Poole).

On the other hand to the same:

on Wednesday on stepping over a fence I had a Thorn run into my leg – . . . an incision has been made to no purpose . . . I have suffered great agony – I am more than lame – for I cannot without torture move my leg from a super-horizontal position. Whether I exaggerate illness or no, remains to be proved; but this I will venture to say for myself, that there is scarcely a *Woman* in the Island that can endure Pain more quietly than I – tho' the Present is scarcely an Instance – for I have had such valuable Lights thrown upon me, with regard to the exceedingly interesting & obscure subject of *Pain* . . . that I am quite in spirits about it. O! how I *watched* myself while the Lancet was at my Leg! – *Vivat Metaphysic* (L419, hitherto unpublished).

On the whole we may hope that he exaggerated but must fear that he didn't.

The present volumes cover the most moving years of "that life-ebullient stream which breaks through every momentary embankment, again indeed, and evermore to embank itself, but within no banks to stagnate or be imprisoned" (*The Friend*, Second Section, Essay xi). They include centrally his period at Greta Hall, Keswick, "a house of such prospect that if . . . impressions and ideas *constitute* our Being, I shall have a tendency to become a God – so sublime & beautiful will be the series of my visual existance" (L33). It is probably safe to say that no house has ever had the views from its windows more worthily described. He even writes of them, "From the leads on the housetop of Greta Hall, Keswick, Cumberland, at the present time in the occupancy and usufruct-possession of S. T. Coleridge, Esq., Gentleman-poet and Philosopher in a mist" (L343). Alas, that so much of hope and delight should have had such an outcome! "Curving round the house almost in a semicircle flows the Greta. P.S. My House stands on the River Greta, which is a literal translation of the Word Cocytus –

> Nam'd, from lamentation loud
> Heard on the rueful stream.

To greet is to lament aloud . . ." (L371). A prophecy to make one shudder.

Emerging from so much, so "inveterately convolved" that anything so consistent as the above sketch feels wrenched out and re-arranged, a reader must pause from time to time to wonder – as the editors doubtless have often wondered – what this whole enterprise is really for. Minute studies, on this scale, of an author's verbal remains are not any inevitable part of human activity. Until recently we have managed very well without them. They would have astonished Coleridge, though his cormorant capacity would have been well-suited to them. Today they may seem so natural that a scholar may pass a whole lifetime in such toils without even asking himself – or indeed ever hearing anyone ask – any such question. That, in general, they serve the cause of truth would not be quite good enough as an answer; it would have to try at least to say what sorts of truth may be expected and, as to these, it is timely perhaps to raise some doubts. Some very plausible answers must probably be rejected: that they enable readers to enjoy and understand Coleridge's poetry, *as poetry*, for example. They do help us to talk and write about it – if we must. But that is not the same thing, as the reflective among teachers of literature realize more deeply with every return of examination seasons.

But perhaps the enjoyment and understanding of poetry as poetry are not the business of such studies. A man's poetry may be merely the bait; the real game to be caught may be psychological or biological. Coleridge certainly is a superb type-specimen. But of what? He has been classified and diagnosed with the uttermost confidence by authorities who now begin to look like useful type-specimens themselves – specimens a lot easier to describe and safer to be sure about. It would be appropriate if Coleridge, whose best philosophic prose discusses method, were to be not so much psychologically as methodologically instructive, if (as was suggested above) we became through him, by example as well as by precept, more aware of the hazards of our judgments. He was a charitable man, severe only on himself – almost disablingly severe. He could perhaps teach us to be more charitable toward others and toward ourselves; and this by showing us how little even the most gifted introspectionist, the most fully equipped analyst, the most ruthless investigator can really learn about himself and thereby about another.

11. POETRY AS PAIDEIA

Among our debts to Werner Jaeger – to whom we owe so much – not the least is for his elucidation of the Greek view of education:

They considered that the only genuine forces which could form the soul were words and sounds, and – so far as they work through words or sounds or both – rhythm and harmony; for the decisive factor in all paideia is active energy, which is even more important in the culture of the mind than in the *agon* which exercises physical strength and agility.[1]

In a period such as ours when so many have supposed that the best that words can do is to deputize in some fashion as some sort of *faute de mieux* substitute for real experience, it is good to be reminded of the priority of language in the development of man and to be brought back to the solid historical grounds for the position whose most influential utterance has been the opening sentence of the Fourth Gospel.

The true representatives of paideia were not, the Greeks believed, the voiceless artists – sculptors, painter, architect – but the poets and musicians, orators (which means statesmen) and philosophers. They felt that the legislator was in a certain respect more akin to the poet than was the plastic artist; for both the poet and the legislator had an educational mission. The legislator alone could claim the title of sculptor, for he alone shaped living men.[1]

Shelley knew what he was saying when he called the poets "the unacknowledged legislators of the world".

But we have an even deeper question to face. It asks who should be included under the ?our? and the ?we? of my opening sentence above. Can Jaeger be justified in setting up a Hellenocentric culture (what today are its bounds?) and in so firmly separating it, as "the ideal which only the Hellenocentric world possesses . . . a concept of value, a consciously pursued *ideal*" (xvii) from "a simple anthropological concept"

[1]   Werner Jaeger, *Paideia: The Ideals of Greek Culture* (New York: Oxford University Press, 1939), p. xxvii.

in which "it is permissible to talk of Chinese, Indian, Babylonian, Jewish or Egyptian cultures, though none of these nations has a word or an ideal which corresponds to real culture". Is this a sort of provincialism? Or is it truly the case that the "educational systems" of nations not in that Hellenocentric world "are in their whole intellectual structure fundamentally and essentially different"? He goes in fact much further. Not difference merely but radical superiority is the essential point. Can he be in fact right in asserting that "The greatest invention of the Greeks was man" and in regarding "the true Greek *paideia*" as "the process of educating man into his true form, the real and genuine human nature"? "Other nations made gods, kinds, spirits; the Greeks alone made men" (xxiii). It is a bold claim. It is also a superb way of inviting us to ask the most penetrating questions about our very selves – including, centrally, about the roles that may be played by poetries in bringing those selves into being.

It will be recognized that such questions are not lightly to be answered. No doubt Jaeger's confidence in part reflects his extraordinary mastery of and insight into Greek Literature and philosophy. But, perhaps too, the surpassing richness and variety of Hellenocentric culture – now spreading so widely, rapidly and victoriously, though in fashions regretable as well as admirable – is sufficient to secure his position. If "we" here can stand for the participants in Hellenocentric culture, ought we to allow modesty to prevent us from acknowledging the truth?

I will revert now to the first point on which I cited Jaeger: the priority of the voice and the word among the representatives of paideia. "Often as the Greeks compared the act of education with the work of the plastic artist, they themselves . . . hardly ever thought that a man could be educated by looking at works of art" (xxvii), and he refers to Winckelmann as having so thought. How often, on what grounds and with what justification people have thought so may be disputable, but the services of language in helping minds become more what they should be will hardly be doubted. We should however, at the same time, recall how much damage to minds language can also be responsible for. Great power, perhaps necessarily, has its attendant dangers. My concern, though, here is narrower. It is to consider what place poetry has and should have in paideia – taken in the sense above defined: the moulding of character by ʾidealsʾ. We may, however, find ourselves having to extend, refine, and perhaps revise our most easily current conceptions of ʾidealsʾ – returning in them nearer to those studied in Greek tragedy.

Poetry as paideia is a high theme to discuss in what seems an evil time for poetry. SEEMS, I say, for we cannot know if it really is so, since we cannot guess what is coming. The picture could change overnight.

But why it SEEMS an evil time for poetry is apparent enough. As a more even distribution of wealth is achieved, SERVICE becomes more costly and rarer. As service becomes rarer we house ourselves in less space – bookshelves become fewer and shorter. As space contracts, BOOKSPACE shrinks. The children we have to teach come to us from relatively bookless homes.

Meanwhile – as "avid absorbents of superfluous leisure" books have lost their status. Cinema and T.V. take up what slack there may be. Moreover, parents are busier than similar parents used to be. There is less time and energy for reading aloud. I do not know one family in which as much reading aloud goes on as the parents themselves enjoyed in their childhood . . .

And in all this diminishment of the book it is Poetry which suffers most. Perhaps Poetry has not, for a long time, had much place in the average home? Perhaps not, but it has had – till recently – an extraordinary potency in the cultivated home. And very likely what matters for the future of poetry is NOT that great numbers should have a rather reluctant acquaintance with some not much esteemed specimens of verse; but that enough people should have absorbed and been so penetrated as children with poetry as to have undergone its transforming power.

As to what happens in the transformation and how it happens, I am persuaded that only close minute study of the modes in which meanings interact with and modify one another in various poetries can lead us toward useful surmises.

12. LITERATURE FOR THE UNLETTERED

Politics has often enough been described as the study, the craft, the art or science of the practicable, the possible. The intention behind the claim is commonly flattering, sometimes self-flattery. It is then an excuse, as a rule, for not doing, for not trying to do or even to experiment with, something which if it were to succeed would be useful. And in politics here we should include not only the handling of suasions, guidance of, contest with, public opinion, but all those multitudinous webs of personal ambitions, dependences, rivalries, jealousies, complots, oppositions ... which, perhaps inevitably, infest the bureaucratic worlds from school levels on up.

These despondent reflections arise here from wondering why the great new media: radio, tape, T.V., casette availabilities ... have not been more variously, more imaginatively, more venturesomely tried out in support of our spiritual inheritance; specifically, as means of helping Literature to have more impact upon those deprived of, unprepared for, access to it. Literature we take here in a wide and a critical sense, as utterance of high quality in whatever genre. In sum, why does professional expertise act as though nothing much of this sort were worth attempting? Plenty of enterprise has been shown in other fields, sometimes too much: TV exploitation of mountaineering, for example, has verged on the gladiatorial.

Physically, these media are among the most alerting instances of how the boundaries of the possible, the frontiers of the feasible, have in our own lifetimes been pushed back. Culturally, educationally, they have been among the most humiliating examples of human inability to take advantage of our new powers – "to the relief of man's estate". The disparity between the new resources and our uses of them is a reproach that has throughout their development been regularly pointed out – without effect. The contrast is indeed grotesque: on the occasion celebrating the twenty-fifth anniversary of British broadcasting, the Bishop of Gloucester told of an old Wiltshire farm labourer and his wife listening to their first broadcast. "Their eyes were almost bursting out of their heads with amazement and every now and again the old fellow muttered under his breath: 'The glory o' God, the glory o' God'." At about that time, I happened myself on an old Welsh Shepherd under Snowdon who had just bought a radio. "'Deed to goodness", he said, "it's grand to hear the pipple coughing and sneezing in Cardiff!"

What might we be offering in place of catarrhal and still more distressing outcomes of atmospheric and cultural smog? Let me risk here some outlines of what might prove practicable: opportunities that have not been explored in the measure that their promise should invite. The appeal in most of them would be to immediate comparison: to the pleasures of trying to see for oneself WHICH of presented alternatives one likes best. Many of them rely on that prodigious mutual control between ear and eye which is the source of the power of writing. There on the screen would stand the sentences, clear and steady in print, while the reading voice (or an alternation of voices) tries out challengingly various ways of saying them.

Such games of choosing or of sitting in judgement while choices are made and discussed presuppose, of course, some fairly well developed ability to read in the audience. I do not enter here on what has been, since 1930, my own chief literary interest: the use of the new media (screen, TV, video-tape) in the initial learning of Reading. Recommendations as to policy and practice in this can be found elsewhere.[1] Neglect of these practicables is the outstanding example of the educators' failure to use our new powers. I will, though, venture a warning. The unrivalled resources of the media for DISTRACTION can very easily lead to that replacing INSTRUCTION. The essential thing is for the learner to be helped in finding our for himself how to learn. He is not so helped by being Pied Piper'd off elsewhere. The etymons of *divergence, diversion* and *amusement* can convey my warning: Whoever will turn up and ponder *verge, verse,* and *muse* in, say, Eric Partridge's *Origins* will find good reasons to be wary: *amuse* has behind it a cow with its muzzle in the air; *not* feeding; bemused, may we say?

To return to what the media might be doing for moderately literate addressees and participants. How could the screen help them to find

[1] See, e.g. my *Speculative Instruments* (1955), Index; *So Much Nearer* (1968), Index; *Design for Escape* (1968), Appendix: all Harcourt Brace Jovanovich, New York. Also, Sheridan Baker, Jacques Barzun, I. A. Richards, *The Written Word* (Rowley, Mass.: Newbury House Publishers, 1971), pp. 61-85.

out more about what literature is and how it works? To find out more
for themselves – not, as with most lectures, just to be told. One of our
major troubles is that people have been led to expect TO BE TAUGHT –
not helped in learning how to learn.

To start with one of the simplest, most easily explored opportunities.
In video tape we have an uniquely flexible means for studying the
cooperations, the mutual control of ear and eye in reading. Consider
how we might be using it to interest more people more fruitfully in how
verse may be spoken, and in learning more about its movement. Here
the first hazard is, of course, the poet himself. Ever since Socrates had
his fun with Ion, the absurdities of poets and rhapsodes as interpreters
of their own and of others' poetry have been an unfailing spring of re-
freshing comedy. There is hardly a move made by Socrates and his
gently, tenderly handled victim which is not highly instructive for our
purposes here. A good reading of a suitably simplified *Ion* could be a
useful way of arousing curiosity about the poet's dealings with his work.
From Socrates' 'loadstone' theory of inspiration on to his conclusion
– which he summarises so astringently in the *Apology* – he is raising
one of the most awakening of all literary questions.

After the politicicans I went to the poets. I took lines from their own writings
and asked them what they meant, hoping to learn something from them.
Do you know: the truth is, almost anyone who was there could have talked
better than they did – even about the very poems they had written themselves. I soon saw that poets don't write from their own wisdom but from
what the gods tell them. Poets say great things but don't know what they
are saying. They are like oracles in that.[2]

Socrates believed in oracles. His ambivalence on inspiration (and his
attitude, almost his devotion, to Apollo) make this a very potent whet
to interest. The puzzles of the poet's pose or calling are unending. So
many of them seem so often, so clumsily, and yet so almost wilfully, to
get in the way of their poetry – reading it unintelligibly, commenting on
it without point or with deliberate distraction, substituting mannerisms
(personality quirks) for matter and so on. They might be wanting to play
their poetry down and steal the show. I recall remarking once – in introducing Robert Lowell to an ADVOCATE audience – that a wise government should make the distribution of poetry very easy but any ascertain-
ment of which poets wrote what impossible. Lowell in reply thought
this the worst plan ever. He was for more and better known poets. And
let the poetry take care of itself!

[2]   Version in Everyman's English from *Why So, Socrates?* etc.

Whatever may be the balanced view in this matter, the various readings of verses presented in print upon the screen should not, in general I think, include that of the poet. Coleridge, at the end of his great penultimate paragraph (in *Biographia Literaria*, Chapter XIV) with which we shall be further concerned, speaks, with a feeling that may have had sad experience behind it, of our need to "subordinate" . . . our admiration of the poet to our sympathy with the poetry". Given the current cult of celebrity, we do well to remember that words it is, not poets, make up poems.

Helen Vendler has wittily described poetry-reading audiences as being "like lemmings: moving in obedience to obscure compulsions" (*New York Times Book Review*, Nov. 7, 1971, p. 1). What we have to do is to replace these obscure compulsions by a comprehending concern. Readings such that hardly a soul in the Hall can take in from the public address system what the words are do not let "sympathy with the poetry" have much chance.

But while avoiding the poet we need not have recourse to the actor. A good reading of a poem should not, ordinarily, be a dramatic performance. It is fine for Ion to tell Socrates that "while reciting a tale of pity, my eyes are filled with tears; when it's a tale of terror, my hair stands up on end and my heart goes leaping". This entertains Socrates and helps him to his joke. "Why, Ion, what are we to make of a man like that . . . Shrinking back in fear though standing up before 20,000 friendly people!" But in general, and for deeply interesting reasons, actors are rarely good readers. And when the words are on view to show us perfectly which they are, there can arise especially a conflict of roles. A reader's duty is to suggest how the lines should be READ (and understood). An actor's business is to represent an ACTION. His training has been for that. But, though we may agree, we should not forget that producers are unlikely to think so. They will believe that the poetry needs pepping up with a performance and that a posturing figure before a color movie of the spring shores of Coniston Lake will be the way to put Wordsworth's *Daffodils* across. We can hardly say too strongly that to bring poetry to the unlettered we must allow the poetry to speak for itself – not bury it beneath adventitious trimmings. We should be exponents – not exhibitionists or undertakers – and, above all, beware of Showmanship.

Suitable readers, I suggest, should be varied in their styles. It will do no harm if some of them are what judges will regard as bad: irrelevant or exaggerated in their intonations: astray in their interpretations, accidental in their stressings and pausings; misleading in their rhythm. Most listeners are still oddly insensitive and over-tolerant as to the handling of the reading voice. Anyone familiar with the resources of musical criticism must be struck by the absence, as yet, of any comparable means of discriminating between readings aloud. It is as if no one thought that such differentiations could matter. Here, good opportunities to compare can do much: faultinesses can bring out by contrast what was unnoticed before. But if ability in comparing is to increase, we should have the better as well as the worse before us.

It is obvious in all this how great can be the advantages of cassette-carried presentations. Most differences being studied require REPEATED experience before they yield full fruit. We should be realizing that technology is now offering us immensely improved means of developing the very discriminations which can be expected to do most people most good. We are not yet benefiting from them and we will not without far more reflective and systematic experimentation than has yet been proposed or planned, much less attempted.

Two arts – the ART of reading poetry and the reciprocal art of listening with discrimination to such reading – can now be developed as never before. They depend upon recognition of the READING VOICE as our prime and indispensible instrument for exploring and comparing meanings. And we have to recognize too the equally indispensible co-operative work of the written notation, of print, in the study of meanings. Those who have proposed the dropping of reading-writing from education know too little both about how meanings have developed and how men have become more human. These thinkers are – it should be said forcibly – inadequately prepared for the role they have assumed.[3]

With cultivation of reading-listening go such minor matters as lineation, insets as rime markers, and the visual arrangement of stanza form. The physical conditions of the screen itself can bring these up: long lines must be broken for it as they need not be on the page. Where they are divided and how placed can make differences which belong with our understanding of line movement. So too with alternative punctuations and the use of capitals and italics. An unpunctuated sonnet started off what followed from William Empson's *Seven Types of Ambiguity*. Simpler problems suitable for the less lettered abound. The point is not so much that a shifted comma can distort a meaning. That is the casualty aspect. It is that punctuation affords exercise in percipience.

[3] These extremities of folly are well described by Sheridan Baker and Jacques Barzun in *The Written Word*.

Still more can comparison of phrasings, of different ways of saying what may profess to be the same thing. I choose, as an illustration a change which has much significance in its own right. It is the "slight alteration" (he calls it that) made by Coleridge in quoting at the end of that same Chapter XIV, from Sir John Davies' *Nosce Teipsum* (1599). As an illustration it is too challenging to be representative of the games of comparing for the unlettered that we are considering. I use it here because I have noticed that suitably simple examples are often disregarded, as mere school exercises, by many who have the talents needed for designing such games.

Coleridge prefaces his quotation with " 'Doubtless', as Sir John Davies observes of the soul (and his words may with slight alteration be applied, and even more appropriately, to the poetic IMAGINATION",

> Doubtless this could not be, but that she turns
>   Bodies to spirit by sublimation strange,
> As fire converts to fire the things it turns,
>   As we our food into our nature change.

In the fourth line Davies wrote *meat*. Perhaps Coleridge (no great carnivore) just remembered the more universal rather than the more robust Elizabethan term. We may recall Walter De la Mare's line:

> Whatever Miss T. eats turns into Miss T.

In the next stanza Coleridge made no change except in the spelling. I will use the original:

> From their grosse *matter* she abstracts the *formes,*
>   And drawes a kind of Quintessence from things;
> Which to her proper nature she transformes,
>   To beare them light on her celestiall wings:

Now come the alterations:

> This doth she when from things *particular*
>   She doth abstract the *universall kinds,*
> Which bodilesse and immateriall are,
>   And can be lodg'd but onely in our minds:

> Thus does she when from individual states
>   She doth abstract the universal kinds;
> Which then re-clothed in divers names and fates
>   Steal access through our senses to our minds.

Divers is one of Davies' favorite words; the next stanza opens with

And thus from divers accidents and acts

which may have prompted *divers names and fates* and the *Thus* above.

There are obviously many points that might be long debated in these changes without any convincing evidence appearing as to whether we should make much or make little of them. We may hold that *individual states* as against *things particular* converts a bare reference to Platonic doctrine into a lively invitation to speculate: *individual*: 'not to be split up', 'living and acting as wholes'; *states*: 'conditions (as in the solid, liquid and gaseous states)' with something of the political meaning of the city state: My mind to me a kingdom is? Again, we may think that *then re-clothed in divers names and fates* is a very bold transformation, a sublimation indeed, bringing in the great questions so much discussed under the heading, imageless thought. Those *universall kinds* in Davies are only negatively contrasted with *things particular* and thus (were other passages in *Nosce Teipsum* left out of account) in some danger of becoming inconveyable. In Coleridge they are given fresh embodiment (in the teeth of *bodilesse and immateriall*) and apparelled in changed *names and fates*: 'new symbols and altered consequences'. It is by these transformed habiliments that Coleridge's universals are enabled to *Steal access through our senses to our minds*. We may think this *Steal* the most significant and intriguing of his adjustments. Are *our senses* here 'necessary channels'? Or are they rather protections, normally preventing access of the Ideas to our minds – needing to be outwitted by the Imagination, as by a smuggler slipping through the Coastguards? Coleridge's "slight alteration" may here seem virtually to be defying Davies' prohibition. It may, however, merely be reembodying meanings of phrase after phrase: 'synthetic and magical power', 'gentle and unnoticed controul' in the account of the Imagination that has just been given.

It may help with what follows to quote from the remarks prefixed to Nahum Tate's edition (1697) of *Nosce Teipsum*. "Written by an ingenius and learned Divine", these comments on the principal poetic composition of Queen Elizabeth's Attorney-General may quite well have had their influence on Coleridge's famous paragraph:

in this, as in a mirror (that will not flatter) we see how the soul arbitrates in the understanding on the various reports of sense, and all the changes of imagination: how compliant the will is to her dictates, and obeys her as a queen does her king: at the same time acknowledging a subjection, and yet retaining a majesty: how the passions move at her command, like a well-disciplined army; from which regular composure of the faculties, all operating in their proper time and place, there arises a complacency upon the whole soul, that infinitely transcends all other pleasures.

Would that the Attorney-Generals of our times could show us as much or solemnize so high a marriage of their Bible and their Plato! We do not enough remember that Lady Jane Grey thought hunting and other female sport but a shadow compared with the pleasure there is to be found in Plato.

As I have remarked, this illustration may ask for a too minute and exacting analysis to be offered to the participants we have in mind. It is too recondite. But it does bring out an important point. The aim of a suitable exercise is not just to explain (or dissolve) difficulties but to heighten awareness of what is happening and thus improve our ability to look into and select from among meanings.

More appropriate for our less qualified students would be comparison of the *Ion* with what is said of "the poet described in ideal perfection" in the paragraph leading up to the quotation from *Nosce teipsum*. Let us try what a controlled paraphrase can do with it, remembering that there can be many such versions using varying degrees of focus. But first, let us see what this "controul" (to use Coleridge's spelling) may be.

We well know what high intricacies of stanza form, meter and rime-scheme can do to the process of composition, and what a variety of less AND more adequate solutions each problem that the poem sets itself can call up. As the conditions being imposed grow stricter selective attention is heightened. With so many possibilities barred out, those that remain undergo closer study. Much of this is a balancing between alternates – thematic, lexical, syntactic, phonologic . . . The effect is to make all the items being balanced grow more distinct. The grounds for rejecting some of them enter in and develop those for preferring others. Every writer who has indulged in elaborate verse knows how many proposals come up which would never otherwise have occurred to him and how many mutual bearings among the meanings that have joined in the game have to be discerned and taken account of. A degree of awareness of all the aspects of these choices can be induced which is beyond anything aroused in an unrestricted free verbal flow. He learns too what an exchange of mutual services the phonologic, the syntactic, the lexical, and the thematic levels maintain.

With, commonly, a dropping of the phonologic components, all this is true – in considerable measure – in controlled paraphrase. The control may take the form of restriction to some specified Word-List, or avoidance of some set of constructions or a limitation of sentence length: such are some of the analogues to meter and rime in the writing of verse. These barriers too cause more proposals to come up for judgment, raise the degree of attention that has to be given to the competing alternates, compel deeper searchings of the successive problems, and lead to a wider awareness of what the phrasings under examination can mean. The analogies between controlled paraphrase and verse writing are indeed remarkable. The stricter the conditions of the task, the more penetrating the task – up to a certain point. Then, as the going gets too hard, the strain imposed by the rules of the game becomes excessive and the job to be done loses precedence.

Let us test these observations out on the Coleridge paragraph. The control here used is that of an adapted Basic English: Everyman's English[4]

ORIGINAL. The poet, described in ideal perfection,

brings the whole soul of man into activity, with the subordination of its faculties to each other according to their relative worth and dignity. He diffuses a tone and spirit of unity,

that blends, and (as it were) fuses, each into each, by that synthetic and magical power,

EVERYMAN'S. The *poet*, if we may say what he is and does at his best, and though no writer of verse may ever, in fact, come up to such a level, puts every power of man's mind and heart into operation with every one of them taking that part in the common work in which it is specially able and has value and authority. He makes the work seem and feel, all through, as though everything in it is needed by, gives support to, and takes support from the rest (is what it is so that the rest may be what it is), he puts things together (as though made liquid by great heat so that they become no longer, in themselves or in their effects,

---

4 Everyman's English. See *Techniques of Language Control* by Richards and Gibson (Rowley, Mass.: Newbury House Publishers, 1974).

| to which I would exclusively appropriate the name of Imagination. | what they would be if separated) by that uniting power for which I would keep the word "Imagination". |

We may pause here to recall that this "subordination of the soul's fa-culties to each another according to their relative worth and dignity" is what is displayed at such length in the *Republic* in terms of the analogy of the three parts of the soul – knowledge, spirit,[5] appetite – with the three components of the state – guardians, guards, workers – As in the key stanza of Donne's "The Extasie",

> So must pure lovers soules descend
>   T'affections and to faculties
> Which sense may reach and apprehend,
>   Else a great Prince in prison lies,

The affections and the faculties here are the intermediaries (the senti-ments or feelings, as we might call them) through which alone that which should rule – the great Prince – can control that which should be ruled. Knowledge cannot by itself reach down to sense (appetite, desire), nor sense reach up to knowledge, without the aid of spirit. Coleridge's account here is a description of Sophrosyne (Temperance). His marked insistence on control may well be a reply to Socrates' mocking account of Ion as being beside himself as though possessed. It will be noted that he returns to the theme of due subordination to be achieved through the "magical and synthetic power, IMAGINATION".

| This power, first put in action by the will and under-standing, and retained under their irre-missive, though gentle and un-noticed control . . . reveals itself in the balance or reconcilement of opposite or discordant qualities: | This power is first moved to its work by conscious purpose and a knowledge of what it is doing, and it is kept under their control throughout – though smoothly and without seeming to be so kept. The Imagination is seen to be at work through the way in which it makes forces or conditions which as a rule, are not able to work together, or are even against one another, give one another room |

[5] "The will (the Platonic Θυμός) which is the sustaining, coercive, ministerial power, the functions of which in the individual correspond to the officers of war and police in the ideal Republic of Plato." (*The Statesman's Manual*, Appendix B.)

	for free play and even get on well together like friends. For example: it makes things able to be the same and at the same time different:
of sameness with difference;	
of the general with the concrete;	be clear examples of general laws and still be no less fully themselves in every least detail;
the sense of novelty and freshness with old and familiar objects;	through it things we have had about us for a long time, and have become used to, seem new — as if then for the first time seen;
a more than usual state of emotion with more than usual order;	feelings become stronger and freer than in most of our living, though their behavior to one another is better; the mind being like a self-ruling, well-ruled state;
judgment ever awake and steady self-possession with enthusiasm and feeling profound or vehement;	the purpose and the ways to it are ever in view and the self keeps itself in control however high or deep or strong the waves of feeling may be;
and while it blends and harmonizes the natural and the artificial, still subordinates art to nature;	and while it adjusts to one another what is natural and what is made by art, still keeps the writer's design from becoming anything more than the servant of natural forces;
the manner to the matter;	makes 'how a thing is said' be ruled by 'what has to be said';
and our admiration of the poet to our sympathy with the poetry.	and puts our interest in what is being made before our respect for or questions about the man who made it.

We have been considering means — by use of the reading voice and by controlled paraphrase — for improving interpretation of short relatively detachable pieces of verse and prose. It will have been noted,

I hope, that the aim has not been the attainment of any substitutable version but the development of a more than usual intensity of inquiry into the original. (What Coleridge described in the poet, that – with "slight alteration" – I have been applying to the reading of sentences.) Let us now pass to a larger question: how can we help people hardly at all acquainted with Literature as the continuing embodiment of tradition? And especially with the great enduring sources of our possibilities of thought, feeling, sentiment, and will, the springs, in fact, of whatever may flow through us?

Probably the most useful suggestion here is offered by the group of metaphors active with *spring*: leap, fountain, season (re-beginning) moving, impelling cause, force, motive . . . the inchoative or, to use one of Coleridge's favorite words, INITIATIVE. There are many subjects, fields of interest and study, in which one sequence, one order, is manifestly and demonstrably more propitious, more likely to lead into sustained advance than any other, it being that order in which what comes FIRST is both, in itself, most intelligible and awakening, AND most helpful in making the following steps intelligible. This is so, for example, in the learning of Reading and of a second language. (And perhaps – though none yet knows – of the mother tongue itself, and possibly of all learning). There is, at least, good reason to think that what is true of these prime studies may prove as true of a controlled initial exploration into our tradition. But, of course, if this best order is to be made effective we must find ways of handing the initiative to the learner himself. Nothing resembling any survey course in the history of literature is being here proposed.

What we must do instead is to prepare special versions of the first great works: the launchings of our culture, the master springs, and arrange them in the sequences that – with due support from the reading voice – prove most awakening. I repeat this word as a reminder that in Shelley's Cave of Inspiration (*Prometheus Unbound*, III, iii, 113), itself a replaying of the Cave of the Nymphs (*Odyssey*, XIII) and not without an echo of *Republic* (514),

> in the midst
> A fountain leaps with an awakening sound.

What we should be doing in this initiation into Literature is devising opportunities for inspiration. In a very deep sense we should be attempting a re-minding.

These special versions – some of them, the *Iliad* and the earliest sources in the Old Testament, for example, will be of Literature which pre-dates writing – must, of course, be designed with due care, with the sort of varied awarenesses, preveniences, and concern, that we expect in say, heart or brain surgery, or from those who stand behind space-vehicle launchings. For what is at stake in these experiments in cultural engineering is plainly of incomparably greater importance than any individual's continuance as living or than the timing of a scientific advance. It is the quality of the human future that they will endeavor to improve and protect. That this is so must, I believe, be admitted by all who know what a great book is. What we offer in this initiation must be rightly chosen and shaped. So too must the conduct of the voices which read them. As to just how the choices are to be made, the versions be written and the inspiration proved, we may fairly appeal to what has been recently learnt of the role of experimentation on an adequate scale in other explorations – spatial and biological for example.

What we will, practically, have most to beware of is – to recur to the theme of my opening paragraph – gain-seeking, distractive ballyhoo. And here is what Partridge in *Origins* has to say about this word.

bally, coll euphemism for expletive *bloody,* owes something to the boisterous village of Ballyhooly (in County Cork) whence AE coll *ballyhoo,* noisy preliminary publicity, whence AE *hooey,* bunkum. See BUNCOMBE).
buncombe, insincere speech – hence insincere talk, hence nonsense; in C20 usu *bunkum,* whence, by abbr, *bunk:* Buncombe, that county in North Carolina which was represented (1819-21) by Felix Walker; persisting in longwinded speech, he said that his electors expected him to 'make a speech for Buncombe' (Webster).

As the current term puts it: *Madison Avenue.* If that were somehow avoided (those that know most about the media will be most doubtful here) a hooey-free enterprise matching in rectitude and scale of effort the sending of a probe to Jupiter could set going what is needed: a planet-widespread awareness of human nature deep enough to keep man from wrecking himself.

Upon what literature might be most helpful it is possible to be fairly specific in exemplification. Any attempt as yet to lay out a full program would be premature, but some main principles of a due selection are evident enough. The two great confluents of our culture (its taproots, if you like), the Hellenic and the Hebraic, must be represented, each with its major internal tensions, since these give to each its own unique propelling drive and create between them their perpetual conflict, collaboration, and mutual control: "the balance or reconcilement of opposite or discordant qualities."

For the Hellenic stream the major internal tension is that between the *Iliad* and the Socratic dialogues, between, we might say, Achilles and Socrates as hero-models for man. In countless ways Homer, "the educator of Greece" embodies the opposites of the designs Plato offers for the individual (man or woman) and for the State. Plato's models, as Werner Jaeger shows so amply in his *Paideia*, amount to the invention (or discovery, if you prefer) of a conception, capable of growth and propagation, of what the human endeavor should be. It is a conception that has stood in such strong contrast to those obtaining in other cultures, over which today it is extending its transforming rule so widely. Plato's design is opposed to the Homeric world – as plus is to minus, and, for that reason, deeply dependent. Without Homer to depart from there could have been no Plato. And within and behind Plato's models much that is Homeric lives on. Nations, for example, remain appallingly Achillean.

We may note, as closely relevant to our purpose, that the Homeric-Platonic opposition corresponds with, and is largely resultant from, the transformation of a pre-literate culture into one that has become extraordinarily responsive to writing, Eric Havelock, (in his *Preface to Plato*) has well described these changes – with a discernment and realization of their consequences which is, as compared with the opinions of Marshall McLuhan, again as plus is to minus. A reflective reader of Plato is, beside an Ion, a system of vastly extended capacities. None the less the new culture can encompass the Homeric order, though its judgment of that will be different. As I write far more than half the human population are trying to accomplish an analogous transition. What proportion of them are failing, and thereby being left mentally nowhere, no one knows. It is most probably huge. They are attempting to pass from inevitably polluted and decaying pre-literate cultures to some sort of substitute carried less by living example and custom than by radio and TV commercials and by cinema – media which are at present providing what amount to travesties, gross wrenchings of derivatives from the Hellenic tradition. And, nearer home than Africa, it is with this dauntingly crucial transition – from pre-literacy to the Ads., from sets of mores conveyed mainly by word of mouth and parental example to what TV, cinema, and pulp offer in its place – that our new megalopolitan populations are supposed to COPE. [Here again, the etymon is not encouraging: *cope*, v (to deal adequately with) ME *coupen*: OF

couper, colper, to hit, strike, from *coup*, a blow, (powerful) stroke . . .
from LL *colaphus*, a kick, a cuff or punch (*ORIGINS*)]. And many
bemused citizens wonder why the crime rate is rising. A F.B.I.-recorded
80% increase in reported rapes in the first six months of 1971 in Washington, D.C. is surely a sufficient portent. The traditional, large personal
channels have been broken and the assaulters now have less than nothing (only minus exemplars) to guide them. (My pen, which seems sometimes to be trying to help with its LAPSUS CALAMI interventions, has
been writing UNLETTED when I intended UNLETTERED! Its point, I take
is, is that WRAGG is not in custody.)

The other great confluent (indeed more often the major stream) of
what was our culture – the Hebraic – is, for very mixed reasons, less
easily outlined. Countless Bibles hide in Hotel drawers and spread-
eaglewise adorn Lecterns in places of worship; but what impact their
contents still have grows ever harder to assess. Nor is it in the least an
easier matter to judge the values, past or present, of most items in their
content. Blake ventured the view that

> The strongest poison ever known
> Came from *Caesar's Laurel crown*

There have been some who have held that "Jacob on his own" might
be a wiser suggestion. And many other odd examples are exalted in
Holy Writ. Much in it has been regardlessly distorted by doctrinal concern. Hardly any of its multifarious ingredients have not been merci-
lessly misused: forced by contending parties to serve opposing purposes
and given by superbly equipped scholars quite incompatible interpretations. None the less – and this is why Coleridge called it *The Statesman's
Manual* – there is no literature and no encheiridion from which more
that most deeply matters has been, and perhaps still can be, learnt. And
this can be admitted even by those ready to charge the Bible for much
that has been atrocious in the conduct of its adherents. Not all lessons
are beneficial. Attempts to restore some knowledge of the Bible through
intelligent reading via the media must reckon not only with its fearsome
powers but with much further probable misuse. The protection is that
no literature better shows how equally compelling opposed views of it
can be.

For example, the greatest confluent of the Old Testament, the Book
of Job, consists of a verse drama enclosed in a folk-tale prose-frame.
First-order authorities have upheld every possible theory of the relations – chronologic, thematic, dramatic, theologic – of the poem to its

frame. All that is agreed upon by all is that both are pre-eminent: each unmatched in its kind by anything else in the literatures of the world. There has been, however, growing agreement among scholars of the last century or so that these two masterpieces are irreconcilably incompatible in the extremest degree. There is a victim, named Job, in both; but these victims are radically opposed in character; one proverbially patient, the other rebellious beyond limit. Moreover, their circumstances and their afflictions are very different and neither knows anything about the other's situation or sufferings. Further, their Afflictors are as diverse as the victims: a Super-Sheik in the folk-tale; a Cosmic Creator in the Poem. Lastly, the endings the two offer are as apart as any can be. None of all which has, however, prevented the Book of Job from being presented and received by pastors and their flocks as a single harmonious work through over a score of changing centuries. And this strange state of affairs, in varying measure, is the case with much else in the literatures comprised in both Testaments.

We would be mistaken, though, I suggest, were we to conclude that such uncertainty makes the greatest works in the Bible unsuited for study by the unlettered, if we can contrive, through reading via the media, to return them (unruined) to the general consciousness. The truth, as I see it, is that we have nothing to take their place. And nothing that can make their successors so intelligible. The Bible, however understood, has been the source in them of too much – excellences and defects alike – for any to read them discerningly without it.

And, we must recall, we must restore and retain the inexhaustible interinanimations (Donne's word) of the Hellenic and Hebraic confluences: the interplay of themes common to both, though with what differences of handling. To consider the brothers' account of injustice at the outset of Book Two of the *Republic* along with Job's arraignment of existence is to be offered a peculiarly entire view of the central problem of living. It is a preparation, to be gained in no other way, for seeing it as later masters, as Shakespeare and Donne, Marvell and Milton, Wordsworth and Arnold . . . have seen it and for facing it as we ourselves must meet it. Squanderers of inestimable energies, let us devote some of them to opening such opportunities to all.

13. SOURCES OF OUR COMMON AIM

Confession is no doubt good for the soul: for the confessing soul and sometimes for some of the souls to whom the admissions are made. It may be well, then, to begin by a mention of what happened in me when I first really resolutely attempted to immerse myself in the *Iliad*. I was by no means completely ignorant of it. There had been some large volumes of the Earl of Derby's verse translation on a reachable shelf when I was a little boy – wide and spacious pages of verse as I seem to recall them – and there had been a Bohn translation in laborious prose rather later: both no more than desultorily dipped into. And I suppose that I would have professed some sort of knowledge of the chief characters and of the action by the time my first serious attempt to read it properly was made. This was, as I now see it, strangely late. I was in my middle thirties and had been a university teacher at Cambridge for some time.

If I linger a little before coming out with the truth here, that should be forgivable. I felt then, and have been more and more conscious of it since, the need for excuses. Perhaps the occasion was too unsuitable. I needed a book – preferably something pocketable – to be absorbed in through a Trans-Siberian Railway journey from Moscow to Vladivostok lasting about twelve days. The *Iliad,* I hoped, would take care of that. There were, it is true, not a few distractions. But thinking of the reading Napoleon managed on his visit to Russia, that did not seem a plea that would stand up. There was also the version I chose: Lang, Leaf, and Myers. It bristled with *thees* and *thous, thereofs, wherebys, haths, doths,* and *-eths* throughout – a "grievous bane" indeed; but, nonetheless and despite all that, how could I have remained untouched by what – however oddly – the pages still were saying? The sad fact I must now be candid about is that I got nowhere, though I spent plenty of hours as the train jolted along, and came out from my reading even more empty-minded than I went in. And with the failure there perked up, I recall, quite ridiculous misconceptions and suspicions of and revolts against I don't know how much of tradition.

In view of what the *Iliad* was to become for me later, and of what it still offers me to pursue, this sheer unmitigated defeat deserves to be recorded. It is worth pondering. Among the adventures that minds may meet, few, it is likely, might better repay observation and reflection than the initial encounters with works that are as yet beyond their measure. What may go wrong, and how could some fruitful transmission be helped? More than is currently imagined may turn upon such inquiries. Looking back now, some random lines from a parody of "Old Man's Comforts" I once read (about 1902 it would be) recur to me. They were written to satirize the inept early conduct of the Boer War; *Clara in Blunderland* was the title of the book, and Balfour's government its target:

> In my youth, said John Bull, t'was ever my plan
>   To win victory after defeat;
> And I certainly thought that the worse I began
>   The better my chances to beat!

However this may be, it is not imprudent to expect that things that may in time come to matter for one profoundly will at first be felt as not only unpromising but as actually repellent, even perhaps corruptive. The early impression is often a measure of the degree of change required in the reader.

When it comes to the new world embodied in a great book, a newcomer's eye has to learn to see. That ordinarily requires not a little active exploration. And the seeing as it develops is going to entail considerable readjustments. These are indeed the sources of its growing attraction.

> Great things are done when Men and Mountains meet;
> This is not done by Jostling in the Street,

wrote William Blake, without stopping to polish up the second line.[1] (Many who recall it substitute "seen when" for that *done by*.) It is safe to say that these Mountains are not those that put their spell upon the modern climber. They are metaphorical and have more to do with Horeb, or Sinai, than with Everest and the Eiger. The great things there done occur

> In your Imagination, of which this World of Mortality is but a Shadow.[2]

[1] *Gnomic Verses*, i.
[2] William Blake, *Jerusalem*.

We shall see below how radically Platonic Blake's conception here is.

Not all the new worlds that great books offer us entail for all readers so much challenge, though many and perhaps most do. There are, of course, a happy few among readers who can sometimes enter a fresh demesne at once and without labor. With Homer and these Mountains of the Imagination together on this page, we may well think of Keats standing in stout Cortez's shoes,

> Silent upon a peak in Darien.

Chapman, though, however "loud and bold" he may be, is, as sampling can soon show, far indeed from making Homer plain sailing for a modern reader.

Having confessed my own humbling repulse, I must in fairness tell the rest of the story. It is bound up with much else concerning the making of the key ideas in great books as widely available as may be. That very Trans-Siberian journey, which was so unfruitful as regards Homer, took me to Peking to teach English literature – to extremely able Chinese students – and to begin myself to learn some of the elementary facts that were to make me, in time, recognize such teaching as a truly impracticable undertaking. The sheer incomprehensibility to my audiences of what I had to offer forced me by degrees back into considering – as I had hardly done before – how I myself had, so I thought, come to comprehend whatever I did of what I was trying to put before them. Though I had been lecturing on English Literature at Cambridge for ten years and writing books largely about meanings and how we may mistake them, I had not, I note now, attempted any at all searching account of what understanding depends on. It was no doubt something to have read for the Moral Sciences Tripos, concentrating on psychology, linguistics, learning theory, and especially on the grounds for assent and belief, but none of that had prepared me at all usefully for what I met. It had not as yet taught me to see how much there was in human learning to be thought about and how little of it all I had noticed.

My Chinese students' difficulties throughout were cultural rather than linguistic. Their troubles in understanding what English-using authors were trying to do sprang from their almost complete unfamiliarity with the ideas, attitudes, feelings, hopes, doubts, wishes, aims, and so forth, on and through which those authors worked. It was not that the students did not know enough words or could not put them together in more or less our sentence forms. They had, in fact, an astounding power of acquiring them. They picked up vocabulary and structure as good flypaper collects flies. But the acquisitions just stuck. They could not grow; they were not alive. They could be used, as a mechanical device for maneuvering meanings, but, alas, the meanings so managed were Chinese and, as a rule, not at all those with which the English work was concerned.

As this sad – and terrifyingly dangerous – situation became clearer, it was natural to ask why there was no comparable obstacle to Chinese advances in the sciences. There was none. As we have seen since then, the Chinese can well keep pace with any nation in techniques: notably, those needed for our joint destruction. What unhappily they cannot do is comprehend the moral-political-philosophical ideas that are commonly regarded in the Western world as our prime cultural treasure, that by which we live. They fail in this just as we fail to comprehend the Chinese moral-political-philosophical principles: *their* prime cultural treasure, that by which *they* live. In terms of conduct, careful, informed and impartial observers can be found to maintain that – by and large and circumstances allowed for – the Chinese are traditionally more moral, more responsible and law-abiding, better citizens, more dependable, and far less given to casual violence than most Western peoples. But these are tricky comparisons; our powers of estimating our own and our fellows' judgments in such matters are, as yet, inadequate.

However, what became apparent as more and more concrete and harrowing illustrations accumulated of the very things I had, in academic abstractedness, been writing about in Cambridge (for instance, in a book called *Science and Poetry,* published in 1926) and as the lessons sank home, was that I must somehow try:

(1) to do something to ease, in time, the task set the Chinese people and the Western peoples of understanding better one another's positions for living, and

(2) by the same means help forward and speed up a supply of persons more competent to meet what were clearly going to be the ever more overtaxing problems of our planet.[3]

(These resolutions took shape early in 1931 when I passed from Peking to Cambridge, England, through Harvard – serving my first term there as Visiting Lecturer. *Ulysses, The Possessed,* and *The Secret Agent* were, I recall, my themes. I was also, with my *Mencius on the Mind,* doing what I could to show how Chinese and Western cultures

[3] For a fuller discussion of this situation, see I. A. Richards, *Design for Escape,* paperback (New York: Harcourt, Jovanovich, 1968).

could be so mutually incommunicable.) As it happened – though this was not as yet at all clearly realized by me – I had a substantial part of what was to become a program as to (1) and (2) already to hand.

BASIC ENGLISH

While C. K. Ogden and I were enjoying ourselves scribbling out *The Meaning of Meaning (The Beading of Beading,* we called it, because we had so many heavy head colds as it progressed through 1918-21), some of the best fun we had was with its chapter 6, on Definition. In the course of this we realized that a relatively small number of words could, theoretically and within describable limits of exactitude, deputize for the rest of the Dictionary. If so, a suitably chosen selection would yield a general-purpose, minimum-cost, but maximum-utility English that could bridge innumerable linguistic gulfs. The huge task of that selection and the provision of a comparably simplified syntax were to become a large part of Ogden's lifework through the next ten years. When I got back to Cambridge, England, from Cambridge, Massachusetts, in 1931, he had his recommendations ready. He had labeled them BASIC ENGLISH (BASIC was then an almost unused word) and was ready to launch his project.

Some day a historian may try to tell what happened. My own account would be that much went amazingly well until World War Two swept away successful and expanding developments in many countries: China, India, Russia, Greece among them. Then, toward the end of the war, Churchill and Roosevelt took up the project. That, for a couple of decades or so, consigned it to the doghouse. Fantastic misdescriptions were concocted and zealously spread by people who knew next to nothing about it. What it had already done and had shown itself able to do were ignored. It became a taboo topic in linguistic and educational circles.

There is much here to interest students of the ways in which professional opinion can resist for a while (even for a long while) possibilities that may disturb their routines. Anyone who reflectively inquires into Basic English[4] will find in Ogden's work a superlatively ingenious,

---

[4] C. K. Ogden, *Basic English: International Second Language*, ed. E. C. Graham (New York: Harcourt, Brace & World, 1968), includes his *Basic English, The ABC of Basic English*, and *The Basic Words*. E. C. Graham, ed., *Basic Dictionary of Science* (New York: Macmillan Co., 1966), published in England as *The Science Dictionary in Basic English* (London: Evan Brothers, 1965), and C. K. Ogden, comp., *The General Basic English Dictionary* (London: Evans Brothers, 1960) are invaluable resources in work with restricted forms of English.

thorough, exact, and comprehensive piece of linguistic engineering, boldly original, scrupulously consistent, and speculatively stimulating in the highest degree. It is indeed one of the most impressive intellectual achievements and its inventor one of the outstanding wits and polymaths of a notable generation. And yet how many who have never bothered to look into it have been content to echo the misrepresentations of others as little acquainted with it as themselves. This tide of fashion, however, has now turned. The needs that Basic was designed to meet have now become too great to be any longer ignored. Yet partisan opposition continues.

For our purposes – making as widely available as possible all over the world the best that has been thought and said – Basic English or variants equally deriving from its fundamental design can serve in three ways, one direct and obvious, the others less so:

(1) By supplying a more economical way into English, giving a greater return and earlier, with less expenditure of time and effort
(2) By enabling the key question: WHAT SHOULD BE LEARNED BEFORE WHAT? to be submitted to new types of experimental inquiry
(3) By offering a clear model or paradigm of the development of the meanings of which a culture consists.

To take these one by one, the first is the obvious advantage. As with other technical matters, its effectiveness can only be discovered through trying it out, but those who do this must study and follow the directives. The point of number two is that with few enough words and minimal necessary constructions, the optimal ORDER OF ACQUISITION becomes an explorable problem. Find the sequence in which what is learned earlier best prepares for what should be learned later: that is the assignment. With Basic, one can experiment in the design of learning sequences in ways not practicable in less controlled languages. In all development – from an embryo's first stages on up to the discrimination of meanings – sequence becomes increasingly the key principle. This should hardly be surprising: "Not only speech, but all skilled acts seem to involve the same problems of serial ordering, even down to the temporal coordination of muscular contractions in such a movement as reaching and grasping."[5] What is true of performance is equally true of growth. And as what is to happen mounts in complexity, we can reasonably expect due sequence, serial order, to become ever more important. Grasping a

[5] K. S. Lashley, "The Problem of Serial Order in Behavior", in *The Hixon Symposium*, ed. Lloyd A. Jeffress (New York: John Wiley & Sons, 1961), pp. 121-122.

meaning in a book is an immeasurably more complex achievement than reaching out and taking up a pencil. This is a spelling out of the implications of UNTIL. Innumerable steps in the growth of organs cannot succeed UNTIL the necessary earlier steps have been taken. And the acquisition of a language is a growth of an organ, literally as well as metaphorically. So too is the acquisition and development of the concepts that the language is to handle.

The third advantage of Basic derives from the fact that most meanings are modifications of earlier meanings, restructurings within them. Robert Hutchins quotes Jean Cocteau as saying that "each great work in Western thought arises as a contradiction of one that precedes it".[6] *Contradiction* here is too strong a word, reflecting a contentious rather than dialectic spirit. It is better to say with Hutchins at the foot of his page, "Every statement calls for explanation, correction, modification, expansion, or contradiction." Of these, contradiction is likely to be least helpful. We may say of it what Alexander Bain said of osculation: "The occasion should be adequate and the actuality rare." Often we will not understand what is being meant unless we can see both what it is a departure from and what it is guarding itself from becoming. A good dictionary is a partial record of these differentiations and interrelationships. All etymology and all history of usage bear this out. Properly speaking, we cannot understand any word by itself. We have to sense how it stands to other words, what it will do when put into sentences with them, which words it can cooperate with and which it must keep away. These things we somehow learn without more than occasionally seeing at all clearly how we learn them. But unless we have learned them, the needed understanding will not occur. And this, which is obvious as it is recorded in dictionaries, is equally true of ideas in the larger sense in which they are what great books embody, organize, and can convey. Indeed it is true, throughout, of the interactions and oppositions among meanings, as is magnificently made clear in the *Syntopicon,* that monumental outcome of superlative discernment, industry, collaboration, and organization.[7] This work shows, as no slighter indication and exposition could, how dependent upon one another are the myriad components of our culture. As its Preface remarks: "each of the great ideas is directly or remotely

---

[6] *GBWW*, Vol. 1, p. 76.
[7] *GBWW*, Vols. 2-3. One would have thought that the virtues of this work, as pointing the way to – and, in fact, enabling – arrangements for making all wisdom available to all genuine inquirers, as the computer age advances, would have been by now far more widely and more effectively recognized than they are. How slow the world is to accept and take advantage of the help it most needs!

related to many others – perhaps to all – through a network of connections radiating from each idea as a point of origin".[8] Could a comparable analysis and presentation be achieved for the Chinese tradition, similar connexities would appear there. And if the fearsome tasks of comparison that translation must raise were faced, man's future would look more secure. The reason the Chinese and the Western people do not understand one another is that the affiliations and resistances, the requirements and exclusions within each of the two cultures are in too many ways too radically different.

My class in Tsinghua University burst into loud applause when the black flag went up telling that Tess of the D'Urbervilles had been hanged (I was reading the page aloud to them). They had been waiting all through the book for the lack of respect Tess had shown for her father to be suitably punished. What Hardy had in mind in writing the book could make no sort of sense whatsoever to them, though, as the applause showed, they were doing their best to admire it.

"The President of the Immortals had ended his sport with Tess." Consider that sentence and how Hardy is able here to use the peculiar forces of its terms. Thanks to its history, a range of possible uses has come to *President* that no word with another history can offer. So too with *Immortals* and with *sport*. It is not, of course, the case that the user need wittingly know these histories. Even Hardy, even his best reader imaginable, may not think of, may not even be in any way aware of, important parts of these histories. The words can work, can exert their powers, without any of that philological knowledge being present and active in writer's or reader's mind. The contexts in which the words have been met, the situations through which their users have learned what the words may do, can operate perfectly without those concerned having any inkling of how it all happens. It is, of course, very unlikely that Hardy and many good readers will not more or less consciously FEEL that Zeus and the Olympians are being brought up-to-date, and that the irony of the contrast between their triviality and the tragic fate of the mortals grows the bitterer when that malcontent family and court is turned into a Corporation. Similarly, many, and Hardy included, may consciously recall,

> As flies to wanton boys, are we to the gods,
> They kill us for their sport.[9]

---

[8]   *GBWW*, Vol. 2, p. xxiv.
[9]   Wliliam Shakespeare, *King Lear*, act 4, sc. 1.

But the force of the word can be felt without Shakespeare coming to mind, just as, for him, the *Iliad* need not have been consciously alluded to. The point is that great ideas and their derivatives have innumerable other channels which bypass the chief forming loci of their use. Needless to say, this does NOT diminish the usefulness of the knowledge of such loci or of an explicit awareness of how great utterances shape and are shaped by later utterances that echo, apply, support, or oppose them. Such explicit knowledge, conveyable through the *Syntopicon* and perhaps through less exacting instruments for which it will serve as a model, may be our best means, indeed perhaps our only means, of restoring the availability of man's intellectual and moral resources at a time when the innumerable other channels mentioned above seem to be (as dismaying evidence often suggests) clogging up.

However this may be, it is certain that my Chinese students, having met *President, Immortals,* and *sport* only through supposed Chinese 'equivalents', inevitably with different histories, could have no sense of how explosive the conjunction of the three English words could be. Their Immortals are not ours – though a formal definition: 'not liable to death', might be the same. Sports, for them and for us, in view of the Hunting Parks in which the Son of Heaven could enjoy diversion, may be more alike – but not deeply. And as to *President,* a foreign importation, as concept and as title, and from the first – with Yüan Shih-k'ai and Sun Yatsen – subject to new and peculiar Chinese uses and vicissitudes, it had no means of linking up with, say, the Yellow Emperor.[10]

---

[10]   It is indeed, even in United States use, rather an odd term with odd episodes in its history and can serve as an illustration of my point above that a word's history can shape its powers without its users knowing that history. Harvard – then more a school than a college or a university – was looking for a successor to its first 'Professor' (Nathaniel Eaton, sadistic tyrant, who had decamped with the funds: a grimly rich story for which consult chapter 17 of Samuel Eliot Morison's *The Founding of Harvard College* [Cambridge, Mass.: Harvard University Press, 1935]; on titles then current, see p. 200). Johann Amos Comenius (1592-1670) was the man chosen. He took too long, however, to make up his mind about it, and Harvard asked Henry Dunster of Magdalene College, Cambridge, to serve as a stopgap. He couldn't be "Professor" or "Master" (in case Comenius accepted), so another title was sought. At Magdalene we have a President whose duty in those days was to defend the Fellows against possibly tyrannic interferences from the Master. (He still supervises guests asked to the High Table and, theoretically, the Master only dines there by the President's invitation.) So Dunster became 'President' of Harvard. He did so well in the end that this title was continued. People forgot why he was so styled, and in time it was only natural that the United States should follow Harvard in having a President. Whence so many other Presidents. No one, however, need know anything of this while recognizing the possible subtleties in uses of the word and the important role in Government that sitting can

TOWARD A BASIC TEXT

To return, however, to the *Iliad*, concerning which this account of my experience in Peking and the development of Basic English will serve to explain how it was that I came to feel I must do something, and could, to reduce what seemed to be the unintelligibilities of the Homeric story. Of course, I should add ,before going into details of that undertaking, that it required some thought of a more analytical kind before I could commence it. Indeed, I had to come, or at least I did gradually come, to an overall view of the poem and of some of the relations it bears to its descendants, its moral and intellectual offspring, chief among which is the *Republic,* on which, as it happened, I began work first.

It is not too much to say that no one can really see the point or feel the force of the *Republic* to whom the *Iliad* is not a living and familiar presence. It is our best starting point in many more senses than one. It was, as Plato said, "the educator of the Greeks", giving them the education against which he conducted the revolt. *Iliad* and *Republic* require one another, as HERE requires THERE, as figure requires ground. Much of the *Republic* (and much else in Plato) is explicit in its rejection of what the *Iliad,* as he thought, was doing to Greece. But much else in Plato is equally that revulsion implicitly directing the influences he was generating. One of the published reasons for Socrates' trial was his being a maker of new gods and not believing in the old ones: those of the *Iliad* and their worse predecessors. In Plato's version of his defense he is made very explicit and as provocative as he knew how to be on this point. It is as though he wished his death to come to him for believing in, and obeying, the god of Delphi.

And so, men of Athens, if you were to say to me, "Socrates, we will let you off, on condition you give up this questioning game of yours; but if you go on with it, we'll put you to death", I would answer "Men of Athens, 1 respect and love you, but I will do what the god says, not what you say. While I live I won't stop pointing out the truth to anyone of you I meet. I'll go on saying. "Look, you are a citizen of the greatest city on earth. Aren't you ashamed to be giving all your mind to money-making and getting on in the world while you don't care a bit about wisdom or truth or the good of your soul?"

If by saying these things I corrupt the young, then these things must be

---

confer (and where you sit and on what: compare Chairman and Throne and the Stool of the African chief).

corrupting. Anyhow I don't say anything else. And so, men of Athens, acquit me or not, but know that I won't change my ways; not if I had to die again and again.[11]

Little indeed of Plato would have been at all what it is without Homer; just as, without Plato, less than we easily suppose in our own thinking – and whether we know this or not – could be as it is. Emerson's story makes the point sharply. He lent a copy of the *Republic* to a farmer who returned it remarking: "That man has a good many of my ideas."

It was, I think, that farmer's reported remark that led me to lay other things aside while I tried to make as intelligible and accessible a version as I could of the *Republic*.[12] That and a realization of the gap between such a farmer – capable of getting so far into himself and into Plato – and most of the newcomers to whom I might lend, say, a Jowett. It was coming home to me that a drop in general sagacity had been occurring, a decline in concern for and power to grasp, reflect on, and use moral ideas. The gulf between the intelligent reader and the traditions by which he still has to live seemed to me to be growing, and too rapidly not to become very soon intolerable. (What has been happening since has not exactly convinced me that I was mistaken.) It was not only the Chinese who could not benefit from Plato. The common man and the average undergraduate seemed to be in almost as distressing a state of need. And I had to doubt whether any of the remedies being tried were powerful enough. To experiment (at first via Basic and then in a slightly enlarged and suppler derivative) toward a more comprehensible *Republic* was, at least, work soothing to the conscience. It made me feel more equal to facing up to the great resolution of Godwin when he said: "The remainder of my time I determined to devote to the pursuit of such attainments as afforded me the best promise to render me useful."[13]

[11] I. A. Richards, *Why So, Socrates?* A dramatic version in simple English of Plato's dialogues *Euthyphro, Apology, Crito, Phaedo* (Cambridge: The University Press, 1964), pp. 23-24.
[12] After various revisions, through decades, finally published as *Plato's Republic* (Cambridge: The University Press, 1966). "It is usually assumed from the start that, keeping an original text in mind, there is going to be *something* queer about a version of it, whether a French version, or a shortened one, or a version leaning strongly toward the views of Professor von Braun, or even a garbled version" (from John Hollander's delightfully discerning discussion, "Versions, Interpretations, Performances", in *On Translation*, ed. Reuben A. Brower [Cambridge, Mass.: Harvard University Press, 1959], p. 221). He adds (p. 222), "Whenever we accept or reject a version of a statement or text, we do so in full recognition of its particular bias or 'limited authority', and never make the fact of the existence of such a bias a point of attack against it." I do hope this is so.
[13] William Godwin, "Autobiographical Fragment", quoted in C. Kegan Paul, *William Godwin*, 2 vols. (1876), 1:76.

Looking more closely into the *Republic* sent me to the *Iliad* again and made me realize more and more fully what a part Homer had in its making. Not only as to its theology and politics. Almost every aspect of human living presented in the *Iliad* comes up in Plato for question and for radical revision, often indeed for sheer reversal. The traits in its heroes that had most successfully invited awed admiration were those that in Plato's eyes most deserved the sternest condemnation. The excessiveness of Achilles, his wilfulness, his temerity, his impiety, the scale of his passions, his momentum as of a mass too vast for any control: all this makes him the perfect image of the opposite of Plato's favorite virtue, SOPHROSYNE, so easily misrepresented by the English word TEMPERANCE. (As Taylor well put it, we must "take care to remember that it is part of the virtue itself that it is not the imperfect self-restraint of the man who holds himself in check ungracefully and with difficulty, but the easy and natural self-restraint of the man who enjoys being temperate".[14] What is happening in the *Republic* and in much of the rest of Plato is the replacement of a traditional model of man by a new model in most essential respects precisely its contrary. To say that Socrates is Achilles turned upside down, an inverted projection of him, would grossly underrate Plato's depth as a dramatist. And it would risk turning one of the greatest of all uncompleted revolutions – the creation of that inexhaustible revolutionary, Socrates – into a sort of trick. Nonetheless, their contrarieties are instructive. Each of these immense and enigmatic figures becomes for us more fully himself by comparison with the other.

These contrarieties, I have no doubt, were largely responsible for my attempt, after making what I hoped was a more easily penetrable version of the *Iliad* – *The Wrath of Achilles*[15] – to fashion an actable play of the trial and death of Socrates: *Why So, Socrates?* But I must tell of that in its due place in this complex story of what resulted from those days of defeat in that Trans-Siberian train. For in spite of worrying about East-West and other communicative distortions, which led me to do a good deal of writing in the following years, and notwithstanding that I worked away at the simplified *Republic*, it was some time before I began on these other projects.

The next determinative moment came when, in the expansive mood

---

[14]   Alfred E. Taylor, *Plato, the Man and His Work* (New York: Dial Press, 1936), p. 48.
[15]   *The Wrath of Achilles: The Iliad of Homer*, paperback (New York: W. W. Norton & Co., 1950).

that followed the end of the Second World War, I was invited to join the Harvard Committee on the Objectives of a General Education in a Free Society. What lovely people were there to work with, and work well together we did! President Conant's Introduction and the committee's *Letter of Transmittal* show well what the participants imagined they were doing. A somewhat wry recognition of the disaccord between the hopes and aims there expressed and the actualities of the worldwide situation in the universities of 1970 belongs to my theme. For me the phrase 'a Free Society' had come to mean the sort of thing Socrates describes at the end of Book 9 of the *Republic*. He has been making up his mythic image of the component powers in man: the many-headed beast, the lion, and the guardian man himself. He comes to its application:

Only when a man is too feeble to control the beasts but has to work for them and please them, only then do we say that he had better be slave to some other man, a man in whom godlike wisdom rules. And this is to give him the same sort of government. It isn't, as Thrasymachus thought, ruling him to his own loss. No, the best is for everyone to be ruled by a wise and godlike power, if possible seated in his own heart; if not, let it act upon him from without; in order that we may all be, as far as possible, like one another and friends, being all guided by the same pilot.[16]

Then follows what is both a founding charter for Western education and the foundation – dependent upon that – of the ideal state; a state, as Glaucon puts it, "whose being is in ideas only, for I do not believe it can have any existence on earth". To which Socrates replies:

Well, maybe its pattern is already there in heaven for him to see who so desires; and seeing it he makes himself its citizen. And the question of its present or future existence makes no difference. He who sees it will live by its laws and by no other.[17]

These are the laws to which the first citizen of this state listens at the close of the *Crito*; they are what he hears "as the worshippers hear the flutes". And this music sounds so within him that he can hear nothing else.

In reality, as was not surprising, the starry-eyed program our committee concocted and prescribed had little relation to the actual courses presented. Some of these were splendid, but very different from what the committee had proposed; their outcomes were thus unappraisable. For me there was a terrifying resultant – responsibility for *Humanities*

16 *Republic* 9. 590.
17 *Republic* 9. 592.

1: *Sources of Our Common Thought*, which meant, to begin with, *Iliad, Republic,* Old Testament. There I was – back, in my imagination, in that Trans-Siberian train – committed to helping whomsoever I could to derive some profit from the *Iliad*.

By this date I had, I supposed, learned an iota or so about it. I had made, very laboriously, my Basic English version of the *Republic* – with many of the most lucid English translations propped up around me and a specialist in the *Republic*, a most resourceful, understanding pupil of Werner Jaeger, at my elbow, and the master, Jaeger himself, to consult when we became too uncertain. That had helped. So too did the propping up of various translations of the *Iliad*. (Since then I have found that the largest available lazy Susan, with the various versions displayed, open at the right pages, can be convenient: a device borrowed from Sir Christopher Wren's installations in the Library in Trinity College, Cambridge.) But it was an enormous class – up to or over a thousand students – with which I had to deal. I knew, I think – if I did not, I soon learned – that for Homer to be at all Homer, with so vast an audience, what you tried to read aloud had to be readable. The rivalry, otherwise – even in those good old times – of naughts and crosses, the *Crimson*, the *New York Times*, the whodunits and the didn't-oughter's, became oppressive. I had, it is true, a resource that greatly helped: a huge screen on which I would always project any passage that to me seemed to deserve especial attention. The screen reminds of the movies and thereby attracts. Moreover, those eye-minded undergraduates were COMPULSIVELY readers. Any scrap of print could close their ears to whatever. Even so, I found that projecting for them Lang, Leaf, and Myers – or even Samuel Butler – would not, often enough, keep them going. I accompanied, of course, the screen display of (alas!) only typescript with my uttermost endeavors in reading. I found out so, how hard most texts are even to read aloud, let alone to listen to. So it came home to me that I must find a version that I could – self- and audience-respectingly – read aloud, and even read with something of the confidence that a rhapsode could enjoy and an Ion[18] exhibit. I began to try out – with my experience of the *Republic* behind me – selected passages.

Selected passages? Here, sadly and reluctantly, I had to seem to dissent from or at least qualify the policy so insisted on by that impressive Advisory Board in the preface to *The Great Conversation*.[19] But I was

[18]   See *GBWW*, Vol. 7, pp. 142-148.
[19]   "One of the policies upon which the Advisory Board insisted most strongly was that the great writers should be allowed to speak for themselves. They should

being unfair. Their recommendations concerned a set of books. My task was a classroom application. Nonetheless, 'digested' and 'mutilated' are strong words with, in at least the second case, highly pejorative implications. Given the levels of preparedness I found in my students, I had to conclude that for them the attempt to read the whole *Iliad* and *Republic* resulted in sheer stultification. Selection is after all the fundamental principle in living. Without it we get nowhere. That integral texts should be available is obviously right. But equally it seemed right that in their approach to such great works, newcomers should be helped in their selection. For students being INTRODUCED to a strange and great new author, more than half his utterance can be to them a hindrance rather than a help. Selection, therefore, is a necessity – indeed, the only hope. (Of course, anyone who has published an abridgment knows too well the non-purchaser who self-flatteringly declares, "*I* need the complete book!" – which he then does not open twice.) Still, selected passages! What an abandonment that can be of the main aim: the transmission, namely, of what the originator had it in him to say! It is the CONNEXITY, the WHOLENESS, of his utterance that most matters, the ACTION (in Aristotle's large sense), the plot (in which each item gets the major part of its meaning from its relations to the rest). Abridgment, then, in a critical sense – selection operating with the most sensitive discernment of relations it can achieve – may reasonably claim to be no mutilation, to be indeed a necessary clarification. Necessary, above all, if we are thinking in terms of billions of readers, instead of some guide-conducted dozen.

Here, as had happened hearteningly with the *Republic*, help came from an unexpected quarter. I had supposed that I would be fighting my original throughout – a daunting prospect. Instead, I found Homer strangely ready, passage by passage, to collaborate. It was as though those alternations of rhapsodes – whose chanted competitive contributions somehow got written down – were, or their audience was, in cahoots with me: what really mattered was rarely in doubt; essential linked up with essential; I had only to drop, almost never to twist even by a degree. The continuity obtainable without strain, merely by omission, often astonished me. From selected passages – as passage reached out to passage – the dream of a single consecutive unitary action began to dominate the design. Could it be, if the right intrusions, excursions, supplements were omitted, that some semblance of an integral, original *Wrath of Achilles* would appear?

speak with their full voice and not be digested or mutilated by editorial decisions" (*GBWW*, Vol. 1, p. xx).

Whether it does or not in the translation I ultimately made, I am the last who could decide. The final drafts settled down during what was for me a strangely symbolic reflex of that first Trans-Siberian defeat. I was on an obsolescent victory-ship (happily filled with a cargo of unsinkable timber) making a twenty-one day crossing from Vancouver to Hong Kong; it was midwinter, and we were several days hove to in mid-Pacific with a number-eleven gale howling and the salt spray freezing where it fell, while the pumps valiantly labored. And – that was the best of it – I was on my way back to Peking. This was in 1950, with the Chinese showing Mao what the sons of Han could again be. The last touches were given and the introduction written high on the Peak in Hong Kong.

Still later, back again in Peking, I found that the clean-up was in full swing. Down in the Forbidden City's drains, clogged by a hundred years of neglect from corrupt officials, and equally up in the very ventricles of the citizens' brains and hearts, the new hope was making its way:

Bliss was it in that dawn to be alive.[20]

Where brutalized War Lords' police had beaten and kicked, a New Order officer gently helped the old water seller whose barrow got stuck in a rut. Something had to be done to calm one's overflowing spirits. The British Council quarters had a spacious court. But its officials were still waiting unhappily for their permits in Hong Kong. Why not try the *Iliad* out in a public reading, newly posted off to the publisher though the top copy was? It was then, in trying to compress its action into two hours, that I found that the poem has five acts and – still more striking – conforms, when so compressed, strictly to the canons of tragedy. Indeed, as so reshaped – with a chorus of alternating rhapsodes to weave in the connective descriptions – the temptation to try to find actors and actresses and essay a dramatic performance was strong. More on this below. For the moment, a one-voice reading had to suffice. In that full courtyard, as the evening light of spring lingered, it was comforting to find that my vocal chords could last out.

Together with this simplified *Iliad*, I had brought with me my near-Basic version of the *Republic*. Its reception by my Chinese students was even more thought-provoking. I took early occasion in my lectures to read key passages. The response from the large class – newly attired in the official student uniforms of Mao's regime – was more than gratifying. Might they, an editorial group came up to request, print what I

[20] William Wordsworth, *The French Revolution, as It Appeared to Enthusiasts*; also in *The Prelude* 11. 1. 121.

had read to them in the College issue of 'Texts of the Week'? By all
means, I replied, but had they not better first check with the Director
about it? Why, of course they would! I still remember their pained be-
wilderment when they came back to tell me that Plato was on the Index.
They could not divine why. Plato had said so entirely, so forcefully,
what they were hoping to live by. Why should they be forbidden to read
expositions of their duties to the State which coincided so well with so
much that Mao was teaching them? Could I explain it? I wished I could.
Under the circumstances there was nothing I could do to help. If their
Director couldn't tell them why they must not read Plato, how should I?

(This episode came back to me some years later during an audience
granted me by Kwame Nkrumah. I had taken along as a commemorative token an inscribed copy of that version of the *Republic*. I thought
it might help to show what a selected English could do for Ghana and
indeed for all Africa. Things had been going well; Nkrumah was displaying all his unmatchable charm. But at the mention of Plato there
fell a perceptible chill, as though his name alone constituted a threat.
That amazing politician's antennae sensed instantly then where danger
lay. His instinct had not served him so well when he set up that more
than life-size graven image of himself in Accra. On its plinth: "Seek ye
first the political Kingdom and all things shall be added unto you." Today, like Shelley's Ozymandias, the statue lies in fragments in the dust.
The inscription bears it witness still.)

The touchstone quality that Emerson noticed in the *Republic* may be
borne in mind when Plato is accused of being the first totalitarian, the
inventor of the police state, and so on. With wrenched texts this view
can be given not a little color. But the more any reader can take in the
book AS A WHOLE, the less can he credit such partial views of it. The
concepts of Man and Justice that it presents are in fact those that best
protect us from oppression, from whatever side it may come and not
least from tyrant trends within ourselves. And this is the chief reason for
working toward a version that will best help as many minds as may to
see it AS A WHOLE: to see it, in its own term – its title being *On Justice*
– justly; that is, with its parts in due relation to one another. It will be
fitting therefore to consider some of the obstacles that have so often
prevented readers from forming this JUST view of it and what can be
done to remove them. Chief among them must be mentioned its great
scale and its extreme complexity. But before looking into these, let us,
as with the *Iliad*, step back for a few moments and try to estimate this
extraordinary thing and its place among the powers shaping mankind.

THE REPUBLIC

No book – except the Bible – has had so much influence, so pervasive and so various, upon the peoples who – since the Middle Ages and until very recently – have been regarding themselves, with some reason, as the appointed leaders of the planet. In a very real sense they have been its creatures. What they have called their ideas have come to them, through whatever channels and in whatever disguises, from its pages. Socrates' words at the close of Book 9, quoted above, have been a true prophecy. These peoples have made themselves citizens of his ideal state and chosen to profess, at least, to live by its laws. By its principles they have attempted or pretended to govern themselves and others. "The greatest invention of the Greeks", wrote Jaeger, "was man." Western man, this is, of course. Other cultures have had their other and very different image makers. The Chinese had Confucius and Mencius to do for them what Plato did for us: give us our model of our true selves. We come short of it, endlessly, but it is of Plato's guardian mind that we come short.

Though we may never have read a word of Plato, or even heard of him, this can still be true. Most of our most serious thoughts have echoes in them of his. Every successful reader of Plato comes to feel that later literature is a whispering gallery. A successful reader is one who, through his reading, knows more about the good and more about himself. And this increased knowledge is Plato's thought living again in him.

It will be granted that to read Plato successfully is not easy. We may recall Whitehead: "If it were easy, the book ought to be burned; for it cannot be educational."[21] But we must distinguish necessary from avoidable difficulties. Part of the avoidable difficulty of the *Republic* is due to the superbly elaborate pedagogy employed. It was superlatively well designed for its purpose. It worked admirably for the scholar-disciples for whom it was written. But, though we are disciples, witting or unwitting, we are not those scholars. The very spaciousness of the book, the broad introductory sketches, the anticipatory hints, the figurative indications, the minor parallels, the skillful arrangements of correspondences and contrasts, the contrived disappointments, the gambits and recapitulations, the returns to deeper levels after withdrawals – all this art can wholly fail, for the modern reader, to have its due effect. Many, for example, have thrown the *Republic* down toward the end of its first book, unaware that the main ingredient of their dissatisfaction is some-

21   Quoted in *GBWW*, Vol. 1, p. 47.

thing that Plato meant them to feel. The long interventions of Glaucon and Adeimantus that open Book 2 show this clearly. They are drawing the bow for the rest of the discussion. The arguments closing Book 1 ARE thin, and Thrasymachus IS overcome too easily. But when the place of these passages in the whole design becomes clear, they are seen to be but a prelude introducing, in summary, much that is to come.

Again, as Plato develops the great parallel between society and mind – the capitals and lower case with which Socrates starts off his reply to Plato's brothers[22] – how many realize that Socrates is going to say of all his figures: "We shall never reach the truth this way."[23] It is a parallel that has shaped many societies and many minds and, with the help of today's and tomorrow's physiology and linguistics, it may well have a vastly expanded future: as we go on to compare language with an organism and both with a state. But its service is in being EXPLICITLY, SELF-ADMITTEDLY, an analogy, and protected, we should hope, by this from being mistaken for an argument. As figures of speech, such analogies are perpetually necessary. They are invaluable as means of exploration, misleading only if supposed to be offered as proofs. The modern sociologist is apt to take his own analyses and arguments so seriously that he may overlook or underestimate Plato's account of method[24] and his hints that in "these things" even a Glaucon (surely the best audience any speaker could have) must be content with no more.[25]

As yet another example of the *Republic's* complexity, we may note the persistent ambivalences of Socrates' position as to the possibility of knowledge. In "these things" must even a Socrates too be content with no more? Must an analogy, a parallel, suffice? Books 6 and 7 present an "outline only" of a program of studies for this first of all Universities that Plato is founding. It is so extensive that it can be read as forefiguring all inquiries ever since, and yet Glaucon is teased and twitted again and again for naïvely taking it as more than a sketch, and a sketch of some preliminaries only. Real knowledge and "the likely story" are deliberately balanced. Probably we are to hold them so – eschewing certainty as guardedly as we avoid crippling doubt. In answering such questions are we not to exercise the very reserves we are asking about? Any recommendation in these matters should remember that it applies to itself.

[22] *Republic* 2. 368.
[23] *Republic* 4. 435.
[24] *Republic* 6. 510-511.
[25] *Republic* 7. 533.

It should be evident that positions so poised raise especial difficulties for translators. Perhaps it is not too much to say that the *Republic*, as it stands in the English versions of the best scholars, is ineffective today for the very reasons that have made it effective in Plato's Greek. The main lines of its thought can so easily become lost among the qualifications and preparations and the polite and (to the Greek) persuasive indirections.

The very familiarity, too, of so many of its ideas collaborates in preventing us from seeing their everlasting novelty. They are like our hands and feet: only now and then do we realize them and how much they do for us. Of all media that could guard us from this awakening shock, a translator's English that attempts to follow the Greek meticulously in minor detail and social tone is the most absorbent. Plato's style deployed endless exquisite devices for meeting attitudes and expectations in his readers that sprang from their milieu. These attitudes and expectations do not arise in us; we have our own. A dummy discourse in English does nothing for either set, however well it is trained to ape the alien delicacies of the Greek. Nor does it help us in taking what Plato said to heart. Versions in nineteenth-century idiom did perhaps help the nineteenth century to realize itself. Today they have the uncanny effect of making Plato seem mid-Victorian. We hardly know which of two remote worlds we are exploring.

This is unfair both to Plato and to Jowett. But the source of these troubles lies even deeper than in the perennial moral strife between intellectual generations. It is the effort to get ALL of Plato's meaning into our English – just that meaning and nothing else – that befogs the translator's prose. It is a wholly admirable effort and ambition from the point of view of scholarship IN GREEK. To try to say it in English IS one of the best means of exploring what the Greek says, though a dangerous means whenever the translator thinks his English has said it. What is needed here is a Socratic inquiry into the words TRANSLATE and SAY. What does a sentence say, the thing the speaker had in mind or the thing some hearer gets? A typical hearer, an ideal hearer, an average hearer, an idiolectic hearer? Such an inquiry would show how hard it is for any translator to know what he is doing, and how he should attempt to direct (and therefore to limit) this 'meaning' he deals with. The meaning, the whole meaning, and nothing but the meaning: that is unattainable, though scholarship rightly makes it an ideal. But when we pass from understanding the Greek as best we can to uttering something partially parallel in English for general readers, the situation is different and another ideal becomes more relevant. We have to realize that different purposes will be best served by different types of versions.

Any version whatever that in a different age is conceived in a different language must depart from that ideal exact meaning. The readings of Plato's friends in his own lifetime departed from it, do what they would, though there was no such refracting linguistic veil between them and his words. Ours must depart far more, at more points and in more dimensions. We can understand this and some of the probable departures more or less clearly. By such understanding we may correct our view. This is what modern scholarship attempts. The fatal thing in this approach is to forget the gulfs.

But there is another means of interpreting our traditional sources, a much more traditional method. And HERE interpreting means spreading out, as in irrigation. It is done by willfully overlooking the gulfs. In all ages Platonists have done this, more or less consciously. They have found in Plato a revealing mirror of their own selves and have made him say for them what they saw. It is this that formerly made him (with the Bible) the field-determinant of the Western mind. Modern historical philology, like other simplifications (or inventions, if you like) that came to power in the eighteenth century, has been extremely subversive in professing to present to us 'the full facts'. It has buried Plato in the dead leaves of a wood that has vanished into trees.

To recover him – our traditional mirroring sun, not any animated waxwork of a historical reconstruction – we have to recognize what we are doing and take, as the philologist likewise does, only what suits our purpose. But our prime purpose, which was Plato's, is saving society and our own souls. This, as the *Republic*, along with other great books, can teach us, is the most inclusive and demanding of all purposes. This should ignore no mode of knowledge, nor should it let any more special mode of knowledge impose its more limited scope. What the greatest school book of all time can teach us, if we let it, is what sort of knowledge it is that can most help us in the conduct both of ourselves and of the state.

All such talk sounds hollow; nonetheless, this is the preeminently searching knowledge that is only arrived at through divergencies, developments, and reconciliations of Reflection. And that capitalized Reflection which Coleridge describes was formulated by him (first as a schoolboy) primarily from Plato, derivatively from Plotinus. In Aphorism 9 of his *Aids to Reflection*, his debt to *Republic*, Book 6, shows very clearly. It is a debt compounded, of course, with an equal or greater debt to the New Testament:

None then, not one of human kind, so poor and destitute, but there is provided for him, even in his present state, *a house not built with hands*. Aye, and spite of the philosophy (falsely so called) which mistakes the causes, the conditions, and the occasions of our becoming *conscious* of certain truths and realities for the truths and realities themselves – a house gloriously furnished. Nothing is wanted but the eye, which is the light of this house, the light which is the eye of this soul. This *seeing* light, this *enlightening* eye, is Reflection. It is more, indeed, than is ordinarily meant by that word; but it is what a Christian ought to mean by it, and to know too, whence it first came, and still continues to come – of what light even this light is *but* a reflection. This, too, is **THOUGHT**; and all thought is but unthinking that does not flow out of this, or tend towards it.

If we hark back to Blake's use of Shadow quoted above, we shall see that Blake's Imagination and Coleridge's Reflection equally derive from Plato. In reading both we have only to beware of *unthinking*.

What such echoes from the *Republic* have to tell us about ourselves, other echoings can tell us about the state. Jefferson, who failed strangely in his reading of the *Republic* and blamed Plato for it, declared that "a Democracy can be preserved only by frequent returns to fundamentals".[26] These fundamentals are here in the *Republic*, which laid them down. Here are both the conditions upon which alone a democracy is possible AND the most damaging description ever written of the dangers to which all democracies are exposed. That this description amounts to a portrait of Hitler[27] is no accident. These things are perpetual, being the price we pay for our failure to become in actuality more nearly what we are in essence. As Pindar put it, "May you become as you have learned you are!"

A version of the *Republic* for the general reader interested in these things may be more faithful to what mattered most to Plato if it restricts its rendering of other things that Plato is caring for. When the lingo that a strict conformity with the Greek forces upon a translator has become so familiar that its strangeness is no longer noticed; when the formulas and constructions translators must use have become by habit a code we decode at sight; when we expect most sentences to read like:

Tell me, in heaven's name, do you not think that such a person would make a strange instructor?

or

I for one most certainly anticipate that a consideration of this question will help us.

[26] Quoted in *The Practical Cogitator*, ed. Charles P. Curtis and Ferris Greenslet (Boston: Houghton Mifflin Co., 1945), p. 553.
[27] *Republic* 8. 565-569.

– when these elaborately articulated garments of simple enough thoughts have come to feel like our skin, then perhaps we will be ready to perceive through English the niceties of Plato's TONES. But I doubt it. I believe the scholar responds to the Greek behind these sentences and that the Greekless get little or nothing of this interplay. English – except through rare and happy accidents – cannot help travestying Greek when it tries to reproduce such things by literal means. Thought, on the other hand, as opposed to tone, can be reproduced to the limits of under-standing. Feeling too is relatively manageable: how Socrates or Adei-mantus feels about a large matter. But not TONE: the intricacies of their attitudes to what has just been said and to its speaker we can guess from content and context, but English refuses to let us be explicit about them without using palpably un-English forms, which for the Greekless de-feat the purpose.

What can be done? The resource with which versions must experi-ment if they are to do what is needed is to omit this attempt, to con-centrate on the thought, leaving tone to be surmised as concomitant to the thought. This is the mode of the English of the Bible, of Bacon and Bunyan, and of modern general colloquial.

The result of shrinking one of the most literal of contemporary trans-lations (Davies and Vaughan) from

Shall you have any answer to make to that objection, my clever friend?
    It is not very easy to find one at a moment's notice; but I shall apply to you, and I do so now, to state what the arguments on our side are, and to expound them for us.

into

        What's your answer to that?
        I haven't one right now. What *are* we able to answer?

and so on throughout, is to shorten our version by about one-third. As this experiment in simplification develops, the bones, as it were, of the book show up so much more clearly that Plato's careful prefaces, pro-gress reports, and summaries become no longer necessary. They become, in fact, barriers to readers, who fail to distinguish the prefaces from the statements. It is possible to streamline the argument still further by cut-ting out all but its active movements; and when we are once launched on that operation the ideal naturally comes up of a *Republic* that would keep whatever has made history but nothing else, and of putting that into an English AS CLEAR TO EVERYONE AS POSSIBLE.

Such a version can be no synopsis or digest. It must keep the dramatic movement, the give and take of the dialectic, the Platonic unction, Socrates' disclaimers of knowledge, the hints of his fate, all his ironies and surprises – for these are what have made and still will make history. However simplified, this must be a *Republic,* and without these it would be nothing of the sort. In practice it proves possible to retain the entire argument, all its essential explanations and defenses, and every detail that has hitherto generated philosophic as well as other discussion, contentious and expository, in agreement and in opposition, and still to reduce its volume to something under one-half.

Why read Plato at all if you are in such a hurry? Well, most readers are in a hurry anyhow, more is the pity. That is what the curriculum and the examination system do to them. Perhaps arranging Plato so that he can be more easily read may help us to become less hurried hereafter. It is not hard, however, to imagine the comments of certain sorts of scholars. This is tampering with Holy Writ with a vengeance, and the vengeance is not unlikely to fall.[28] But if Plato's thought flows again more freely in more readers through such a version, its boldness will be justified enough. And if we will think less of that ideal 'exact meaning' to which the scholar properly aspires and think more of the 'actual understandings' to which living and largely baffled readers attain, Socrates himself, I believe, would be ready to clear such adjustments from charges of impiety. But to be fully useful, this pruned and adapted version should not only make it easier for a NEW READER to see what Plato was saying. It should help even the student who has worked faithfully through a complete translation with notes. With minor points absent, the great limbs of the argument should show the more clearly.

Whoever attempts such abridgment must feel pang after pang of regret for what he leaves out for the sake of the clearer movement of the whole. But our aim (as Plato might say) is not to make our rendering of this or that phase or section or interest especially happy but to make the whole thing as good an exposition as possible of the arts of ruling and being ruled.

Misunderstandings in matters as important as those with which the *Republic* deals can be dangerous. Readers who have not realized that the book is an inquiry into justice, or who agree at heart with Thrasy-

---

[28] In fact, the worst that has come so far was from no less a figure than Sir Richard Livingstone himself (cf. *GBWW*, Vol. 1, p. 48). He wrote me, in a kind and most indulgent letter, that I was playing Beethoven on the harmonium. I was not alarmed or surprised. My version had been doing a thousand things which in terms of scholarly and pedagogical orthodoxy in these days are not done.

machus, are very ready to call it reactionary. But more comprehending readers know better. They have seen Socrates set up the very concepts of Man and of Justice that we most need when liberty is threatened either from without or from within. Lacking these concepts – though like Boëthius we forget what we are – we should be defenseless, fer example, against the manipulations of a blind social science[29] and its servants among the educators. But these defenses now need an active existence in every mind. What was written for aristocrats of a city-state has in fact become the prime text for world citizenship. Other versions – valuable and indeed essential for other purposes – need to be supplemented by a version given the clearest, most universally open form attainable.

THE *ILIAD*

Plato on the *Iliad* had, I think, prepared me for what I found, among my undergraduates in the Humanities I course, to be an extremely widespread response to Achilles. It was best expressed by: "God! How I hate that man!" as one of them put it. Wildly unjust, of course, imperceptive and undiscerning; nonetheless as deep-seated as it was frequent. To attempt some redress – with Plato on Achilles coming up within a month – was a good way of engaging newcomers to both in useful self-explorations. I expect I tried a good many different lines, direct and indirect. These General Education students were, all but a very few, unfamiliar with such reading. Most of them were very soon even as lost with it as I had been in that train. What they needed first and MOST was controlled exercise in thoughtful skipping. How to construct a catena of passages through which an overall ACTION could come alive for them: that was the prime task. It had to be an action they could follow both intellectually and emotionally, one that would allow Achilles – as the first truly mysterious man, the first problem-character in our tradition – to grow in them.

I have written at length – in the preface to *The Wrath of Achilles* – on some of the aspects and the outcomes of this search. I can avoid repetition here by using a device for selecting and presenting synopses that I did not hit upon till much later when I had to have it for that two-hour *Wrath of Achilles* reading in Peking. It is that of looking for, selecting, and extracting a minimal dramatic form, an irreducible framework of plot on which might be hung such other selected episodes as

[29] *Republic* 6. 506.

would not obscure (but would heighten) the essential indispensable action. But before embarking on this somewhat complex analysis and construction, this adventure in the playwright's craft, let me say something more about other strains of response in my Harvard undergraduates and in other readers.

Not all were repelled by Achilles. Some identified with him and exulted in just what antagonized the others. And some, of course, found themselves of two minds – shrinkingly sympathizing with his slaughterer's heart. Most people, I suppose, are simultaneously of all ages: have a long series of past selves, can be infants, small fry, youthful, mature, ageing, at any moment, their past and future personae ready to pop up (as with Plato's Many-Headed Beast) at call and not in any manageable fashion. Certainly the *Iliad* showed itself to be "one man's meat and another man's poison", and sometimes it was that in the same mind at all but the same moment. I do not have 'protocols' available recording my students' responses. I did not foresee occasion to use them. I have however a collection of phrases from final-examination blue books written by freshmen after a term's work at Harvard, much of it on the *Iliad* and *Republic* read in various uncut and unsimplified versions. I noted them down as evidence of what seems an almost customary response, a cultural habit of blaming the text, its editors and publishers, as well as its teachers, if there is anything in its pages that "fails to hold the attention", "is not immediately intelligible", "requires thought", or "doesn't make sense right away", and so on. Among them they give an impression that more of these entrants to higher academic studies than we may suppose are torn between a belief acquired from their schoolwork that everything ought SOMEHOW to have been made easy for them – failure in this being a sort of fraudulent betrayal – and a shrewd, native, almost biologic conviction that everything (apart from the exam game) REALLY is an utterly uncrackable combination, either arbitrary – formed by an unknown, unpredictable will – or irrational: put together by forces ungoverned by intelligence. In any case the widespread resentment that difficulty arouses is remarkable.

These responses to Lang, Leaf, and Myer's *Iliad* or to Paul Shorey's *Republic* may be compared with an account of how *The Wrath* has been taken when read by younger people and discussed in school classes. For example, I have this from a white beginning teacher, wished into a forty-three-teacher all-black school in Alabama. She is reporting to her college instructor:

My ninth-grade English class had about the most wonderful literature book possible, and included in it was I. A. Richards' version of the *Iliad*. Because of all kinds of reasons hingeing on this being a Negro school in the South, these students were far behind any kind of national or even Southern ninth-grade par, so it took all the way until late spring to get up my guts and the confidence of the class to attack such a problem as the *Iliad*. But they loved it. Even the people who couldn't read were fascinated enough, while the rest were talking about what was going on, to be quiet and listen and then were able to retell the stories themselves. Gosh, and I just sat there amazed, listening to people talk about whatever book they had read the night before.

First of all, they loved the gods and goddesses and loved it when they could pronounce all those big new names without a hitch. And the most wonderful thing was that they just totally accepted them. They didn't have any hang-ups about how gods didn't really exist in the world – like I was afraid I was going to have to figure out and explain what Aphrodite really meant in all men's lives. But not at all. They were just mad at old mean Athene for telling Diomedes not to dare fight with any of the other gods, but he could wound Aphrodite if he wanted to, and were sad and happy when Aphrodite ran to her mother and Dione wiped the wound away and comforted her. They didn't find it a bit unbelievable for gods to come pick men up off the battlefield or appear to men in different forms. I guess the only 'philosophical conceptions we came to terms with' were how mortals hate Hades the most because he never changes his mind and how gods and mortals both hate Ares because he doesn't care what side he's fighting on, just so he's fighting.

Another thing were epithets. I never said a word about them in class. I'm sure no one even knows what the word "epithet" means. And yet, whenever they were writing in class, books closed, they would automatically use them; that is, the five or six really turned-on people would – man-killing Hector (that was their favorite), thunder-throwing Zeus, and even ox-eyed Hera.

When we first started reading it, I made a pretty big deal of similes – what exactly were being compared to what and why – because that seemed a good way to make a 'more-aware reader' and they liked racing to see who could figure it out correctly first. Well, by about Book 16 I never had to mention the word simile again. . . . For the rest of the year, no matter what they were writing about – whether it was about something that happened to them last summer or a story using as many forms of "lie, lay, sit, set" as possible or describing a trip – there would always be in almost every paper something compared to a hungry lion, or a raging river, or a man coming upon a snake. (Back reading the *Iliad,* they'd always find that simile "very funny.")

You made me love the *Iliad* in Hellenic Heritage and I guess I read it, I mean, I can even remember reading it and thinking how wonderful it was, but I think I thought that because you'd already convinced me that it was wonderful. But this year it seemed incredible that I'd ever read it before, and I certainly didn't respond to much then, except what you said.

The big problem teaching here was that in every class there were maybe 10 people who could read fine, 10 on fourth- to sixth-grade level, and 10 who couldn't read at all, so the problem was keeping all these different levels interested and behaving at one time. They were just sitting there misbehaving in my classes, though ready to read and write and think once they got the idea it was fun.

It is a nice question whether these ninth-grade Alabamians or our recent exegetical Homerists more truly represent the *Iliad's* audiences throughout the ages. Possibly Homer has never been understood (as opposed to enjoyed) before our times. If so, we may picture him in Elysium consulting with Shakespeare, Milton, and others about such a new turn of events.

Let us now see what a minimal plot for a *Wrath of Achilles* might be like, keeping both the scholar and the newcomer in view. In essentials, it is the same sort of inquiry as that needed in reducing the *Republic* to an accessible form or that of making a dramatic presentation of *Euthyphro, Apology, Crito, Phaedo*, attempted in my *Why So, Socrates?* – to which, after discussing a nuclear *Iliad,* I will turn. But the *Wrath* (as I will call it) aims at a more dramatic elimination of all but necessities. The episodes, movements, nuances, touches omitted – for the sake of bringing out the indispensables of the PLOT with the maximal clarity – will be regarded as being, for purpose, audience, or occasion, possibilities of DRAMATIC enrichment. The minimal form can thus be conceived as a nucleus, a central core or, better, stem, out from which various DEPENDENT activities or branches may, if dramatic gain outweighs risk of confusion, be developed. Diagrammatically, it might look something like this:

ETC.

The ETC. represents the total *Iliad*. Of course to the unifying Homerist of today hardly a phrase in all that will be without its important contribution.

By setting our problem up this way, we gain, I believe, certain advantages: (1) freedom; (2) clarification as to what we are attempting; (3) spotlighting of the CHOICES we are considering; (4) reminders of the audiences to which our efforts are addressed. As Reuben Brower well says, "We read from a particular point in space and time."[30]

To set to work. Let us suppose that our minimal plot turns out to have five acts, each act having one or more scenes. The PAUSING of the action between the acts and between the scenes will be as significant as pauses are in all utterances. These pauses do, in fact, determine how the play is divided. The action – PRAXIS, in Aristotle's term[31] – and its necessary UNITY, on which Aristotle so much insisted, are what this inquiry seeks to clarify. Each choice-point will bring up that REFERENCE TO THE REST OF THE ACTION, that mutual relevance of components, which Aristotle also stressed with his "organic" metaphors. "Plot", he says, "is the first principle, and, as it were, the soul of a tragedy."[32] If we recall that Aristotle selects as "the transcendent excellence" of Homer this very unity of action, studying what it stems from will seem worth more than usual trouble. My references are to books and lines in the Loeb Classical Library *Iliad,* and the quotations are from *The Wrath of Achilles.*

Act one

The Greeks are in council. To them enters Chryses, priest of Apollo, to ransom his daughter, Chryseis (1. 17-21). The Greeks shout assent, but Agamemnon sends him harshly away. He withdraws in silence to pray to Apollo, who looses shafts of the plague on the Greeks – "till the fires of the dead were burning night and day". On the tenth day Achilles (not Agamemnon) calls the Greeks together, proposing that they ask some seer why Apollo is doing this. Kalchas says he will tell them, if Achilles will protect him from Agamemnon. Achilles replies that he can and will. Kalchas then declares that Agamemnon must return Chryseis to her father, without a ransom. Agamemnon furiously refuses, unless the Greeks give him an equivalent prize of honor. Achilles proposes that they do so when they have taken Troy. Agamemnon then demands Achilles' own prize of honor, the girl, Briseis. Achilles threatens, if so, to sail away home, and Agamemnon then declares that he will come to Achilles' hut and himself take away Briseis.

[30] "Seven *Agamemnons*" in *On Translation,* ed. Reuben A. Brower, p. 171. His essay demonstrates this dependence most persuasively. Many other essays in his volume are highly pertinent to our theme. And it has an admirable bibliography.
[31] *Poetics* 6.
[32] *Poetics* 6.

The first choice-point now arises: should we include in the minimal action the following episode?

Achilles is putting his hand to his sword to end Agamemnon (and the *Iliad*) when Athene, unseen by others, arrives and seizes Achilles by his golden hair. She orders him to put up with it but to tell Agamemnon what he thinks. Achilles obeys; as regards the gods he is notably docile.

Splendid though this is, it seems to me an episode, not a movement in the main action. It belongs to a numerous class of Olympian interventions, most of which yield an action different from, wider and far more intricate than, the MINIMAL plot. Certain of these interventions, by Zeus and by gods and goddesses who are acting as his messengers (Hermes and Iris), and by Apollo in sending the plague, do belong essentially to the action. As to those of Thetis, that Achilles' mother is a goddess is an essential element in his CHARACTER. He would not be the same man, and the action of which he is the prime source would not be the same, if her role were to be omitted. But her dealings with Zeus (and Hephaestus) need not be included.

To continue with this summary of the action: Achilles reviles Agamemnon and commits himself to withdrawal from the war. Nestor attempts to make peace between them, but without effect. Achilles returns to his hut. Agamemnon does not, significantly, go there himself but sends two heralds to take Briseis, and unwillingly she goes with them. And there (in l. 348) ends, I suggest, what I am calling Act One.

Act two

This, I suggest, consists essentially of the embassy in Book 9. The Rhapsode describes the council and Agamemnon's weeping as he rises to propose that they give up the war and sail home. Diomede declares that whatever Agamemnon does, he and Sthenelos will stay on and take Troy. Then Nestor intervenes, reminding Agamemnon of what he did in Act One and of the need to win Achilles back. Agamemnon agrees and declares his readiness to return Briseis along with adequate gifts. Nestor selects, as the best ambassadors, Ajax and Odysseus. With them goes Phoenix, Achilles' tutor.

They find (and this could be Scene Two) Achilles playing the lyre and singing of heroes to Patroclus, who sits in silence waiting for him to end (9. 191). Achilles greets them most cordially and hospitably. (A remarkable amount of eating and drinking takes place that night. Much of it, no doubt, is ritual: ambassadors will sympathize.) When the moment for speeches arrives, Ajax (the "beef-witted lord" of Shakespeare's Thersites, in *Troilus and Cressida*) signs to Phoenix to begin. But Odysseus knows better. His great speech has ever since been THE model of diplomatic approach and suasion. Throughout he is watching the effect of his every sentence on Achilles, changing his note accordingly. He was there (with Nestor in an earlier embassy) when Peleus sent Achilles (with Patroclus) to join Agamemnon's war. He heard what Peleus then said and tries that. When he sees that the list of Agamemnon's offered gifts is not working, he reverts swiftly to the piteous plight of the Greeks and to what Achilles could do to the vaunting Hector.

Achilles' reply is, of course, one of the greatest master passages in all poetry and as probing a search for self-knowledge as can be found, endlessly repaying study. It begins with a stiff rejection of the diplomatic art: "Zeus-born son of Laërtes, man of many designings, now I must say what I have in mind and what I will do, so that you may not sit before me and argue this way and that. I hate—like the gates of Hades— a man who says one thing and has another in his heart" (9. 309–14). There follows the negation of the very value of honor which turns (so wounded he is in his own self-esteem) to speaking of Briseis, his prize of honor, as though she were his wife. "Why has Agamemnon brought all these fighters here? Because of fair-haired Helen? Are Agamemnon and Menelaus the only ones who love their wives? Does not every man in his right mind love his dear one – as I loved mine with all my heart, even though I took her with my spear?" (9. 338–42). In view of what I suggest could be the last line of the *Wrath*, "Achilles in the innermost room, with fair-faced Briseis at his side", this must be allowed some weight among the confluents of the action. Now comes savagely ironic mockery of the Greeks and a disdainful glance at Hector – all but anticipating what is to be his end. Then wounded honor strikes up again: scornful refusal of Agamemnon's gifts, with his offer of one of his daughters in marriage ironically treated again: "No, let him give her to another, to some man like himself and more of a king than I am!" (9. 392). His twofold fate – long happy years in his homeland, but without honor, or an early death with immortal fame – hangs in balance before him. He ends by advising the Greeks to sail home too. But it is clear that he does not know his own mind.

They sit in silence, and here another choice-point comes up: should the long speech from Phoenix that now follows be included in the action? It tells us much of the spoilt childhood of Achilles and has the great passage on Prayers that walk in the footsteps of Sin. Nonetheless, for a MINIMAL action it can be omitted, though certainly it should be one of the first enrichments to be added.

Ajax sums up. The "beef-witted lord" shows himself to be a diagnostician: "Let us go, for Achilles has worked up his anger. Any man will take a great enough price whatever the wrong done him. As for you, Achilles, you have made your heart hard because of one girl only, when we are offering you seven, the best there are." Achilles, surprisingly, almost agrees: "But my heart swells with anger to think what Agamemnon did to me before everybody. . . I will not take up my arms again till Hector comes to my own ships with fire. Then, I think, he will be stopped, however much of a fighter he may be."

Act three

Our selected minimal action resumes when Achilles, watching from his great ship how badly things are going for the Greeks, sees Nestor drive by in his chariot with Machaon, the surgeon, wounded (ll. 599). That moves him. "A surgeon is of more value than many fighting men" (ll. 514). He sends Patroclus running to Nestor's hut to verify and report. Nestor, at the end of a speech which makes him a prototype of Polonius, suggests that Patroclus put Achilles' armor on and take the Myrmidons out to drive the Trojans back to Troy. Patroclus runs back weeping, exactly as Agamemnon weeps at the outset of Act Two (Book 16, opening). This distresses Achilles, who asks what can be the matter? Is there bad news from home? Can it be the Greeks he is sorrowing for – being killed, all for their own fault? Patroclus (in many ways the most attaching character in the *Iliad*) rebukes Achilles grandly and asks for the armor in which to go out against the Trojans in Achilles' place. Achilles replies with what he has said already about "What Agamemnon did to me before everybody. . .". Then he pretends he has ended his anger and grants Patroclus his wish. "But take this to heart. Come back again when you have cleared the ships. Do not go up against Troy or you will make my honor less." Then, HOMERICALLY – there is no other word for it – he foresees what is to happen: "One of the gods that are forever may come down from Olympus against you – for dearly does Phoebus Apollo love them." Now occurs the supreme instance of HUBRIS, the type specimen of it: "O father Zeus, and Athene and Apollo, O would that not one of the Trojans, not one of them all – *nor one of the Greeks* – might escape death, if only we two together might throw down the sacred walls of Troy" (16. 97–100). He is beside himself. More extreme alienation can hardly be imagined.

The worst then naturally happens. The feats of Patroclus and his end – at Apollo's hand – can be briefly recounted by a Rhapsode. Then Antilochus, Nestor's son, brings the crushing news to Achilles (opening of Book 18). Achilles' behavior when he receives it may be described by the Rhapsode while the actor representing Achilles mimes it. It is this behavior that is selected by the Socrates of the *Republic* both in Book 3 and in Book 10 to illustrate what a man struck by terrible news should NOT do. A good man guided by reason will take such blows of fate less hardly than other people. It is best to keep quiet as far as possible because we are not certain what is good or bad in such things, and to take them hardly does not make them any better. The Achilles of the action of the *Wrath,* however, moans so loudly that his mother, Thetis, hears him. She comes up from the sea bottom, takes her son's head in her hands, and asks, "Has not Zeus done as you prayed?" Achilles tells her that Patroclus is dead, that Hector has his armor, that his own heart will not let him live on. But first he must kill Hector. She replies: "You will be short-lived, then, my son: for after Hector's death, yours will come quickly."

Here, in the middle of Act Three, comes what Aristotle called the PERIPETEIA. In the *Poetics* he defines a Complex action as one in which the change is accompanied by Reversal of the Situation (PERIPETEIA) or by Recognition or by both,[33] and he goes on to describe Reversal of the Situation as a change by which the action veers round to its opposite. Recognition, he says, "as the name indicates, is a change from ignorance to knowledge, producing love or hate between persons destined by the poet for good or bad fortune. The best form of Recognition is coincident with Reversal of the Situation, as in the *Oedipus*."[34] His account equally well fits this crucial turning point in the *Iliad*. Indeed, we may wonder, in view of his immense admiration for Homer, that he did not use this illustration. Recognition combined with Reversal, he remarks, will produce either pity or fear. These two are, of course, his defining marks for tragedy. Previously he has spoken of "pity and fear" together.[35] Here he separates them.

It has become customary, in discussing tragedy, to tie these up to-

---

[33] *Poetics* 10.
[34] *Poetics* 11.
[35] *Poetics* 6.

gether, to relate pity with fear, as joint necessary components in the tragic effect, and to make the 'proper purgation' an outcome of their combination and opposition. Certainly here, with Achilles down in the dust, the set and direction of his energies veering as he recognizes what he has been and what a change must now come, pity and fear are very intimately conjoined. Antilochus in tears holding Achilles' hands for fear he will cut his throat, the women crying aloud around him, and Thetis, too, feel both together. And in scene after scene that follows (Achilles' Lycaon speech is perhaps the clearest single example), there is the same tension between them. This is indeed the pervasive quality of the *Iliad*.

In this moment of reversal (or should we call it here REDIRECTION) it is interesting to note how deeply symbolic Achilles' armor can seem: "Patroclus is dead whom I honored as no other, even as my own self. And Hector, who killed him, has taken his armor – armor that the gods gave to Peleus on the day you were married to him." The armor can represent Achilles' very being, including his semidivine prowess. Hector, in killing Patroclus and in taking the armor, has deprived Achilles of his own self. That his own death will come quickly after Hector's seems fitting to him. "Let it come, then, for I was not there to help Patroclus . . . *or any of my brothers-in-arms that Hector has killed*" (this is indeed a new Achilles speaking), "but was here by the ships, a useless weight on the earth: I that in war am such as no other of the Greeks." Because of all this, "now would that war itself might end among gods and men, and anger that sweeter far than drops of honey swells like smoke in men's breasts. Even so did Agamemnon anger me." That anger is passed, swept aside and replaced by a greater anger: "But now I will go to look for Hector, who killed the man I loved . . .". His goddess mother reminds him of his new sense of responsibilities – "It is well to save your friends from destruction" – and of his need for armor: "In the morning I will have new armor for you, made by Hephaestus."

In the morning she brings the armor: shield, breastplate, helmet, and leg guards. She puts the arms down before Achilles, and they ring loudly in their glory. All the Myrmidons shake with fear, and no man has the courage to look upon them. But when Achilles sees them, rage for battle comes on him again, and his eyes burn like flame. The wish "that war itself might end among gods and men" is forgotten. All through the *Iliad*, 'evil war' turns to 'joy of battle' as lightly as an aspen leaf trembles.

By the side of the sea Achilles goes shouting loudly, and the Greeks come to the place of meeting, happy because Achilles is coming back into the war. Among them are the wounded Diomede and Odysseus – helping themselves with their spears – who sit in front. Last of all comes Agamemnon, wounded too. This is the physical image of the turning point in the action. Achilles rises and speaks: "How was it better for us, Agamemnon, for you and for me, to rage in such high anger about a girl. Why did not Artemis kill her among the ships with an arrow on the day that I took her at Lernessus?"

Agamemnon, too weak to rise, answers from where he sits. He too has not been himself. He was not to blame, but "Zeus and Fate and Erinys that walks in the dark. Here in the place of meeting they made me blind on the day I took his prize of honor from Achilles." And he offers his gifts again. Achilles replies, "This is no time for talk. There is work to be done." But Odysseus wants to make sure. So he takes men, goes to Agamemnon's hut, and brings them to Achilles' ship, all of them, with the seven women skilled in needlework; and the eighth is fair-faced Briseis. And she, when she sees Patroclus dead, throws herself upon him. "Patroclus, friend to my unhappy heart. You were living when I went from this hut and now I find you dead. So evil comes upon evil. My husband, to whom my father and queenly mother gave me, I saw cut down before our city, and my three dear brothers with him. But when swift Achilles killed him you would have stopped my tears. You said you would make me Achilles' wife and that he would take me in his ships to Phthia to a marriage feast among the Myrmidons. Endlessly I cry aloud for your death for you were ever kind." And the other women add their cries. For Patroclus truly they cry, but each for her own sorrows too.

With this, Act Three, the Act of reversal and return, ends.

Act four

The next great movement of the action – through the death of Hector – opens with the going out of Achilles. Achilles' implacable fury mounts and mounts. Nothing can assuage it, as he kills Trojan after Trojan. Old Priam's youngest and dearest son, Polydorus, is the first to be named. There he is, foolish boy, letting everyone see how swiftly he can run, when Achilles takes him with his spear point. Just how much of the horrors of this slaughter should be included presents us with another choice-point. If actors mime these episodes as the Rhapsode narrates them, the degree of realism they are permitted would be a matter to be watched. Homer spares us little. Here with Polydorus: "Through him went the spear and he fell to his knees moaning and a dark cloud came over him as he held his bowels to him with his hands." (There are almost no two woundings alike in all the *Iliad*: a remarkable feature in so formulaic a composition.)

Achilles cuts the Trojan armies in two. One part he sends running back to Troy. The other "like locusts before a grass fire flying into water" come to the banks of the deep river Xanthus and leap in. Achilles leans his spear against a tree and follows them with his sword. When tired of killing, he takes twelve young men living out of the water to be a blood price for Patroclus. And then he meets Lycaon, another of Priam's sons, coming up out of the water. Lycaon runs in under Achilles' lifted spear and prays to him with words feathered like an arrow. He has been taken earlier by Achilles and ransomed, and his prayers should be sacred. "Hear me out and do not kill me. My mother was not Hector's mother. I am only the half-brother of the man who killed your friend."

But the voice that replies is pitiless. "Fool, offer me no such words. Till Patroclus fell, it was my pleasure to have pity on the Trojans and many of them I took and sold overseas. But now, not one of them may escape death, least of all any of the sons of Priam. No, friend, you die with them. Why do you sorrow so? Patroclus died, who was better far than you. And do you not see what sort of man I am – how beautiful and tall . . . but over me too hang death and fate. There will come a dawn or eve or midday when some man will take my life in battle – with the spear or an arrow from the string." Achilles hits him on the collarbone by the neck, and all the two-edged sword goes in. Then he takes Lycaon by the foot and throws him into eddying Xanthus to go on his way.

These are preludes to the death of Hector, but they seem to me essential to the action. Much immediately preceding Hector's death, famous and deeply moving though it is, seems episodic, as regards the *Wrath*. I have, in fact, a play with an action centering on Hector to which his full meditation, the flight round Troy, and Athene's trickery are indispensables. But to the action of the *Wrath* belongs, I suggest, chiefly, that deadly fate holds Hector outside Troy, while the defeated Trojans, like helpless fauns, are wiping the sweat off them within the city, as the Greeks approach. It is the old Priam who first sees Achilles running, like a prizewinning horse, toward Troy. "And to Priam he

seemed like the star which comes out at harvest time – bright are his
rays among the armies of the night – the star men name the Dog of
Orion. Brightest of all, he is but a sign of evil." This belongs, as building up Priam toward his part in Act Five. How much of it is needed or
is dispensable enrichment is a director's problem. Priam beseeches
Hector to enter the city, but Hector is lost in self-accusations. It is almost as in a dream that he sees Achilles coming upon him in his waving
helmet with the great Pelian spear lifted. Away he runs, with swift-
footed Achilles behind him. The heartbreaking list of Hector's most
familiar landmarks of childhood, culminating with "the wide stone
basins where the wives and daughters of the Trojans washed their
clothes of old in time of peace before the Greeks came to Troyland"
would have to be given by a Rhapsode as Chorus. "By these they run –
a good man in front but a far stronger man at his heels. And the prize
they run for is no bull's skin, or common prize for the swift-footed, but
the life of horse-taming Hector."

We omit the Olympians' discussion, seething with irony though it is.
And the details of the chase. Also, and with anguish: "When they came
a fourth time to the springs, Zeus lifted up his golden balance and
Hector's fate went down; and Phoebus Apollo left him!" How that has
echoed on! Also and most regretfully, Athene's ruthless and abom-
inable cunning in taking on the semblance of Deiphobus, Hector's
brother, come out to help him, and letting him sickeningly down at the
turn of the fight. But their preliminary exchange must be included:
HECTOR: "I will run from you no longer, Achilles, but kill you now or
be killed. Let this be our agreement before all the gods as witnesses"
(all the gods ARE there witnessing all): "if Zeus lets me outlive you and
take your life, I will give your body back to the Greeks, after taking
your armor. And you will do the same." ACHILLES: "Talk not to me of
agreements, Hector. Between lions and men there is no swearing of
oaths . . . Now you must pay for all my sorrows for my friends you
have killed." (Perhaps, for Achilles' sake, we should substitute Patroclus for those friends.)

At the climax of the fight: "As a star comes out among the stars of
the night, star of evening, the most beautiful of the stars of heaven, even
so came the light from the bronze of Achilles' spear as he lifted it looking for the place most open to the blow." Hector is in Achilles' own
armor taken from Patroclus, and Achilles knows it well. There is an
opening where the collarbones come into the neck, and through that
Achilles strikes. They have their final exchange: ACHILLES: "Little you

thought, you fool, of me when you took that armor from Patroclus . . . The Greeks will give him his funeral but throw you to the dogs and birds." HECTOR: "By your life and knees and parents take the gifts my father and mother will offer you and send my body back so that the Trojans and their wives may give me to the fire after my death." ACHILLES: "Pray me not, dog, by knees and parents. O that I could make myself cut up your flesh and eat it raw myself . . . There is no man living who can keep the dogs from your head, Hector." HECTOR: "I know you for what you are, and knew it before. The heart in your breast is of iron. See that I do not bring the anger of the gods down upon you on the day when Paris and Apollo kill you, strong though you are, at the Scaean gate." He dies; his spirit goes from him down to the house of Hades, crying out sadly. Then ACHILLES: "Lie dead there; I am ready for my own death whenever Zeus and the other immortals send it."

One last movement completes Act Four. Achilles takes that armor off Hector. The Greeks run up to wonder at Hector's beauty. And all who come near wound him with their spears saying one to another, "Hector is softer to handle now than when he burned our ships." ACHILLES: "This man has done us more damage than all the rest together. But what am I thinking of? Patroclus waits at the ships for his funeral. Even if in the house of Hades men forget their friends, even there I will not forget him. Back, sons of the Greeks, to the ships, but we will take this man with us." So, with a huntsman's knack, he cuts the backs of Hector's heels, puts thongs of leather through and ties them to his chariot. Dust goes up from Hector's dark hair outstretched and his head that was so beautiful; for now Zeus has given him over to be shamefully handled in his own land where he was born.

Act five

Scene One, the burning pyre of Patroclus. Achilles among his Myrmidons lies moaning by the side of the sounding sea in an open place where the waves wash in. He falls asleep and dreams: the ghost of Patroclus stands at his head and says: "You sleep and have no more thought for me, Achilles. Not in my life were you unmindful of me; but now in my death. . . . You too, godlike Achilles, are fated to be killed under the walls of Troy. Hear now, if you will, my request. Let our bones lie together as we were brought up together in your house." Achilles answers: "Why, my brother, do you come to tell me this? I will do all. But stand nearer. Though it is but for a little, let us throw our arms about one another and give full way to our sorrow." He stretches out his arms, but the spirit, like a mist, goes under earth, feebly moaning. Achilles leaps up clapping his hands together. "See you! Even in the house of Hades, the spirit is something – though the life is not in it. He was wonderfully like his living self!" He falls asleep again beside the pyre. Enter Agamemnon and other chiefs who waken Achilles. ACHILLES: "First put out the burning pyre with wine. Then take up the bones of Patroclus, separating them carefully from the rest." (There is need for this; many have been the sheep and cattle burned with Patroclus. Four strong horses Achilles has killed and flung upon the pyre, moaning as he did so. And two of Patroclus' nine house dogs, and, as climax, the twelve brave sons of the Trojans he had taken out of Xanthus and killed with the sword – "evil work of his heart's designing", comments the Rhapsode. There might be a temptation to mime and describe some of this; it belongs to the action.) Achilles goes on: "Then let us place his bones in a golden urn with a double roll of fat around them till the time when I go myself down to the house of Hades. But build no great mound till then. Later you may, those of you left among the ships when I am gone."

The others go off to supper and sweet sleep, but not Achilles. All night he turns this way and that by the side of the waves, ceaselessly moaning, and, as Dawn comes on the water, he takes out his horses and chariot and drags Hector three times round the pyre.

Scene Two, Olympus, gods and goddesses in council. Apollo speaks: "Hard-hearted and cruel you gods are. Has Hector never burned thighs of bulls for you? Have you no care to save him, dead though he is, for his father Priam and his people who would burn him in the fire and give him his funeral? No, it is Achilles you would help, a man out of his mind, without pity or shame in his heart... Let him beware that we do not become angry with him." Zeus sends Thetis to Achilles. She takes a motherly view. "My child, how long will you go on eating your heart out with sorrow. Good for you would be even a woman's arms. You have not long now to live. I come from Zeus who says that the gods are angered with you, he more than all, because you have not given Hector back. Give him up now and take a ransom for the dead." ACHILLES: "So be it; let the ransom-bringer take him, if so the Olympian wills." Zeus has sent Iris with orders and comforting words to old Priam. He is to go – with a herald only, an old man to drive the mule wagon – to Achilles' hut.

There are many inviting scenes here. One between Priam and Hecuba. She upbraids him; he must be out of his mind. Another between Priam and his remaining sons; he rages at them in a vein that vividly reminds one of streams of abuse in *Kim*. These might be of use to build up Priam, but a good actor would not need them. They belong rather to play with a purely Trojan action centered on Hector: later extracted and easily performed in the Loeb Drama Center, Harvard. In the present action, Priam, with Hermes' help, comes to Achilles' hut.

In this final scene, Priam, alone, goes in and finds Achilles with two Myrmidons waiting upon him. He has just finished a meal, and the table still stands at his side. (It might all have been designed for acting, so clear and adroit are the stage directions.) Priam comes in without being seen, kneels and clasps Achilles' knees, and kisses the terrible hands that have killed so many of his sons. Achilles wonders as he sees Priam, and the two Myrmidons also wonder and look at one another. Then Priam, in prayer: "Think of your father, O god-like Achilles, of your father who is even as I am, at the sad doorway of old age. It may be that those who live near him trouble him and that he has no one to keep war and destruction from him. Still, when he hears that you are living . . . But I – unhappy I am. My sons were the bravest in all Troy, and the last of them and the bravest, Hector, that himself guarded Troy, you killed but now as he fought for his country. So I have come to the Greek ships to win his body back with a ransom too great to be counted. Achilles, fear the anger of Heaven, think of your own father and take pity on me . . . I have made myself do what no other man has done and stretched out my hands to the face of him who killed my sons."

In Achilles this wakens a desire to sorrow aloud for his father, and he takes the old man's hands and gently puts him aside. The two then sorrow together: Priam for Hector and Achilles for his own father and now again for Patroclus. And the sound of their moaning goes up through the house.

Achilles' three following speeches show us a supremely dramatic transformation. It comes, though, by stages. At the end of the first, which contains "How did you have the heart to come to meet my eyes? Your heart truly must be of iron" as well as the "two urns stand on the floor of Zeus" passage which Plato reprehends,[36] he tries to soothe Priam: "You too, Priam, we hear were happy in times past . . . But

---

[36] *Republic* 2. 379.

give the pain in your heart some rest . . .". Priam answers: "Say not to me, Achilles, be seated" (he is still at Achilles' feet), "while Hector lies uncovered among the huts. Give him back to me quickly and let me look upon him . . .". That nearly blows up everything. "Anger me no more, old man!" cries Achilles, with eyes of flame. "I am minded myself to give Hector back, for from Zeus the word came to me by my mother. And well I know that it was not without help from some god that you came here. No mortal man would be brave enough. So move my heart no more, or I may still sin against the will of Zeus and not even here under my roof will you be safe, for all your prayers." He is still barely in control, though he is coming to know himself better.

He springs out like a lion to attend to matters: to look after Priam's horses, take care of the herald and bring the ransom in, and have the women wash and oil Hector's body, keeping it out of Priam's view. Otherwise Priam might cry out on seeing it, and Achilles then might be moved to anger again and kill him.

Achilles' last long speech, made when all is ready and the body in the wagon, is to persuade Priam to supper. "Even Niobe, tired out with weeping, took food at last. Somewhere now high up in the lonely mountains where the rocks are, where, they say, the nymphs sleep, there, though turned to a stone, she still thinks of what the gods did. So now, father, let us take food. You may weep over your dear son, later, as much as you will, in Troy." Then they look and wonder at one another: one so beautiful and tall, the other so kingly.

Priam and the herald are put to bed in the place of honor. One last question: "How many days do you want for Hector's funeral? How long must I hold back the Greeks?" Priam asks for eleven days – to get enough wood in, sorrow, give the funeral, let the people feast and build the mound. "All this, old Priam, will be as you have said." Achilles is whole again. SOPHROSYNE has returned. "I will hold back the battle for as long as you want."

He takes the old man's right hand in his to keep him from any fear, and they go to their rest: Priam and the herald in the front part of the house with wise thoughts in their hearts; but Achilles in the innermost room, with fair-faced Briseis at his side.

The action of the *Wrath* is ended.

Such approximately was the two-hour version of the *Iliad* I read and mimed as best I could that spring evening in Peking to that crowded courtful of Chinese, for all of whom it was utterly new. I had opportunity to work it over again later. The Ford Foundation gave Harvard a TV professorship, which I was invited to occupy for two terms. Eight fifteen-minute spells, one each week, had to take care of the whole poem. (The second term I tried readings of eight great English poems with the words on the screen.) I have never worked harder in my life. So much planning, so much measuring, so much practising of various voices, so many concomitants, so much adjustment to camera, lighting, settings, and continuity. I suppose it was worthwhile, for even now, twenty years later, I meet complete strangers who speak of that TV *Iliad* excitedly without recalling who did it. I used for the characters, archaic Greek sculpture. They held the eye and relevantly helped me to make clear who was speaking. How I longed at the time for the relative freedom and the experimental flexibility of film. Possibilities of trying a film reading – enriched and relaxed, with a variation of voices – or even of making an acted film presentation hung in the air for some time. But the local NET station, WGBH (Boston), went up in flames, and one of the two kinescope copies that had been made of my readings helped to feed them. The other, which had been sent to Harvard for their files, proved unfindable when I inquired about it. This account, here presented, is my somewhat delayed attempt to explore the problem again. I am more than ever persuaded that the *Iliad* contains an action (and a second Trojan plot as well), and that working this out is, at least, a useful exercise. Classroom discussion of what belongs or not to a central Achillean action is as good a way as I can imagine into deeper investigation of the *Iliad*. I am inclined to believe that on this at least Aristotle would be in agreement.

The same, with significant differences, is true of the parallel play: the above mentioned *Homage to Hector*. That brings out sharply the wide differences between the ethos of the Greek camp and the ethos of the well-ordered city with its rich domestic and familial concerns. It is perhaps a commonplace to remark that Homer's women seem our contemporaries as compared with his men. Andromache and Hecuba support this and, however different she is from them, so does Helen: the other character in the *Iliad* as enigmatic as Achilles, concerned with self-discovery, though infinitely more self-critical throughout than he. By contrast, Paris, as a character, is extremely well understood by Hector. There is nothing very deep in him except his luck and charm – too deep to be plumbed – and Aphrodite's passion for him, divinely inexplicable. It seems fitting that it should be frivolous, pleasure-loving Paris who – though after the ending of the *Iliad* – sped the "arrow from the string" causing Achilles' death. He has Apollo's help, as though Apollo had had his further intentions when he deserted Hector.

WHY SO, SOCRATES?

A very different Apollo this from Socrates' god of Delphi, god of the swans which Socrates evokes an hour or so before his death. Any bout of dramatic analysis and construction whets the appetite for another. I think it was the overwhelming fun I had had fumbling with threads of plots in the *Iliad* – that and an awareness of the significant contrasts and mutual relevances – that set me to making, if I could, a four-act play: *Why So, Socrates?* from *Euthyphro, Apology, Crito, Phaedo.* The general conditions of the problem were the same. Add nothing whatever to the original. Only find in it – without, I could hope, distortion – an ACTION with beginning, middle, and end, such as would have an Aristotelian unity and closure. And also to present it in a version linguistically simplified enough to be serviceable in school classrooms, as well as for radio or film or TV cassette presentations to forthcoming world populations. (Designs, these, that most educators, I find, shake off as easily as ducks do the raindrops. But such remarks may not be the best way to further these projects!)

One merit of such a play would come from the tension with the *Iliad* it could set up, if taken as a due sequel. I had the *Republic*, in simple form, already, as a staging of the main clashes between them. But the *Republic* called for a more dramatic presentation of Socrates; in fact, for the crucial Socratic action to balance that of Achilles. I could not, of course, explicitly and consciously look for these things in dissecting out the action. Otherwise there would be many risks of wrenchings. I had to let the greatest familiarity I could achieve of the full texts combine of itself with my best dramatic sense of what, in Aristotle's terms, could with most plausible possibility, follow from and prepare for what. Especially, I had to beware of stretching interpretations, even more than of importations.

As before, with the *Iliad* and the *Republic*, help came most from the books themselves. As one came a little nearer to what appeared to be their essentials, these seemed, more and more, to link up, join hands, and participate. The action I sought was there, offering itself for presentation if I could only disengage it. And what I must disengage it from clung to it so because – once the action was disengaged – so much of the rest could be enrichment. But let me come now to detail.

I suppose I thought I knew the *Euthyphro* fairly well. I had found it, off and on through decades, a somewhat baffling sequence of tricky maneuvers and remained unconvinced that Socrates, where the argument appears to become really strict, was clarifying much. Then coming back to it from the *Apology* – for which a PERFORMABLE version had not been too hard to make – reading the *Euthyphro* as a designed prelude to Socrates' trial changed everything. Socrates' interlocutor then becomes a superficial, insensitive, and breathtakingly vain foil to a Socrates resigned to facing – with his unbreakable courage – a situation of the utmost danger. So far from this visit to the King Archon's office being merely a setting for a philosophical discussion on holiness and piety, it provides a deeply penetrating contrast between two sincerities and two types of religion, between a Socratic and a fanatical (one might say a more than Deuteronomic) piety. The argument is not designed to show anything beyond the fact that two such sincerities – one so complex and so self-searching, the other so simple and so unacquainted with doubts – cannot meet. Each of the definitions over which Socrates perplexes Euthyphro can be taken in at least two very different senses: one trivial and silly, the other profoundly suggestive. The silly sense Euthyphro uses, the profound sense Socrates could entertain. But not in this dialogue. Here Socrates is strangely playful throughout. It is as though the prospect of his coming encounter with his 501 judges were raising his spirits. He is clearly under no illusions whatever as to the risk he runs. Perhaps he has just freshly resolved not in any way, on any account, by any concession, to reduce it. Perhaps he already sees in this grand climactic encounter with the Great Beast an opportunity to be more himself than ever. Curiously, he can remind us of Achilles going out in his new armor. There is an "impetuous valor" and a moral joy of battle.

Here, from Book 6 of the *Republic,* is Plato's description of what happens

when the masses crowd together in public meetings, in the Assembly, at a trial, in the theatre or the camp, crying out full throated that some of the things done are bad and others good. At such times will not a young man's heart, as the saying is, be moved within him? What private teaching won't be washed away by such a river? Taken up by its current he will say as they say, do as they do, be as they are.
Adeimantus: There is no help for it, Socrates.
Socrates: And, moreover, we haven't yet pointed out the chief force at work.
Adeimantus: What is it?

Socrates: What these trainers and Sophists, the public, back up their words with if the words alone haven't the desired effect: punishment, fines, loss of rights and death.[37]

Need we doubt that in writing this, Plato would look back to Socrates' trial, at which he was present and doing what he could, terrified and amazed, perhaps exalted, at the way in which his hero was behaving? That behavior was precisely the reverse of what the Socrates of the *Republic* goes on to describe. Instead of placating the Great Beast, the historic Socrates flouted and annoyed it.

Socrates: As things are, if anyone anywhere comes to good, that must be through some sort of heavenly inspiration. For there is not, never has been, and never will be any keeping to true values and virtues for a soul which gets the opposite education public meetings give. It is as if a man were learning the impulses and desires of some great strong beast, which he had in his keeping, how to come near it and touch it, and when and by what it may be made most violent or most gentle. Yes, and the cries it makes under which conditions, and what sounds from its keeper and others make it angry or quiet. And after getting this knowledge by living with the great beast long enough, he names it "wisdom" and makes up a system and art, and gives that as his teaching – without any knowledge as to which of these opinions and desires is beautiful or ugly, good or bad, just or unjust. But he fixes all these words by the tastes of the great beast, and names what pleases it "good," and the things which made it angry "bad," having no other account to give of them. And what is necessary he names "just" and "high," never having seen how very different are *what must be* and *what should be*. So he is not able to make that clear to another. By heaven, won't such a man give the young a strange education? Have you ever heard an argument to the effect that whatever the public praises is good and beautiful, which wouldn't make you simply laugh?
Adeimantus: No, and I am not looking for one.[38]

This passage may help to bring out a relevance of the ARGUMENT of the *Euthyphro* to what Socrates is going to do before his judges. That the gods approve it does not make an act holy any more than being pleasing to the Great Beast makes it good. And in the *Crito* and *Phaedo* the same point is pressed home in an increasingly dramatic fashion. What is so, is to be settled, not by what people say, but by what the careful, critical, responsible thinker can SEE to be true – in that strangely safe and simple sense in which we SEE that it is beauty that MAKES beautiful things be beautiful. This is the intellectual vision that Coleridge's Aphorism 9[39] is speaking of.

---

[37] *Republic* 6. 492-493.
[38] *Republic* 6. 493.
[39] See p. 185 above.

There are opportunities here, of course, for the greatest and most continuing mistakings in the history of philosophy, for all the differings that have made the Doctrine of Ideas a battleground. *Why So, Socrates?*, as a play intended for every sort of performance via all available media, does not pretend to resolve any controversy. It couldn't. But no presentation of Plato's Socrates could possibly omit what is, in these four dialogues, their kingbolt. The *Euthyphro* is nominally and explicitly a quest for the Idea, the form, the universal, the essence, of holiness, piety, religion, spoken of as a single ἰδέα 'principle',[40] then as an εἶδος 'idea',[41] and an οὐσία 'essence'.[42] As Taylor points out, Euthyphro not a philosophic mind) understands all this without any need for explanation, though it is talked of in the technical language of 'theory of Forms'. Taylor concludes that "from the very first Plato represented Socrates as habitually using language of this kind and being readily understood by his contemporaries".[43]

There is, however, a safe and simple and familiar sense for such words, which can be used without (perhaps) committing ourselves to anything more recondite than an evident fact which all will allow. This is that things and events recur; they can be the same and not the same, the same in some ways and not in other ways; they can be instances; we can ask what they are instances of and be intelligibly answered. For instance, in the last sentence the word THEY recurred. It (the word THEY) appears there three times. Three THEYS occurred. What is that IT? What are these THEYS? Common sense is content and at ease with a division between occurrences (which we can note and count, compare, distinguish between, contrast and relate) and what they are occurrences of. We need not, and most thinking does not, try to go further, though we are well aware that we can only note, count, and compare occurrences by SOMEHOW using something of another order of being, something they are occurrences of. But, as it is so well brought out in Chapter 96 of the *Syntopicon*, on the Universal and the Particular, if we try to go beyond that SOMEHOW, we step onto the philosophic battleground and are involved at once in what "seems to have the character of a professional secret". It is as if we were to try our hand with the spear against Hector. The safe and simple and familiar sense keeps well this side of that SOMEHOW. It is the sense that Euthyphro so readily understands.

40 *Euthyphro* 5.
41 *Euthyphro* 6.
42 *Euthyphro* 11.
43 Taylor, *Plato, the Man and His Work*, p. 149.

For dramatic purposes, this sense is all that is needed. What the last paragraph has presented are points we can SEE in the sense in which we see that beauty makes beautiful things beautiful and whiteness makes whites be white. Nothing (perhaps) follows from this evident, allowable fact. But for Socrates – and friends of the Ideas, in general – enormously important outcomes have seemed to ensue: promise of immortality and at the least a new scale of intellectual and moral ambition.

It is usually assumed that to understand a play we do not NEED to adhere to, actually believe in, accept and assent to any of the philosophical positions of any of the characters.[44] Nor need we actually participate in their emotions and disturbances. Some sort and degree of imaginative entertainment is normally sufficient and necessary. Given that, a source of our respect for good drama is the balanced conduct of response and reflection it invites. There is to be SOPHROSYNE in the good reader, in the good playgoer, whether the characters exhibit that virtue or not. And what became clear as I tried to bring the four dialogues together into one continuous Aristotelian action was that, with Socrates as the overwhelmingly dominant character, the theme of the play would be maintenance of SOPHROSYNE itself, and the action, as a result, would be Simple. I need look for no Reversal of the Situation and for no Recognition. Socrates knows himself too well for redirective changes to take place. In fact, the force of Act Three, the *Crito*, comes from Socrates' calm resistance to very strong pressure for Reversal. As regards Recognition, we may be less certain. Socrates, in Plato's pages, never stops thinking; there is development throughout the *Phaedo*. The nearness of his death gives a living freshness to his view of the philosopher's attitude to it, as well as a heightened awareness that he is likely to be indulging in idle talk to encourage himself and his friends. Naturally the friends want to moan – the Achillean "desire to sorrow aloud" is strong within them. Parts of Socrates' discourse – stretches omitted in my play as dramatically inoperative – were probably a means chiefly of diverting if not distracting them. I had to cut them to let the action develop.

So too in Act Two, the *Apology*: I had to cut anything that could not be conveyed dramatically or that requires special knowledge if it is to be understood, such as the bulk of the cross-examination of

---

[44] I am by no means securely convinced that this is true for most of the meanings of ADHERE and its synonyms, and I would hold the matter to be philosophically indeterminate unless and until these meanings become far clearer. There are, of course, schools and movements in the theater that will think such remarks much out-of-date.

Meletus. Most of these decisions did not seem doubtful or difficult; there were more than enough dramatically valid motions waiting to be used.

Time pressure, however, was troublesome. Total performance time for an unrehearsed reading over Station WGBH with parts distributed among eight readers was 73 minutes. My recollection is that some of it went too fast. Separate Acts, READ and in a measure mimed, have been, I am told, fairly successful. As I took Socrates myself, I am in a poor position to judge. I have lively memories of doing Act One, the *Euthyphro*, with Dan Seltzer in the pulpit of the Old North Church in Boston. A lady afterward accused us of presenting an IRRELIGIOUS play. Local schools have seen readings of the other Acts: Two and Three are the easiest. I recall that, in my inexperience, I did not anticipate the queer sensations that nearly overcame me when I had drunk the poison.

Two topics in *Why So, Socrates?* invite comment: Socrates' attitudes to suicide and to Apollo.

In the *Phaedo* he comes very near to giving his audience at least a strong hint that he has deliberately used the verdict of the judges as a means for ending his life: "Maybe it is not unreasonable to say that a man must not kill himself until God sends some sort of compulsion on him like this that is upon me now." Certainly his behavior at the trial seems calculated to bring that verdict about. Even if Xenophon's explanation, forty years afterward, that Socrates provoked his own execution in order to escape the infirmities of old age be "absurd" (Taylor's description), it nonetheless shows that there had been people who wanted some such story. Infirmities, no, but there might be other reasons. Taylor and John Burnet hold that Socrates forced the judges' hands and point to the words that follow his sentence: "You are really killing me because I wouldn't say the sort of things you would have liked to hear . . . I had much rather die after such a defense than live on after the other sort of defense . . .". Something about this may remind us of Achilles on his twofold fate (indeed, a current Homerist presents Achilles as virtually willing his own death[45]). When the first judgment of the Court was announced, Socrates could see clearly that he had only to be modest and reasonable (in the judges' eyes) to have

---

[45] "It is safe to say that the baffling vision of self-destruction with eternal glory was native to Greek air, and that Homer was the first to frame it in the symbols of poetry and canonize it for the succeeding ages of the Hellenic, and especially the Athenian mind" (Cedric Whitman, *Homer and the Heroic Tradition* [Cambridge: Harvard University Press, 1958], p. 220).

some light penalty replace that of death. Instead, his counterproposal was so infuriating that the balance against him leaped by eighty votes.

Socrates: I am not pained, men of Athens, that the vote has gone against me. For many reasons. Among them is the fact that I was not surprised. I am more surprised that there were not more votes against me. It seems that if thirty votes had gone the other way, I would have been acquitted. My accusers propose the punishment of death. What ought I to propose in its place? What I deserve, isn't that right? Well, what do I deserve? What ought I to undergo or pay – for never resting; for turning away from what most men care for: money and property, military office and public life; for keeping out of things in which I should have been no use to you or to myself and for giving myself up completely to doing the greatest possible good to every one of the citizens? I tried to make each of you care more about becoming better and wiser, than about what he can get, and to care more for the state itself than for its possessions. And what does a man like that deserve – a poor man too who needs time and support to do this for you? How about giving him his meals free in the Prytaneum as if he were a winner in the Olympic Games? That would be more to the point for me than for one of you who may have come in first in a chariot race. You don't need free meals, but I do. So if I am to suggest something to match what I deserve, here it is.[46]

This is certainly asking for it. Why? The gentlest suggestion is devotion to a cause: in Socrates' eyes a cause so great and so sacred and so exacting that any accommodation, however slight, to the Great Beast would have seemed its betrayal. "Be soople, Davie, in things eemmaterial!" so his mentor advised David Balfour. To Socrates what happened at his trial was too material to admit of any yielding.

Just how serious Socrates is being is uncertain enough at enough points to make most judgments feel hazardous. It seems fitting to be in two minds, then, about his attitude to Delphi. No doubt his audience, and men of Athens generally, had good reasons for not regarding the oracle with friendly or with trustful feelings. If so, the great play Socrates makes with its answer to Chaerephon's question would be a sharp preliminary irritant. Indeed his introductory injunction: "Don't cry out now and shut me up if I tell you a very strange thing", shows that he knew he would anger them. On the other hand, what he does to test the oracle – "Why does he say I am the wisest of men? He can't be lying. Apollo can't do that" – the tone of his references to his mission – "Men of Athens, I respect and love you, but I will do what the god says, not what you say" – and other passages suggest that he feels in some peculiarly close relation to Apollo. At the beginning of the *Phae-*

[46] *Apology* 36; *GBWW*, Vol. 7, p. 209b-c.

do, when his friends visit him, it appears that he has been writing verses, among them an ode to Apollo. Later, at the central crisis of the discussion, when Simmias and Cebes are whispering together,

Socrates (noticing it all): If you have difficulties, don't shrink from coming out with them and take me along with you, if you think I can help at all.
Simmias: Socrates, here is the truth. For some time Cebes and I have been in doubt and each of us has been trying to get the other to ask you a question. We want your answer, but we didn't want to trouble you in view of your present misfortune.
Socrates (laughing gently): Ah, Simmias, a hard time I would have with other people if I can't make even you two believe that this isn't to me a misfortune. You seem to think that I am more irritable than usual today. Evidently you take me as much less of a prophet than any swan, who, when he feels that he is going to die, sings his best in his joy at going to the god whose servant he is. Silly death-fearing men say the swans sing for sorrow, mourning their death. But no bird sings because it is hungry or cold or in trouble – no, not even the nightingale or the swallow, who, men say, sing for grief. No more do the swans. Being Apollo's birds, they have prophetic vision. And I myself, I think, am a fellow servant of the swans, belonging, I too, to Apollo. And I go out from life with as little sorrow. So ask what questions you please, for as long as the officers of the Athenians will allow it.[47]

Belonging, I too, to Apollo. Simmias clearly does not think this merely whimsical. He says: "Either we must discover the truth, or, if that is impossible, we must take whatever doctrine seems soundest and ride through the seas of life on it as on a raft. That is, if we cannot sail more safely upon some divine revelation."[48] Prophetic vision? Divine revelation? Some sort of heavenly inspiration? Socrates makes no further comment here and concerns himself with the arguments that Simmias and Cebes advance. But there is the libation to some deity he would like to pour. That might be what we could call mere piety: the sort of thing Euthyphro knew all about. It hardly seems likely. And there are his last words: "Crito, we owe a cock to Asclepius. Don't forget!"[49] Asclepius, god of medicine (who may be curing Socrates of the disease of life), was son of Apollo, and the cock was sacred to both. These ritual acts can remind us, moreover, of the Homeric background from which the life and death of Socrates were so deeply a revolt and a departure.

[47] *Phaedo* 84-85.
[48] *Phaedo* 85.
[49] *Phaedo* 118.

14. POETRY AS AN INSTRUMENT OF RESEARCH

Poetry may seem to have got into bad company in my title: "Poetry as an Instrument of Research".

INSTRUMENT: bad enough! A horrid array of forceps, scalpels, stethoscopes, electrocardiographs, and psychogalvanometers, is conjured up. But RESEARCH – worse still, whether you pronounce it re-search or resürch. That intellectual treadmill, offered us as the next step – step, step; step, step, step STEP IT UP THERE! – for Poetry! What has poor Poetry done to suggest such a sentence?

Far be it from me to conduct any such inquiry. On the contrary, it is what poetry has been showing signs of doing that makes me try now to sketch a suitably new (though equally an ancient and indeed original) role – role, aim, ambition, function, fate – for poetry.

Take another look at these words: INSTRUMENT and RESEARCH. The most decisive instruments we use are words: words with their meanings, of course; without its meanings a word is but a noise, or a mark on paper. With its meanings a word is as much an instrument as a camera, say. Somebody takes a photograph of you. What his camera gets is not, of course, you. It is only something which may make you say: 'Good Lord! Is THAT what I look like!'

So it is with our words. And, as we do not think very much perhaps, of any photograph of ourselves – so we should not take too seriously any picture of things, of other people or of ourselves, indeed, that words may seem to be presenting. (No, not even this snapshot of poetry which I am trying to offer you now.) On the other hand, consider how little there is – without words and their meanings – that we can form or keep any clear ideas of at all.

So much for poetry as an instrument. It is a use of words, a way of putting them together to give us – what? I am bringing up that obnoxious, that all-but abusive word RESEARCH, here, as a useful pointer; to research, the Dictionary says, is 'diligently to examine, to search again, to regard anew". To regard what? Whatever may seem worth while.

Talking like this does not bring anything presently, wholly and livingly within our awareness – to be examined, enjoyed, realized, appraised, undergone: whichever it may be among the varied invitations of poetry. It is another use of words which can do all that. All that is for poetry: not for such prose as this. What such prose as this may attempt is to discuss (what a word!) what poetry today can do which it could not, perhaps, do a few decades ago.

Consider what fantastic and, until recently, unthinkable enlargements of human powers we are being faced with daily. Need I list them?

Everyone thinks of only too many of them without prompting. But may I add to speed and population records, anaesthetics, television, and the guided-missile, a few developments whose benefits and whose attendant perils are not so immediately obvious.

I will pick four among many that would be possible: four enlargements of human possibilities which should, I suppose, matter more than space travel to poetry and its public. I say "matter more" because they concern every man's attitudes to anything. Space-ships and their passengers' adventures are, I have found, relatively cramping. My four recent expansions of possibility are in logic, in methodology, in linguistics, and in pedagogy. Not a promising list, you may think. Let me try thumbnail sketches of what I have in mind.

In logic, the last thirty years or so have shown that the kind of rigour in proof – the self-contained perfection – that traditional logicians have taken as the very aim of their study is not obtainable. This does not make logic any less useful in criticizing bad arguments; but it does remove some of the logical limits to possibility. It does not make ordered thought or discourse any less orderly; but it does show that the order which logic studies cannot have the completeness or the independence that was supposed. In a way it restores logic to the condition of a tool, rather than a completely autonomous master study.

This liberation from self-imposed limitations is more than matched by the licences to adventure that came to Physics when Niels Bohr launched his Complementarity Principle. More than one methodology, more than one set of assumptions – however incompatible they may be, formally, with one another – may yet co-operate with mutual advantage. And no one knows in how many studies other than Physics the same new methodological possibilities may be found.

In Linguistics as it grows more self-critical, as its metalingual analyses question its own procedures more reflectively, it looks as though a similar freedom to use seemingly incompatible assumptions together can be to the good. Incompatibility (a logical notion) is being re-interpreted. What language successfully DOES is being given again due precedence over rulings as to what it cannot do. And more is being found out about how it actually works. In particular, the complexities of the interplay of words with one another and the resources these open up are being more variously and subtly recognized.

Words get a large part of the peculiar charges or flavours they carry from the networks of partial agreement, partial synonymy, connecting any word with others in these ramifying, flexible ways. We often feel of a word well used that no other word could possibly replace it; and in fact no other word is linked into just that partial synonymy net.

Add to this its rhyme-field, the other words which sound more or less like it, and, of course, its peculiar dealings, through these various sorts of linkage, with other words around it, through their linkages, and we have the beginnings at least of an account of the mutual control which all the parts of a poem may have upon one another. What keeps every word in a good poem to its duty, what makes it do what is required of it, is the rest of the poem. The words in that order govern and explain one another.

All this may look more like a regimentation for poetry than a liberation. But no. Poetry, so conceived (and this way of conceiving it need not conflict with some other ways: recall the complementarity principle again), can release a poet into larger freedoms. Instead of having to express himself, say, he finds himself serving a possibility of the language – as that has been, is, and shall be used by discriminating people.

I have just sniffed somewhat at 'self-expression' as a poetic aim: but there can be excellent self-expression doctrines of poetry as well as very bad ones.

For this intra-linguistic translation view of meaning – the view that the meanings of words are controlled through the other words which can replace them – a poem becomes a representative of the language, showing what the language can do with a situation and using the poet for this purpose. Thus the poem becomes an independent sort of a creature. This is something a poem ought to be able to say better than prose can. So here is a poem trying to do so. It comes from my *Goodbye Earth* and is called "Retort". What it is a retort to is the poem which precedes it there, a poem in which the mind has complained of being possessed.

A poem's not on a page
　　Or in a reader's eye;
　　Nor in a poet's mind
Its freedom may engage.
　　For I, a poem, I
　　Myself alone can find
　　Myself alone could bind.

I, though I take from you
　　All, all I have to sing,
　　Am all an empty ought
Spinning itself its clew.
　　Burning up what you bring
　　To search out what you sought,
　　I work on out from naught.

Eyeless, a source of seeing,
　　Careless, a fount of care,
　　An unrecorded vow
Is all my core of being.
　　Yet, neither here nor there
　　And with no then but now,
　　Your life I disallow.

I sing, who nevertheless
　　No accents have or breath.
　　I neither live nor die.
But you whom I possess . . .
　　You, you know life and death
　　And throughly know; so I
　　What void I fill thereby.

Thence to pedagogy: most repugnant and unlikely field from which
to look for new, unthought of enlargements of the spirit. Strange –
isn't it? – that we are prone to think so, seeing what enlargements all
who hear these words have already undergone through teaching! None
of us would be expressing any views at all without it.

My point here, however, can be put briefly. Whatever successes
teaching as yet achieves are slight in comparison with those which become possible as the question "What should come before what?" is
really explored, systematically and closely. There is an order, a system
of steps, to be found in every study by which the learner's mistakes
can be cut down to the fewest and his powers accordingly encouraged
to their height. The thing is to avoid confusing and stultifying him as
the sequences currently employed cannot avoid doing. The finding of

this most propitious order is important above all in the elementary stages on which later progress depends. The most advantageous sequence has been, on the whole, probably found for mathematics; we begin to have something like it for second languages and for the teaching of reading. A similar order can be found for other subjects as soon as we wake up to what is needed and to what we might gain from it.

One gain to the poet would be this: a greatly enlarged and enlightened audience able to read, take in, and enjoy poetry. Another might be a better preparation for writing poetry. For, if we ask "What sort of an order is propitious?" the best answer can be given in the words of an old description of a good poem: "one in which what comes first prepares best for what follows, and what follows confirms and completes what has gone before".

After these thumbnail sketch-maps of vanishing frontiers, what could, might, should be the upshot for poetry? There could be countless upshots, of course; the overall outcome could be an immense release. Before I spell out one or two, let me spike a misapprehension. I am not saying that poets must get up this logical, methodological, linguistic, and pedagogic stuff and write about it. They may if they will, but there is no must about. There are no musts of that sort for poetry. To quote Coleridge: "Let us not pass an Act of Uniformity against poets". I would add: "or against poems either".

No: but I will opine that the most deeply influential and vivifying poetry is likely to be as responsive to these intellectual releases as the best poetry of Dante, Donne and Pope was to the intellectual breezes of their day.

How would such responsiveness appear? What might it be like? My guess – in a matter which, above all others, can only be shown by the fact – is that a sober balance of responsibility and audacity might be a mark. More freedom AND more power: both daunting, unless we can rise to them. All these enlargements I have been describing have appalling risks attached; freedom and power always have.

"Responsibility and audacity" – not a bad substitute phrasing for, not a bad intra-linguistic translation of, 'prophetic inspiration': as in Amos, Hosea, Isaiah, Blake, or Shelley at their best. Do not be put off by mention of Shelley here. Have you re-read him – with eyes which really looked into what, at his best, he was about?

As for form: I would expect – somewhat apprehensively, being familiar with the way in which true prophets always surprise – a kind of quiet and smooth, highly organized, highly economic, highly elegant (in the mathematicians' sense) spare, subtle, and feline poetry. It need not be ABOUT the condition of the world or coming events – unless timelessly necessary reconstitutions in ourselves can best be symbolized so: in terms of deprivation and renewal. The perennial encounters of the accidental and the essential lend themselves to that sort of dramatic handling.

I am inclined to predict that, as regards rhyme, metre and stanza form, these prophets will be intricate, their poems difficult – to write, but not necessarily to read. Studies that linguistics and criticism are beginning already show how much our words depend for their powers on other words which normally do not come into clear consciousness – other words which may sound like them or which could follow them. I am not here discussing depth-psychology or psychoanalysis – whose influence on poetry may not continue. I am talking of the control – over every word we ever say – of other words we might have said: the penumbral awareness of our choices. We are underestimating, all the time, the complexity of the choices behind even our simplest remarks. The poet is, among other things, the adept in such choosing. Rhyme and metre are the invaluable, traditional means (which can still be much developed) of imposing a more exacting search upon the working poet, a search into the possibilities of the language for the situation with which the poem is grappling. Robert Frost much enjoyed telling Carl Sandburg once that, as to free verse, he personally preferred to play tennis with a net. Coming poets, I fancy, may play on smaller courts.

Such poetry, I think, will not be easy. It will invite and reward study. There will be plenty of popular poetry – current song hits – which do not invite and do not reward study. The kinds of poetry I am discussing will, consciously or unconsciously, be concerned with making new sorts of people: remaking, renewing the poet himself and his public. That is not often done in a flash. Most poems which could do it require repeated intimacy with them. Relatively few readers at present are capable of this. That is why a prospect of many more and far more able readers may matter much to future poets.

Wordsworth, in his essay supplementary to the preface of the *Lyrical Ballads, 1815,* quotes a good remark on this as "made to me long ago by the philosophical Friend" (that is, Coleridge), whose poetic genius he had, one might say, manslaughtered. Here it is: "Every author, as far as he is great and at the same time *original,* has the task of *creating* the taste by which he is to be enjoyed." The thought was Coleridge's, no doubt; but it was Wordsworth's vanity which made him apply it so confidently to himself. Coleridge, apart from his rather morbid idolatry of Wordsworth, would, I think, have preferred to widen his remark. "All poetry", he might have said, "in so far as it is unfamiliar, has to initiate its readers into the means by which its end is to be discerned and pursued."

After all, what Poetry has done for people in the past, and could do again, is worth the trouble. "Homer was the educator of Greece", as Plato said: he was a most unpropitious educator, Plato thought, and we can in some ways agree with that. For better or worse, "Poets are the legislators of mankind" – as Shelley told his friend Peacock, who had pretended to doubt whether we really need any more poets.

We do need more poets and better poetry, if poetry is our means, our instrument, for regarding anew the changing world and our changing selves: seeing thereby what we have to be and do.

15. WHAT IS SAYING?

What follows has to be peculiar.[1] It is about ways of saying things. So its sentences have to be peculiarly about themselves – always being sent back to their own ways of saying things . . . about saying things.

At first all this may make you feel as if you were being asked to keep looking into your own apparatus for looking. You feel for a while that you are getting mental eye-ache. But that wears off quickly as you notice that what you are doing is comparing different ways of saying whatever-it-may-be and that this comparing is a game you have been playing all your thinking life. It is a game about which you can go on finding out more and more. And, as a result, you come to play it better.

To ease the strain, most of this chapter is put in the form of a dialogue, a discussion between the Author (A) and his Reader (R). The question discussed is: WHAT DIFFERENT SORTS OF WORK MAY A SENTENCE BE DOING? What is being discussed is something you very often know as much about as anyone does. But you may not know that you know it.

If you like, you can take this CONVERSATIONAL form as no more than an internal dialogue, a 'dialogue of one': one mind, your mind, questioning and answering itself, conversing[2] with itself, developing its

[1] *peculiar* is itself a queer word. Its base is the Latin *pecu*, 'livestock'. Hence 'money', cattle widely being early wealth. *pecu* has *peculium*, a diminutive (i.e. word describing a small specimen of the thing) meaning 'small part of herd, given to slave looking after it, as his own private property'. Hence *peculate*. That part of English through which the rest of the language must be explored may be thought to be peculiarly English, deserving of peculiar attention from the student.

[2] *converse* is an interesting word in itself and in its relations with *convert*. The sense 'talk with' is relatively recent. Dr. Johnson: 'to convey the thoughts reciprocally in talk'. The *-verse* element, means 'turning' this way or that. The religious sense of *conversion* looks back to Plato, *Republic*, VII, 518: "The natural power to learn lives in the soul and is like an eye which might not be turned from the dark to the light without a turning round of the whole body . . . of which there might be an art . . . of turning the soul round most quickly and with the most effect." That is what education, for Plato, was to be.

thought by alternate moves much as in walking we put our weight
first on one foot, then on the other.

A. Do you feel clear about the difference between: (a) WHAT SOME-
ONE HAS IT IN MIND TO SAY and (b) HOW HE SAYS IT?

R. At first sight, yes: (a) is something he might say in different ways;
(b) is the special way he says it.

A. Why do you say "at first sight"?

R. I'm not quite sure. Perhaps it is because as I go on thinking about
it I don't see how I know what (a) is apart from (b) what he says.

A. You feel like the Bishop?

R. What Bishop?

A. He was on a train and he couldn't find his ticket. The Conductor
trusted him and said, "Never mind. It's all right, My Lord." "No,
it isn't! It's not all right!" replied the Bishop. "How do I know
where I am going to without it?"

R. Poor old thing. But it is a difficulty, isn't it? How do we know what
it will be before it is said?

A. Sometimes that is difficult. But very often can't we see from THE
SITUATION THE SPEAKER IS IN what he will be most likely to say?

R. Maybe, too, from the sort of person he is. There are people who
never say anything surprising and there are others who . . . , well,
you never know what they won't say.

A. And won't you add the sorts of people they may be talking to?
There are people you can't say anything surprising to – because
they wouldn't take it in if you did, or so it seems to you.

R. The situation the speaker is in? Doesn't that include whoever he is
talking to?

A. Does it? Are you sure about that? As a rule, of course, we are
talking to someone, but sometimes . . .

R. Sometimes we are talking to ourselves.

A. That's true, but sometimes people are just talking and it doesn't
matter who is there or who is listening or not listening . . .

R. You mean they just go on . . .

A. And aren't even listening to themselves.

R. Isn't that more often true of writing?

A. Probably; there can be all sorts of ideal and imaginary audiences
for writers, possible readers who may come along sometime, posterity, and all that.

R. But in this situation the speaker is in, don't you have to include
what he is talking about?

A. Yes, and what else?

R. Maybe we had better put in what he is trying to do?

A. Right. And with that we have a lot to look into. Let's see: we have
(1) the situation he is in, (2) the sort of person he is, (3) who he's
talking to, (4) what he is talking about, and (5) what he is after. It
is quite a packet: all that behind WHAT HE SAYS.

R. There is another trouble about those words: WHAT HE SAYS. They
could mean just the sounds he makes – what a tape could record;
or they could mean all you have just been summing up.

A. Yes, and there are other troubles here too. There's the sound as
what the tape gets and the sound as what his voice produces (which
often aren't closely the same, it depends on where the mike is).
And then too there's what various people may hear him as saying,
which may sometimes be way off. That's a difference which has
killed plenty. And again, there is the difference between his utterance and the part of the language it represents.

R. That last seems a bit obscure.

A. It's all right. Any number of people can say the same thing. Actually all their utterances of it are different, for they are different
people with different bodies and voices and minds. No two of the
utterances can be strictly the same. But linguists, while noting the
differences as minutely and finely as seems worth-while, can agree
as to what words in what sorts of cooperation with one another
make up what was said. That, what was said, is a part of the system
of possibilities of the language. It is the part of it an individual utterance represents. Is that clearer?

R. Yes, but I have still a further puzzle. The words AND the ways they
work together may be the same – as far as the grammar goes – I
see that, but still what is SAID by them may not be the same.

A. But when you say different things, don't you have to use different
ways of saying them?

R. Can't we make the same words say different things?

A. We agree that we can.

R. Well then, we CAN say different things without using different ways
of saying them.

A. You see what has been happening here. We have been using ʷsay
different thingsʷ and ʷuse different waysʷ, BOTH OF THEM, in different ways. We've been illustrating the very thing we were talking
about. Can you get any further in seeing how?

R. I think I can. But it may be easier to see how it is than to say it.

A. Shall we try? How about this: ᵂsay different thingsᵂ MAY = (a) attempt a different communication or (b) pronounce different words. ᵂuse different waysᵂ may = (b) pronounce different words or (c) have something about a communication different.

R. You know, you are making me think it is a miracle when people understand one another.

A. And yet it sometimes seems so easy.

R. Nothing to it. Easy as winking. However, we all know that we can say things as simple as "Hi!" or "Good afternoon!" so that "Hi!" may mean anything from what a smile means to "Here, stop that!" and "Good afternoon!" anything from a welcome to "Let me hope I'll never see you again!"

A. And there are all sorts of smiles too, aren't there? Would it help if we tried separating: THE WORDS WE USE from THE TONE OF VOICE IN WHICH WE USE THEM?

R. ?Tone of Voice?: that would be things like ˢʷlaughinglyˢʷ, ˢʷsweetlyˢʷ, ˢʷcuttinglyˢʷ, ˢʷthreateninglyˢʷ, and so on.

A. And so on and on and on. There would be any number of tones of voice, a whole study, the sort of thing actors ought to be good at. People differ in this. Some get enormous power from using tones. Others hardly have any tones or notice them, let alone employ them.

R. And aren't there people who scarcely notice anything else? They don't take in what you say becaue they are off on how they think you are saying it!

A. There would be different sorts of tone: ˢʷgrufflyˢʷ isn't in the same group with ˢʷcoldlyˢʷ or with ˢʷbreathlesslyˢʷ. And some of these things have names, some haven't Someone said the other day that a man spoke "grumly" to him. Do you make that one out?

R. Would it be a sort of cross between ˢʷglumlyˢʷ and ˢʷgrimlyˢʷ?

A. That's it, and with a taste of ˢʷgrumbleˢʷ about it too, perhaps. But to go back to our words and tones division, we would have to do more with it. What about Questions and Orders as against Statements? You may have noticed that about the time you brought in ˢʷHiˢʷ we switched over from WHAT IS SAID to HOW IT IS SAID.

R. Out of facts into social relations. Another sort of communications. Do you want to go into the word-order we use in questions?

A. Shifting word-order is one way of asking questions. *That is a man. Is that a man?* and so on. But there are others. And we can make *That is a man.* into a question easily enough without changing the word order.   "That is a man? Why I thought it was a baby or a turtle! Or some sort of insect!"

R. You give it a special lilt, a questioning intonation.

A. No doubt, USUALLY, there is a special intonation we use, a rise of pitch at the end perhaps. But you may doubt if it is as uniform as the books sometimes say. People may have a variety of ways of doing these things. And given a strong enough setting we can go beyond formal intonation patterns. Don't nurses in hospitals often know when patients are asking a question or asking for something without there being any tone?

R. Two senses of ASKING, those.

A. Can you think of some more?

R. What about "I'm asking you" when someone is a bit steamed up and feeling important, or "I ask you!" when he wants sympathy?

A. And "He was asking for it" when he was inviting trouble – doing something likely to get him into it.

R. And isn't there a way of seeming to be asking a question when you are really telling someone something or telling him to do something?

A. Is that what you are really doing here and now?

R. Maybe. Yes, it is.

A. There are all sorts of polite or disguised or indirect, round the corner, requests, suggestions, directions, directives, instructions, orders, commands. Some, as you said, look like questions: "Tommy, don't you want to go and get Mother her what-not?" Some look like statements about the future; prophesies, we'll call them. "You will lock up before you go." or "I'll get you to . . ." Some are like flat general statements: "All students observe the following rules." Many of these are ways of making the chain of command (who gives orders to whom) less visible. Sometimes it may be to spare the feelings of the giver or the receiver of the order, or it may be to make obedience seem more natural or more by consent than by compulsion. Conversely, what sound like straight imperatives can turn into nothing more than encouraging cries – as with spectators cheering on their side at a game.

R. So the Indicative, Interrogative, and Imperative of the Grammar books aren't quite what they profess to be.

A. Formally, they can be separated. Indicative: *I do.* Interrogative: *Do I?* Imperative: *Do it!* but, with the aid of varying intonations and given strong enough special settings, each of them can be used to do the work of the others.

R. I wonder if that is true of *Do I?*

A. Suppose you are wondering about something you think you do, wondering if you really do it or not, don't you find yourself using *Do I?* not so much to ask a question as to state to yourself a doubt or give yourself a direction? Do I really think so much about that? If you make a genuine question be something which has a genuine answer – one normally NOT KNOWN TO THE QUESTIONER – then won't you conclude that a large proportion of seeming questions are really being used as statements and directives? The questioner knows the answer and is trying with the seeming question to wake up the action side of his mind. You'll have noticed that we've been using interrogative forms here: *don't you find?* and *won't you conclude?* as a way of stating and directing – asking them as Rhetorical Questions, as the old books used to call them.

R. Is there really a deep difference between statements and these others? And if so what is it?

A. That's the deep question. What do you think yourself about it?

R. Well, that a lot, perhaps most, of the things people tell you are just ways of pushing you around.

A. A good many are, but not all and not most. It shouldn't be too hard to see which are which and it would be wonderfully useful. Shall we look into this – taking care not to push one another around or push ourselves around?

R. All right. It won't do any harm to try.

A. We can start perhaps a bit of a way back, in 399 BC, when Socrates is talking to a young man with only a little beard named Euthyphro. Euthyphro thinks he knows all about the gods and Socrates is busy showing him that he doesn't. Euthyphro takes all the old stories about the gods' fighting against one another quite seriously. Socrates won't. He thinks the gods know what is right and wrong and are of the same mind about it. So they won't fight. But Euthyphro is sure they do.

SOCRATES: Let's take a good look at what we are saying. Haven't we been saying that the gods, Euthyphro, grow angry with and fight with one another?

EUTHYPHRO: Yes, we said that.

SOCRATES: And what causes this anger and fighting? Look at it this way. If you and I don't agree about how many pigs we have, would we fight about them or count them?

EUTHYPHRO: Of course we would count them.
SOCRATES: And as to the sizes and weights of things, we measure and weigh? We don't fight?
EUTHYPHRO: No, of course we don't.
SOCRATES: But what sort of things *do* we fight about? Maybe you haven't an answer right off. Let me put one forward. Isn't it about what is right and what is wrong? Aren't these the questions people get angry about and fight?
EUTHYPHRO: Yes, Socrates, that's how it is.[3]

A. What do you think of that? Do you agree?

R. He does seem to be distinguishing facts from what are not facts.

A. And how does he do it?

R. Things that can be counted and weighed and measured give us facts. Other things don't.

A. Counting and weighing and measuring are all ways of COMPARING, aren't they?

R. Comparing – are they?

A. Yes. When you count: one, two, three, four ... you are comparing the number of the things with the number of numbers you have said. And when you weigh?

R. You look at the scale and see where the pointer is pointing.

A. The scale does the counting for you. And if you haven't a scale?

R. You could make a balance ...

A. And a balance is a machine for comparing weights. What about measuring?

R. A tape measure or a measuring rod is a way of comparing lengths.

A. So these are ways of comparing?

R. But what has all this to do with difference between statements and other ways of saying things?

A. Statements are the results of comparings. Other sorts of things said don't have to be that.

R. Oh!

A. Is it like this? In a statement there are two things: (a) what you are talking about and (b) what you are saying about it.

R. Or them.

A. About it or about them. *Your right hand has five fingers.* Try it on that.

R. My hand is what you are talking about and what you are saying about it is that it has five fingers.

---

[3] From *Why So, Socrates?* A dramatic version of Plato's dialogues: *Euthyphro, Apology, Crito, Phaedo* by I. A. Richards (Cambridge University Press, 1964).

A. And that it is a hand and that it is yours and on your right and that they are fingers and that there are five of them.

R. All that is in (b) is it? In what you are saying about it? What's left of (a)?

A. It's still what you are talking about, however much or little you may be saying about it.

R. All right, but how does this help?

A. It is the beginning of a list that may help us to keep things clearer about how the things we say may be the same or different. We are going to be asking about different ways of saying the same thing – as we call it. This list will help. These two, (a) and (b), are headings One and Two: One (a) – what we are talking about; Two (b) – what we are saying about it (them).

R. What are the others in the list? How many of them are there?

A. Perhaps seven in all will be enough.

R. Five more. What is next?

A. Heading Three? It hasn't got a good name of its own. You'll have to find or invent one. It's like this. Sometimes one way of saying something makes what's being said far more vivid, actual, real to you than another. It brings it home to you. You feel you REALIZE it, have it PRESENT to you, know it. But with the other ways you seem only to know OF it – not to know it.

R. I'm not sure that I quite get that. It isn't the difference between being really INTERESTED and not caring much about it?

A. Not quite, though that is what it can feel like. You can be deeply, indeed burningly INTERESTED in whatever-it-is, and yet some ways of saying even very important things about it leave you with a sense that it's unreal, not present to you at all, or very little.

R. Is it like having it sharply focussed or blurred?

A. Yes, it is very like that, but it's not just that. Some ways of saying things go dim under this Heading Three, by trying too hard to focus it all up dead sharp.

R. Dead sharp, yes, stuck there with no depth or life in it.

A. Would ˢʷvividityˢʷ be a good name for Heading Three? Or what about ˢʷnear or far offˢʷ? Would that be a good way of describing it? Might we simply use the metaphor of DISTANCE and say that something well said was held at the right distance for it: Not brought too near to the viewing mind and not left too far away?

R. I begin to get some dim idea of Heading Three now.

A. And wouldn't everything you have to say have its proper distance:

the degree of reality, livingness, actuality, that is most suited to it!

R. So it isn't always the better for being more vivid.

A. You don't think it is, do you?

R. Go on to your other four.

A. You are right. They all, Heading Three most of all, become clearer when you have them all in mind together. Heading Four should be very familiar. Isn't it VALUE?

R. Value?

A. Yes. And isn't it positive or negative? Can't the way a thing is said be trying to send it up or down on a value scale, trying to make us think the situation described is fine or frightful?

R. Give it a (+) plus or a (–) minus, play it up or run it down?

A. But wouldn't you agree, too, that people aren't always boosting or downing things, advertising or disparaging them? Don't they sometimes try honestly to say just how good or bad things are?

R. How things ARE? Or how they seem to them?

A. Aren't these the same?

R. Well, are they? And wouldn't this anyhow come under Heading Two: what we are saying ABOUT it or them?

A. Yes, except that THESE are the things people fight about. These values are the rights and wrongs Socrates thought the gods agree about, although men don't – at least not yet.

R. You mean valuing isn't like other sorts of comparing?

A. Yes. And it looks as though you see why. We are all very much at home with all that comes under Heading Four.

R. It seems so. What's the next?

A. The next one covers that pushing around business and it is just as familiar. (In fact, we have been over part of the ground already in talking about directives that look like statements or questions: "Don't you want to get me my bag, darling?") Only here again, we haven't a good ready-made name yet. How about calling it ?IN-FLUENCING?: making the people talked to DO something or NOT DO it through the way in which you say what you say.

R. You mean, political speaking?

A. That's an enormously important example, certainly. But if you watch, you'll find a component of influencing in most utterances. People are trying all the time to get things changed.

R. It is different, is it, from VALUING?

A. It can be very different. You may value something highly and yet talk of it so as to stop people from wanting it. Or, the other way round, you may not really think very much of it and yet give it all the sales talk you can concoct. People are always doing these things. But this isn't really a good way of describing this Fifth Heading. It isn't what you privately think or feel that comes into the question but WHAT YOUR WORDS WILL MAKE THOSE WHO HEAR THEM THINK OR FEEL. Above all, it's what your words will make others DO or NOT DO that matters. Your own wishes, etc., apart from what you say, don't need to come in.

R. So under Four it is how much or how little we really value whatever it may be and under Five we are persuading people to do this or that about it?

A. Yes, and persuading ourselves too. You remember that we began with a speaker or writer, a hearer or reader, as a man IN a situation. Well, he can either adapt himself to the situation or adapt it to him. When he persuades other people to do something isn't he trying to adjust the situation? When he persuades himself, isn't he probably adjusting himself to it?

R. Right enough. And what is Heading Six?

A. Fitting together all that is being done under Headings One to Five, adjusting them one to another so that they don't get in one another's way.

R. More adjusting.

A. Yes, but here it is a matter of adjusting one's own various efforts to deal with the situation TO ONE ANOTHER. You can see there can be a good many conflicts between

1. SELECTING what you are talking about (You might have chosen to talk about all sorts of other things.)
2. SHAPING what you are saying about it (them).
3. KEEPING it – as you talk of it – at the right distance from the viewers' minds,
4. GIVING it the right value (+ or –) that suits the case,
5. MAKING it so that the required action (or inaction) is promoted?

Heading Six covers the managerial work needed to let all these component efforts go forward smoothly together.

R. Where does WHAT FOR come in?

A. You have asked it, the key-stone, the topmost question. Of course, that is the Seventh Heading. "Of course", by the way, pretends to be and often is a typical bit of management (Heading Six) but, as we all know, of course, it can be other things: a little gesture of modesty, a recognition of the audience's claim to intelligence, an aggressive warning: "Differ from me if you dare!" or a self-comforting precaution against panic depending on the other words active (in the setting, in the then play of oppositions and collaborations) along with "of course".

R. But what's the answer to my topmost question?

A. Isn't there always something you are trying to do? Even if it is only trying to find out what it is. Whenever you say anything, haven't you always something you are saying it FOR?

R. Sometimes that something isn't very much.

A. Maybe. But don't you remember Confucius? "What to do?" said Confucius, "Indeed, I do not know WHAT TO DO with a man who doesn't ask himself that!"

R. Asking that isn't the same as answering it.

A. Are you really so sure it isn't? Asking it open-mindedly may be the same as finding the answer. This keystone question: WHAT IS IT FOR? isn't just one in a bunch along with the other questions. It is inside them all and holding them together. Look, we began with Heading One (1) What are we talking (thinking) OF or about? What selects that? We might be talking about all sorts of other things.

R. What selects (2) What we say about it or them? We might say all sorts of other things.

A. Go on.

R. What selects (3) How near up or far off what's said should be?

A. What it has to do, what it's for.

R. And it can be wrong.

A. It very often is. The whole thing can be wrong.

R. The valuing (4) and the influencing (5) . . .

A. And the managing (6) . . .

R. And the What for? The purposing (7), what is being done and what's being attempted . . .

A. Yes, it can be and often is all wrong.

R. And what can we do about that?

A. That's the point; an open-minded asking may be the answer.

R. Then it still is up to us?

A. Let us suppose so. Look! Why don't we make a picture of these seven?

R. A diagram of how they work together.

A. Let's put them round in a sort of circle with "What for?" – the Purposing – in the center.

R. And leave them all open to one another.
A. With one starting off.
R. And two following.
A. And three underneath it all.
R. And four, Valuing, beginning the return.
A. And five, Influencing, moving on up.
R. With Management at the top.

A. Because six has the job of supervising, of seeing that the other jobs which 1, 2, 3. 4 and 5 are trying to get on with . . .
R. Work out together.
A. Don't get in one another's way.
A. Don't get in one another's way. Did you ever read Plato's *Republic?*
R. Why do you ask?
A. Because not-getting-in-one-another's-way is Plato's account of Justice.

16. WHAT IS BELIEF?

My difficulty with beliefs is the simple-seeming one that I do not know what they are. But it is possible to play so many conjuring tricks with the word "know", that I had better explain, if I can, just in what sense I do not know what a belief is before discussing the consequences of this particular kind of ignorance or skepticism. Incidentally, the sorting and caging operations needed to keep the word "know" from betraying us in this discussion are so much the same as those needed for "believe" that they will help us later. Moreover, these possibilities of analyzing and separating different senses of such key-words as "know", "believe", "truth", "love", and "self" supply, for me, both the grounds of a very wide skepticism and the hope of turning the skepticism into a constructive movement. Skepticism is so often associated with despair that it is worth while to insist at the beginning of a skeptical article upon its hopeful possibilities.

I invite the reader to consider the remark, "I do not know what a belief is", in a spirit of neutral curiosity. I invite him to set aside the combative tradition in which such remarks are usually discussed, and to look before he leaps to any conclusion as to what it MUST mean – to look rather lingeringly for what it MAY mean, and to consider the very important differences between these possible meanings. In especial, I would like him not to suppose that I MUST know what beliefs are if I am to try to say anything about them. Imaginings of what they MAY be will do quite as well. I wish to suggest at the same time that there is hardly any remark of general interest which we can make that does not need to be examined in this way before we can use it – except for crude polemical purposes.

First, there is the sense in which to know what a belief is would be to know its ultimate nature. In this sense, evidently, we do not, any of us, know what ANYTHING is. So this is not the kind of ignorance which is troublesome with beliefs. In fact, this seems a singularly supportable kind of ignorance that troubles none but metaphysicians.

Next is the sense in which not to know what a belief is, is simply to lack some piece of available information. This kind of ignorance, again, is not, I think, the kind which is troublesome here. For this kind of ignorance is easily removed. If a Tibetan, for example, does not know what an oyster is, we can send for one and explain it to him and for all necessary purposes he will then know what an oyster is.

Close to this, is a sense which may concern us here. A man may not know what a belief is through the lack of a necessary kind of experience. The blind man who does not know what a color is has often been cited in this connection. But with the blind man we can easily decide that he is blind without using his ignorance of colors as evidence of his blindness, and moreover we know so much about vision and about colors that we can understand his ignorance and explain it once we know he is blind. (And the same applies to color-blindness.) So the parallel is weak. No one can suggest why it is that certain people, belonging to a cultural tradition which has had much to do with beliefs, people in all other respects normal, as far as we can tell, and enjoying the full range of normal experience, should show this ignorance. No one can explain why they should lack the necessary experience, or, here is the main point, just what experience it is which is necessary and lacking. It remains, however, possible that, if we knew much more psychology than we do, we might be able to give some explanation of this kind and so straighten out the parallel with blindness. Later on I shall sketch some conjectures of this sort. So for the moment we may leave this case of the man who does not know what a belief is because he has never had any.

More to our purpose is the man who does not know what a belief is because he does not know which, among the mental states which he does enjoy, are beliefs and which are not. This may be thought to be the same case as number two above. The man needs a little teaching, we may say. He should consult a dictionary or get a better-informed friend to instruct him. But if he replies that he has done this conscientiously and that the information which has been given him is insufficient to enable him to decide what a belief is, we shall, with our next step in trying to understand his trouble, come nearer to our main problem.

There seem two plausible interpretations (not incompatible) of this skeptical state. He may be in the same case as a man who does not know what an AFANC is. Consulting the dictionary he discovers that an AFANC is a fabulous Welsh beast – and, of course, he does thereby get to know, in a sense, what it is. But he is entitled to say that, for his purposes, he still does not know what it is. The description 'a fabulous Welsh beast' is too indefinite for him to be able to decide whether, for example, he has ever seen an AFANC, or whether there are or have ever been any AFANCS. The authorities, he notes, are divided as to whether an AFANC was a beaver, a crocodile, or a dragon. In brief, the dictionary definition is adequate for the purposes of Welsh folklore, but not for zoology. Similarly, the man who does not know what a belief is may say that such definitions as he can obtain may be adequate for logic or theology but not adequate for psychology or for his personal problem of deciding whether he himself has ever had any beliefs or not.

This brings us to the second interpretation of his difficulty. The definitions available may work fairly well as parts of the systems of abstract psychology to which they belong. But they may still be held to be inapplicable to our actual mental states – insufficient to allow us to identify one of our own or our neighbor's mental states as a belief, and reject another. Add to this the large number of psychological theories that are current – all using the word belief but in very different ways – the queer mixtures of these theories that most people have compounded, and the extreme VAGUENESS that is prevalent in these matters. We shall then have the outline of the excuse a man may offer who says he does not know what a belief is, and that, when other people say they believe something, he does not know sufficiently what they are doing to be able to agree with them OR dissent.

But, someone will say, it is easy to point to beliefs that all men share, and whatever the exact account of them may be, all men can easily identify these beliefs in themselves and so unambiguously settle what a belief is. I agree that there are an infinitude of certainties that all men share – all the certainties that belong to that routine of expectation on which our life depends. But I should argue that these certainties differ in a number of all-important respects from any beliefs that are ever subjects of interesting discussion. These certainties of expectation, for one thing, are being ceaselessly verified in our lives, verified in an exact sense which leaves no room for discussion about it. By an artificial extension of the technique of prediction and verification we get science, which, so long as it remains science, also gives no scope for dispute. Where it turns into speculation – not yet ripe for verification – there is, of course, plenty of room for discussion, just the same kinds of discussion with the same kind of ambiguities that play about the other beliefs that I am contrasting here with certainties. But these certainties, which we can identify in ourselves, are not discussable (as opposed to conjectures about them) just because they are so certain, so universal, and so unambiguous. For example, my certainty that if I dive off the summit of the Matterhorn I shall soon be in pieces. If this is called a "belief" it is, along with all similar "beliefs", quite uninteresting. I could make a list of such "beliefs" that would run to a million words and nobody would find a word to say against one of them. The only "beliefs" that would provoke discussion (let us give them a capital B to mark them off) are Beliefs that a majority of the world's inhabitants would, if they could understand them, dissent from. The only exceptions to this last might be, perhaps, a number of Beliefs of a character too vague to be susceptible of examination.

This odd state of affairs (odd when we consider the confidence with which Beliefs are discussed) is partly due to the provincialism of human traditions hitherto. As comparative studies extend (they are only embryonic at present) we shall recognize that Beliefs are products of tradition and circumstances to a degree which we cannot as yet reconcile ourselves to admitting. We may also become more ready to inquire persistently into the question, "What is Belief?" As we know, the best minds (in these matters) have given the best part of their best energies to the questions, "What should we Believe?" and "Why (on what grounds) should we Believe?" I cannot find that any comparable attention has been given to the question, "What is Belief?" ("What are we doing when we Believe?") It is at least arguable that this is logically the prior question; that it must be answered to some degree before the other questions can be profitably taken up.

Any definite answer to it will seem a long way off to a student of comparings, but a surmise as to the general form of the answer may be worth venturing. The basis for such a surmise lies in analogies with questions about other items in popular or traditional psychology; Love, for example, or Knowledge. Each of these much-argued items can be admitted (more easily than Belief) to be an OMNIUM GATHERUM including many very different kinds of things. If we consider the way in which we learn to use these words and to think with their aid about what we mean by them we shall see no reason why this should not be so, and fairly good reasons for thinking that it is so. And the same reasons hold for Belief. The psychologist, in fact, when he is sticking to his business, has no use for the term Belief except as marking a collection of materials for analysis. The analysis cannot yet be carried very far, only far enough to suggest that under this heading, Belief, both in popular and in sophisticated use, are to be found an extremely heterogeneous set of mental states, processes, and conditions. So diverse indeed that it may well be doubted if there is one among them which deserves the name – one, that is, which its possessor may name Belief with a decent likelihood that other people will really more than vaguely understand him.

Such an extreme surmisal may be unduly skeptical; but the arguments for the view that Believing covers a variety of very unlike mental events can be made, I think, as sound as any argument in psychology. Sound enough to put the burden of proof – that there is some one definite, recognizable mental act, specific in its nature and frequent in occurrence, which is to be called Believing – on to anyone who maintains it. A general consensus of opinion that there is such an act will clearly not do as a proof, for, as we have seen, the question is, "What are we being unanimous about?"

So much for my initial simple-seeming difficulty that prevents me from having any confidence that I know what a Belief is. It also prevents me from any steps which might encourage any Beliefs I might happen to have – that is to say, any attitudes and so forth that I treat (or that treat me) otherwise than as the hopes, fears, desires, devotions, renunciations, aspirations – that I do not call Beliefs. In what follows I shall mean by Beliefs just such feelings, attitudes, settings of the will, concentrations of attention, and so on, but given a kind of secondary sanction by being called Beliefs, being confused through the prime ambiguity of this word with truth-assertions, and being thus afforded marked privileges in the parliament of their fellow-sentiments. And, when I say that I am, so far as I know, without Beliefs, I do not mean that I am devoid of these sentiments, but that in me they are without this special secondary sanction. I fancy that this situation I find myself in is shared by a good number of my generation – those, at least, upon whom a speculative interest in language has taken effect. Even some who are nominally Believers in creeds are not, I imagine, in a very dissimilar position. The difference would be that whereas they are wishing to Believe, I am not. This difference may be worth exploring.

It has often been alleged that without some Beliefs life would be intolerable or worthless – that Beliefs of one kind or another are an unescapable need of human nature.

If the Sun and Moon should Doubt
They'd immediately go out!

I would reply that certainties (of the kind instanced above) are, of course, necessary. But these certainties are of the same kind in mice and men, only more numerous and elaborate for man as his life becomes more artificial in its conditions. But the necessity of Beliefs either for mouse or man is another matter. I should be inclined to admit that for some types of mind (which are the result of a special training and tradition) life may be more difficult, and especially more difficult to live finely, without Beliefs. But against the view that this need goes deeper than can be explained by an acquired mental habit I would point to the Chinese, among whom what are recognized as their finest types of humanity seem to have for centuries refrained from Believing more studiously than their fellows. "Ah! But they were avoiding bad Beliefs!" someone will say. I agree, but I want for the moment only to damage the opinion that Beliefs OF SOME KIND NO MATTER WHAT are a necessity for the mind.

"What an inexplicable frame of mind is belief!" said Darwin. It is perhaps rather less inexplicable now than in his day: sixty years of psychology have done a little toward clearing up the tangle. For it is in the image of a tangle – the threads of our different interests, needs, sentiments, rubbing against, hitching upon, twining round one another – that we can most easily picture the problem. We will assume, here, that metaphors are not psychology. But in terms of this metaphor, a Belief may be imagined as a point where a thread of interest (an imagining, a feeling, a desiring) has caught improperly upon other threads, so that in the incessant running of the threads it is given checks and pulls which do not properly belong to it, and would not occur to it if the mind's economy were in perfect order. For example: a feeling, let us say, that a story creates in us would be altered in various ways if the story were actually true. But our proper interest in whether the story is true or not may and usually does belong to quite another system from the interests that give the story its feeling. If these interests catch in one another, we can be easily convinced that the story gets its value from its truth, or conversely that it must be true because we feel as we do about it. Add to this our amazing virtuosity in conjuring with the various senses of truth, and we have the typical conditions for a set of Beliefs about the story.

This is an over-simplified example, of course. The 'catching' of independent interests in one another evidently cannot be demonstrated. It is merely a plausible sort of hypothesis to account for observations we all constantly make about each other's Beliefs. But the main point I want to make with its aid is that the value of the story may be and often is quite free from any implications with its truth standing. It may get a little adventitious force from being taken as true, but this extra force may very well not be an improvement in its value; in any case taking it for true exposes it to risks. As Matthew Arnold said, "we have attached our emotion to the fact and now the fact is failing it". If the fact fails it the emotion is, quite unfairly of course, apt to be damaged.

To take a different kind of example. A man setting forth a plan – say the Five-Year Plan – is very likely to get his admiration for the plan implicated in his opinion as to whether it will be realized in fact. He comes to Believe in the Plan. I should argue, and those who do not Believe in the Plan will probably agree with me, that success is more likely if his inspiration from the plan and his judgment of practical possibilities do not get intertwined, and he does not Believe that it MUST come true.

These instances are too easily seen through by the non-Believer. They have to be to serve my purposes here. In cases of more interesting beliefs the intricacies of the tangle are likely to be beyond all tracing. I want only to suggest that the same kind of 'catching' or snarling of lines of interest which would work just as well or better in freedom from one another may be suspected in all Beliefs. And the more adequately we can imagine the natural complexities of the mind and therefore the opportunities for snarling, the stronger our suspicion will grow. Psychoanalysis has helped us immensely here.

I suggest, then, that there may be reasonable ground for not wishing to Believe anything. Those who say, "I am convinced", and think this should recommend their views may be a little naïve. And in making this suggestion I am not overlooking the immense value of Beliefs to certain types of minds. The ages of faith may have supplied invaluable ingredients to human nature. I think it very likely that we should be today infinitely the poorer without them. I wish only to discourage the assumption that the type of mind which needs Belief is necessarily the finer. Often it seems to be, and if this were usually so, at present, there would be nothing to surprise us. For our tradition encourages such minds and serves them with all its treasures.

But I began by remarking upon the hopeful possibilities of skepticism. The kind of questioning which, for me, dissolves the traditional landmark, Belief, into a cluster of undeveloped problems can be applied to almost all our mental landmarks. Truth, Knowledge, Beauty, the Will, the Good, the Self – with all their satellite terms – fade out. Under a persistent analysis they appear as merely fictions – devised to suit changing needs and owing their seeming solidity to their systematic interlocking ambiguity. A moment comes when any persistent inquirer will be forced to echo Trumbull Stickney:

> Sir, say no more;
> Within me 'tis as if
> The green and climbing eyesight of a cat
> Crawls near my mind's poor birds.

But, looking back, the picture that human history presents is not one which needs no mending. Our mind's poor birds have not served us so well that we must fear to disturb them. And in any case they are being disturbed whether we like it or not. The hope of skepticism is that it may uncover behind these fictions more of the actual forces by which we live. Then, with a more conscious control, we may better order our lives.

17. THE EVER-NEW DISCOVERY

I have borrowed my title from an old XVII Century book – Charles Hoole's *New Discovery of the Old Art of Teaching School*. I am hoping to lead up to the point that the chief new discovery of old ways which every teacher has to make for himself in the little world of his classroom is how to reconcile authority and freedom (thus reconciliation through Reason) – the very problem that is tearing the great world up by the roots just now. In brief it is the very old and always new discovery that our profession has the world's one hope in its care.

Let me start with my favorite quotation from Hoole:

It is not only possible, but necessary to make children understand their tasks, from their first entrance into learning; seeing that they must everyone bear his own burden, and not rely upon their fellows altogether.

And let me oppose to that one of the voices of authority, Ruskin. This is from *Munera Pulveris*:

The essential thing for all creatures is to be made to do right; how they are made to do it – by pleasant promises, or hard necessities, pathetic oratory or the whip – is comparatively immaterial.

He adds a footnote here:

Permit me to enforce and reinforce this statement with all earnestness. It is the sum of what most needs to be understood, in the matter of education.

Well, there we are: "the sum of what most needs to be understood in the matter of education".

Now what would be some of our reflections on that? May I formulate three of them?

1. The first concerns the phrase "made to do right". We'd agree, I take it, that the essential thing is FOR THEM TO DO RIGHT. We might differ about what the right things are. But the word "made" is the

point we are likely to boggle at – the compulsive implications brought out by Ruskin's mention of the whip.

2. Our second reflection would raise the question: can human beings be made to do right – in any but a very external sense of "right" – by any of Ruskin's agencies – pleasant promises, hard necessities, pathetic oratory or the whip? If we are to take these words "to do right" as seriously as we must if we are to agree that "the essential thing for all creatures is to do right" must we not add to this list of alleged educational agencies something which Ruskin doesn't mention?

3. Our third reflection would be on what this very different thing is. In fairness to Ruskin I should add something from his very next sentence which shows that Ruskin, of course, – who that knows his Ruskin could doubt it? – really remembers more about human nature than the sentences I have quoted would suggest. He says, "To be deceived is perhaps as incompatible with human dignity as to be whipped." What is this thing in human nature, on which human dignity depends, that he is alluding to here? It is UNDERSTANDING, is it not, the distinctive power of the mind – what Aristotle called man's FUNCTION? Remembering that, we should want to rewrite Ruskin's footnote and say that the sum of what most needs to be understood in education is that nothing, by whatever means it is induced into a mind, which is not UNDERSTOOD really promotes its growth as a REASONABLE, that is as a HUMAN, being.

You may have qualms about this – but we are not saying that everything is to be FULLY UNDERSTOOD (what is ever fully understood?) but only understood in due measure so that it takes its place in a growing fabric of understanding.

To quote another new discovery of the old art, this time from Locke:

So much as we ourselves consider and comprehend of truth and reason, so much we possess of real and true knowledge. The floating of other men's opinions in our brains, makes us not a jot the more knowing, though they happen to be true. What in them was science is in us but opiniatréty.

What we have to ask ourselves incessantly is how much in our teaching, and in the learning our charges get from us, is science (in Locke's sense of real knowledge), how much opiniatréty? This is a daunting question, which, like such things, may most trouble those who least deserve to be troubled by it.

Turn back now to Locke's "consider and comprehend" and Hoole's "understand their tasks". Both imply that the tasks, the truths and reasons, must be in such an order that they CAN be understood; and that we can SEE WHY we have to do them. That SEEING WHY – with all its struggles and errors, false steps and recoveries, its clouding and clearing – is understanding, and the urge to its growth is the motive through which the human being becomes more human.

It is only in so far as we SEE WHY that we are truly free. If we don't see why, WE don't act, we are only acted upon. As Locke said, "A man could not be free if his will were determined by anything but his own desire, GUIDED BY HIS OWN JUDGMENT" (II, xxi, 71). "Liberty is a power to act or not to act according as the MIND directs." The emphasis has to be on MIND, mind you; it's not as the wishes lead but as the mind directs. It's not following our own desires but being GUIDED BY OUR OWN JUDGMENT that makes us free. So without a developed power of judgment, no one can be free. Before a certain point of development no child can be free. And as creatures endowed with original sin we, none of us, are entirely free. It is the degree of our freedom which matters.

To return, after this note on freedom, to Hoole's point that the children are to understand their tasks from their first entrance into learning. Understanding the tasks includes entering upon them freely, in this sense, seeing why they should do them. To quote a yet earlier new discoverer of the old art of teaching school, here is Plato on this point (Republic, 536).

Socrates: All these arts, geometry and the like, which are to make them ready to see why more fully, are to be given them while still young but not forced upon them.

Glaucon: Why not?

Socrates: Because it is not wise to make a free mind work like a slave. Forced bodily work does no damage to a body, but nothing learned through force from without takes root rightly in the mind. So, my friend, don't keep the young at their work by force but by play, and then you will see better what their natural powers are.

Glaucon: There is reason in that.

When Socrates says "takes root rightly in the mind" he doesn't mean 'becomes fixed'; he means 'becomes able to live and grow'.

So, ideally, children are to SEE WHY they have their tasks, or at least to see why they cannot yet see why.

But SEE WHY, like UNDERSTAND, is a tricky expression and my argument will fail unless I clarify the expression. You will see why I have to in a minute. To see why is to be aware of and take note of a cause. And as Plato and Aristotle pointed out – thereby founding this part of the old art – there are different sorts of causes. It is final causes, or reasons, which matter here.

For example, you may be wondering why you are reading me now. It would not be a good answer to say, "it's because you opened this book at this page", or, to be more minute, "because rays from little black marks on a sheet of paper are making certain patterns on your retinas, which lead to certain patterns in your coordination centres which lead to certain motor responses, etc., etc." Those wouldn't be good answers, or rather they are good enough in their way, but it's the wrong way.

Those are efficient causes of your reading, but it is final causes we see when we really SEE WHY. The final cause is understanding.

Another example: in such a matter the bigger it is the better. Just now, I think the United Nations SEE WHY (in this most important sense) they have to fight. But the Germans, I see, cannot – because there is no final cause, in this deep sense, for their fighting. The United Nations, that is, are fighting for the realization of man, to make it possible for man to become MORE HUMAN rather than less human. So they are free men, however much they have to submit to discipline and do what they don't want to, in fact loathe and dread and abhor.

It is alarming how many people identify freedom with doing what they like. I was looking over a lot of Seventh and Ninth Grade attempts to say what being free is the other day and only one child in one hundred got beyond "doing what one wants to". Very dangerously crude views are current, almost dominant, on this. If we take the philosophy of democracy seriously and are to defend it in the schools we certainly ought to recognize this as a key point. To clarify general ideas on freedom is one of the most urgent specific tasks of education, and if I go on to discuss what such clarification involves I won't be stepping out of my way a bit. "It is not only possible but necessary for TEACHERS to understand their tasks, from their very entrance into teaching." And this is the task of the hour for us.

No one can understand what education tries to do without understanding what freedom is and what authority is, or without seeing why and how you can have neither without the other.

How are we to teach this? How are we to see why it is so ourselves and help others to see why in their turn?

It is little use reciting the great formulas: F. H. Bradley's "moral obedience is free obedience to a law recognized as right" or Coleridge's "He alone is FREE and entitled to the name of gentleman who knows himself and walks in the light of his own consciousness" or Tennyson's "Self-knowledge, self-reverence, self-control" or the Prayer Book's "Whose service is perfect freedom". These are fine reminders, but we have to have visited and lived in that intellectual country before they mean as much as they should. And, of course, being able to talk well about freedom is not the main thing. It is being able to live freely – a harder matter – but still to be able to talk rightly, in so far as it helps us to think more clearly, is a part here of the aim of education.

We have all heard lately plenty of praise of freedom and talk about it generally. That is part of the difficulty. It is in some danger of being buried in words. So it is very modestly and with a full awareness that what I say may be but opiniatréty, not science, that I make these suggestions. It seems to me that much depends upon THE ORDER in which the groups of ideas that are required in a doctrine of freedom are reflected upon and discussed. We'll agree, I think, that a doctrine of freedom requires adequate ideas about

1. Human nature: what man is and might be.
2. Right; or the good for man, what he should be.
3. Causes, in more than the two senses I was illustrating a few minutes ago.

It is worse than useless, I would say, DISCUSSING freedom and authority, democratic principles and the rest of it, if the persons in the discussion have quite different sorts of conceptions under all these headings. That sort of thing leads to nothing but confusion worse confounded. Whenever I've had to listen to it – as we've all had to lately – I've been forced to believe that I wasn't the only one who "found no end in weary mazes led". The indispensable prior examination and understanding of the notions bandied about in the discussion had not been undertaken.

Here let me mention a parallel that haunts me. I've been much concerned in recent years with teaching English as a foreign language – to Chinese or South Americans say – and therefore with the problems of Broken English. Like a good many other things, once a person's English has been well broken, it is a hard job putting it together again for him. Especially if the fractures are complex and of long standing. Well, it is possible, if English words and constructions are taught IN

THE RIGHT ORDER – first things coming first and opportunities for confusion carefully eliminated and postponed – it is possible, I say, to
prevent his English from ever being broken. There is an optimum order
in the steps of studying English which prevents untold unnecessary
muddling.

Similarly, I believe, though it's still harder to find, there is an optimum order in the steps by which the doctrine of freedom may be
taught. I believe we are all of us suffering from a higher kind of Broken
English – or rather Broken Thought – in our arguments about Democracy, Freedom, and the rest of it. And that this could be avoided if
we studied the words and ideas that must enter into these discussions
in the proper order.

Or take another parallel. We all agree that we shouldn't teach the
calculus before we teach addition, don't we? Well, I think we jump
into discussions of Democracy and so on before studying as they must
be studied the much simpler ideas – clearer because separated – which
must enter into the discussion. The result is that we get into a dis-
heartening tangle of mutual misunderstanding and perhaps even feel
there is something fishy about the whole thing. At best we may say
that the problem needs more analysis. And to say that is itself a sort of
defeatism since few hope to get the reasonable hours needed to give it
that analysis. We lose our courage and the way is open for every sort
of faithlessness.

All this I suggest is unnecessary. The tangle comes because we have
not studied the threads before we start tying and then trying to unravel
the knots. The chief threads I suggest may be studied under these three
questions: What is human nature; What should man be; What different
sorts of causes are there. I have said a word or two about causes. Let
me finish with a few words on the other two questions, trying to suggest with them how simply these questions might be handled. This
then is a sample of exposition for your criticism. It is compressed, of
course. I am doing in five minutes what should have leisurely and
repeated sessions in class.

First, as to human nature; or what makes man man?

I cited earlier Aristotle's word FUNCTION for this: man's function
is intelligence, understanding, the power to see why. Of course FUNC-
TION is a poor word for our purposes here. It is better to talk about his
TASK, or WORK as a man; WHAT HE DOES, HIS BEING, HIS END, WHAT HE
IS FOR, or HIS BUSINESS.

It is well to use all these alternative phrases; one may strike where another fails. That which they all may be made to mean is the thing we are after. Let us call it man's proper work as man. And in using such a phrase as WHAT MAN IS FOR, I suggest we should not bring in HERE the question 'Was he made?' and the analogy with man-made things. That is a point for another discussion.

Whether or not he was made or just grew (and whether or not BEING MADE and JUST GROWING are here in any way different, if we consider them deeply enough), man as man has his own proper work, business, being or nature, which nothing else has. It is this which makes him man; and this is reason, the mind, intelligence, understanding, the power to see why.

So much, at this stage, on human nature. Now for what man should or ought to be, and the words GOOD and RIGHT. And here we can go openly to the Aristotle I have been glossing upon: to the *Nichomachean Ethics* (1, 7, 9).

To say that the highest good, or the best thing, is being happy is only giving it a name. That does not make clear what this best thing is. Possibly we may get at *that* by seeing what work man has to do, *as* a man. For a good flute player or painter or workman of any sort is one who does his work well. In the same way, it may be that a good man is one who does *his* work well, if man, as such, has any work to do.

And certainly he has. The wood-worker and shoe-maker, as such, have work which only they do, or which they do best; so is it possible that man is without any work which is naturally his to do? Again, the eye, the hand, the foot and all other parts of the body have their special work to do, so it is probably safe to say that man, as man, has some work of his own, more than all this, to do.

What then may this be? It is not the simple act of living, for even plants do this, and we are looking for something which only man does, or which man does best. After this comes the sort of living which has sense and feeling, but the horse, the cow and all other animals have this. The only other sort of living is that which is guided by reason. Living may be guided by reason in two ways: by keeping rules or by seeing why the rules are so and taking thought. This sort of living, again, may be looked on in two ways: as acting, or as being; as doing well or as being good. We take it here as *acting*, because it is doing a certain sort of work. Man's work, then, is what his mind does guided by reason . . .

So we may say that man's work is a way of living, a way of acting not only of being. It is done by the mind in harmony with reason. A good man is one who does these things rightly and well – in view of what sort of work it is. Putting these thoughts together, we get this statement of what is good for man or being happy. It will be: using all the powers of the mind well, in the way that is best and most complete . . .

Well, that is how Aristotle sets up his starting point. I don't see why we shouldn't take our starting point there and give it to our pupils too, far down in the grades, if only we are careful enough and leisurely enough with it. Why shouldn't they have that conception of happiness early – in place of other conceptions of happiness they are more likely to have. It is more interesting than those other conceptions even to very undeveloped minds – more interesting because it gives them a better chance of understanding their tasks, both the specific tasks of the schoolroom and the general task of man, which is to become fully human.

One last word about authority. With such a starting point, I conceive, no conflict, no broken thoughts about the opposition of freedom and authority need arise. That the recognition of authority is any bar to freedom is no part of any sane democratic principles. Nor is any claim that one man's opinions are as good as another's. The freedom we have to seek is the freedom to be guided by reason in following authority – and the ultimate source of authority is intelligence – man's proper task, embodied it may be in "the best that has been known and thought in the world".

Freedom and authority, as I said at the start, are reconciled in every well-run classroom. To reconcile them is the teacher's proper task as teacher. And thereby he has an immense lesson to offer the warring world.

Mr. T. S. Eliot in his last great poem but one, *East Coker*, has the lines:

> The whole earth is our hospital
> Endowed by the ruined millionaire

(May that millionaire be Adam, who endowed us with original sin.)

Man will never win happiness, till he rediscovers and takes to heart another portion of the old art – the truth, fellow children, that THE WHOLE EARTH IS OUR SCHOOL.

INDEX

abridgement, 179
Adam, 249
addressee, Chapter 1 passim, 19, 20, 33
addresser, Chapter 1 passim
advertisement, 19, 22
alliteration, 69
ambiguity, 10, 12, 237, 241
Amos, 219
anti-Coleridgeans, 130, 131
Aristotle, 49, 74, 82, 83, 89, 108, 179,
    193, 197, 206, 207, 211, 243, 245, 247,
    248, 249
Arnold, Matthew, 164, 240
art of listening, 153
art of reading poetry, 153
asceticism, 107
asking (see also question) 226
association, 26
Attar, 55
Augustine, 82
authority, Chapter 17 passim

Bacon, Francis, 100, 187
Baker, Sheridan, 32, 150, 153
Bain, Alexander, 171
ballads, 65, 66, 116
Bartram, William, 137, 138
Barzun, Jacques, 32, 150, 153
Basic English (Everyman's English), 4,
    7, 8, 9, 157, 169, 170, 171, 173, 175
    advantages of, 169, 170
    misdescription of, 169, 170
beauty, 241
behaviourism, 24
belief, 73-74, Chapter 16 passim
Bentham, Jeremy, 130
Bible, 156, 163, 164, 182, 185, 187
    misuse of, 163
binary correspondence, 40
binary opposition, 39-40

biography, in poetry
    relevance of, 113, 114, 115, 132, 144
Blake, William, 102, 122, 163, 166, 167,
    186, 219
Boethius, 130, 189
Bohr, Niels, 216
bookless homes, 148
books, loss of status of, 148
border ballads, 60
Boston, Massachusetts, I. A. Richards
    at, 212
Bradbrook, M. C., 103, 106
Bradley, F. H., 246
broken English, 247
broken thought, 246, 247
Brower, Reuben, 1, 2, 17, 175, 193
Bruner, Jerome, 29
Bunyan, John, 82, 187
Burnet, John, 212
Butler, Samuel, 178

Cambridge, I. A. Richards at, 165, 167,
    168, 169, 178
Cambridge, Massachusetts, I. A.
    Richards at, 169
Campion, Thomas, 106
Carey, Henry, 63
cassette, 149
cause, 246, 247
    efficient, 245
    final, 245
celebrity, cult of, 152
centrifugal lines, 40, 41, 47
centripetal lines, 40, 41
certainty, 236, 237
Chapman, George, 167
Child, F. J., 59
Chinese, 167-169, 172-173, 175, 180,
    181, 205, 239
    index, Plato on, 181

Churchill, Winston, 169
cinema, 148, 162
classroom, 133, 206
Coburn, Kathleen, 115, 128, 133, 135, 136, 137, 138, 141
Cocteau, Jean, 171
code, Chapter 1 passim, 38
cognitive ability, growth of, 33
Coleridge, Derwent, 138
Coleridge, S. T., 45, 69, 80, Chapter 9 passim, Chapter 10 passim, 152-160, 163, 185, 186, 209, 219, 220, 221, 246
Coleridgeans, 130-131
colloquial, 187
combination, 6
communication, Chapter 1 passim, Chapter 2 passim, Chapter 15 passim
comparing, 2, 6, 7, 24, 25, 35, 46, 154, 237
  meanings, 38
  principles of, 6, 7
complementary principle, 216, 217
composition, 6, 7
  process of, 157
conative function, Chapter 1 passim
Conference on Style, Bloomington Indiana (1958), 1
Confucius, 182, 232
conscious comparing, 35 ff
contact, Chapter 1 passim
context, Chapter 1 passim
  of situation, 11
contiguity, 26, 30
control, 2, 4, 5, 24, 27, 220, 241
  self-, 246
Coomaraswamy, Ananda, 90
creative artist, 133
creative process, 77
creativity, 74, 133, 142
creeds, believers in, 239, 240
crime rate, 163
criticism, 45, 220
Croce, Benedetto, 80
cultivation of insight, 34
culture, 147, 149

Dante, 78, 100
Darwin, Charles, 239
Davies, Sir John, 108, 154, 155, 156
decoding, 13
deep structure, 47

definition, 8, 169, 235, 236
De la Mare, Walter, 154
democracy, 245, 247
democratic principles, 246 ff
depiction, Chapter 2 passim
depth psychology, 220
Derby, Earl of, 165
descriptive linguistics, 39
design, sequence of, 33
dialectic art, 71
dictionary, 171
didactic poetry, 104
discussion, 236, 237
Donne, John, 48, 49, 76-84, Chapter 7 passim, 95, 97, 109, 124, 158, 164
Drury, Elizabeth, 77, 78, 83
Dryden, John, 77 ff
dynamical object, 11

East-west, distorted communications, 176
Ebreo, 91
education, Chapter 2 passim, 45, 74, Chapter 11 passim, Chapter 12 passim, Chapter 13 passim, 218, 221, 242, 246, 249
  conative and affective aspects, 18
  demand that learning be made easy, 190
  ideas, order of in, 246, 247
  learning to explore meanings, 24
  pedagogic prepossessions, 45
  task of, 21
efficient cause, 245
elimination of distraction, 34
Eliot, T. S., 58, 59, 82, 249
Emerson, Ralph Waldo, 50, 175, 181
emotion, 240, 245
emotive function, Chapter 1 passim
Empson, William, 122, 153
enactions, 29, 31, 32
encoding, 13
energy, 146
English, see education
Everyman's English, see Basic English
evil, 27
examinations, 144
exegesis, 36
exploratory activity, 31
extension, 10

facts, 73
factors in language, Chapter 1 passim

Fairfax, Mary, 104, 111
faith, 74, 240
figures of speech, 183
film, 30, 207
final cause, 245
Fitzgerald, Edward, 55
Fourth Gospel, 146
freedom, Chapter 17 passim
Fricker, Edith, 142
Frost, Robert, 220
function of language, Chapter 1 passim

Gardner, Helen, 90, 92, 94
general semantics, 36, 37
Genesis, 102
Germans, 245
Ghana, I. A. Richards in, 181
Gibson, C. M., 31, 157
Gilbert, W. S., 101, 102
Gloucester, Bishop of, 149, 150
Godwin, William, 138, 140, 175
Goldsmith, Oliver, 63
good, 27, 241
Graham, E. C., 169
grammar, as a school of subject, 45
Gray, Lady Jane, 156
Greek culture, 146, 147, Chapter 13
   passim
   tragedy, 147
Grierson, Herbert, 88, 92
Griggs, Earl Leslie, 133, 137, 139

Halle, M., 6, 26
happiness, 108, 248, 249
Hardy, Thomas, 172
Hartshorne, Charles, 28
Harvard, I. A. Richards at, 168, 169,
   190, 206
Hebraic culture, 161, 163, 164
Hellenic, Hellenocentric culture, see
   Greek culture,
Hitler, Adolf, 115, 186
Hollander, John, 2, 175
Homer, 60, 87, 115, 160, 162, Chapter
   13 passim, 221
Homeric-Platonic opposition, 162
Hong Kong, I. A. Richards at, 180
Hood, Thomas, 66
Hoole, Charles, 242, 243, 244
Hopkins, Gerard Manley, 110
Hosea, 219
humanity, Chapter 17 passim
humanities, 187

human nature, 246, 247
human possibilities, enlargement of,
   216
Hutchins, Robert, 171
Hutchinson, Sara, 116, 138, 142
hyperbole, 104

iconic use of signs, 27, 29
Iliad, see Homer
imagery, 29, 45
imagination, 154, 158
immediate object, 11
import, 112, 113
incompatibility, 217
individual, 155
influencing, 230, 233
initiative, 160
insight, 34
inspiration, 151
instruction, 150
instrument, 215, 221
intelligence, 247-249
interest, 229
interinanimation of words, 58, 61,
   Chapter 6 passim, 90, 164
interlingual transposition, see
   translation
interplay of words, 217
interpretation, 48, 83, 104, 114, 163
   in teaching, 8, 10, 11, 23
intersemiotic transposition, see
   translation
intonation, 225, 226
intralingual translation, see translation
Isaiah, 219

Jaeger, Werner, 146, 147, 162, 178, 182
Jakobson, Roman, Chapter 1 passim,
   Chapter 2 passim, Chapter 3 passim,
   66
Jeffress, Lloyd, 170
Job, 115, 163, 164
Jones, Lawrence, 39
Johnson, Samuel, 78, 80, 107, 132, 222
Jonson, Ben, 78
Jowett, Benjamin, 175, 184
judgment, 244

Kawamoto, Shigeo, 43
Keats, John, 103, 109, 167
Kittredge, G. L., 59
Kings, First Book of, 60
knowledge, 10, 33, 35, 132, 134, 135,

158, 173, 185, Chapter 16 passim
'about' v. 'know how', 44
increase in, 132
self-, 246
Kökeritz, Helge, 42
Korzybsky, Alfred, 36, 37

Lamb, Charles, 128, 136, 139
language, Chapter 1 passim, 35, 72, 76,
　113, 147, 160, 183
　acquisition, of, 33, 219
　ordinary use of, 23
　uses of, 18, 19, 22
Lashley, K. S., 170
learning, 29, 33, 150, 160, 243, 246, 247
　theory, 167
legislator, 146
Lerner, Daniel, 47
lexicology, 36
liberty, 244
linguistic analysis, 48
linguistic knowledge, 35
linguistics, 26, 35, Chapter 3 passim,
　71, 72, 75, 167, 169, 183, 216, 219,
　220
linguisticians, 17
literature, passim
　introducing students to, 178, 179
　transforming power of, 167
　value of, 129
literary research, 132, 133
literary semantics, 1, 5
literary studies, 132, 133
Lloyd Thomas, M. G., 103, 106
Locke, John, 243, 244
logic, 6, 131, 134, 216, 217, 219, 236
　limitations of, 216
Longfellow, H. W., 115, 118
Lowell, Robert, 151
Lowes, J. L., 59, 137

McLuhan, Marshall, 162
Malinowski, Bronislaw, 11
man, 247
　future of, 172
　function of, 247-249
managing, 231, 233
Marvell, Andrew, Chapter 8 passim,
　164
mathematics, 6, 23, 37, 73, 219, 220
matter, 82
Maurice, F. D., 129
Mau Tse Tung, 104, 180, 181

meaning, Chapter 1 passim, Chapter 2
　passim, 101, 153, 156, 167, 168, 184,
　215, 217, 248
　complexity, 171, 172, 184
　musical, 26
　referential and metalingual, 38
measure, 228
media, 149, 150, 162, 164, 184
Mencius, 182
message, Chapter 1 passim, Chapter 2
　passim
metalanguage, 38
metalingual function, 3, 4
metaphor, 36, 43, 45, 71, 74, 75, 81,
　82, 83, 160, 166, 193, 239
metaphysics, 23, 89, 234, 235
metaphysical poetry, 81, 83
methodology, 216, 219
metre, 220
metrical scheme, 69
microlinguistics, 13
Mill, John Stuart, 75, 130
Milton, John, 47, 81, 98, 99, 124, 164,
　192
mind, 108, 183, 244, 248
misunderstanding, 247
moral obedience, 246
Moscow, I. A. Richards at, 165
mother tongue, learning, 160
mountaineering, 149, 166
Muir, Edwin, 59
musical criticism, 153
musical meaning, see meaning
musicians, 146

New Testament, 185
Nkrumah, Kwame, 181
noise, 105
nominalists, 24
non-believer, 240

object language, 38
Odyssey, see Homer
Ogden, C. K., 11, 28, 169, 170
Old Testament, 161, 163
opiniatr\u00e9ty, 243, 246
Oppenheimer, 134
opportunity, 164
orators, 146
original sin, 244
Osgood, Charles, 13

paideia, Chapter 11 passim, 162

painter, 146
pantisocracy, 142
parallelism, 43
paraphrase, 2 ff, 47
  controlled, 157, 158
parapsychology, 25
paronomasia, 66
Partridge, Eric, 150, 161
Peacock, Thomas, 221
Peking, I. A. Richards at, 167, 168,
  172, 173, 180, 189, 205
pedagogy, 216, 218, 219
peripeteia, 197, 211
persuading, 231
phatic function, 3, 4, 9, 16
Philips, Ambrose, 60, 62, 63
philology, 185
philosophy, 72, 83, 134, 146, 147
phonetic analysis, 47
physics, 6, 82, 216
physiology, 183
pictorial representation, 29
picturing, 27, 31, 32
Pierce, C. S., 1, 2, 8, 9, 11, Chapter 2
  passim
piety, 214
Pindar, 130, 186
pity, 197
plastic artist, 147
Plato, 44, 49, 71, 72, 74, 78, 80, 83, 89,
  91, 92, 93, 97, 103, 105, 109, 110,
  116, 122, 141, 151, 152, 155, 156, 158,
  160, 162, 164, Chapter 13 passim,
  221, 227, 228, 244, 245
  on Chinese index, 180-182
Platonism, see Plato
playwright, 19
plot, 193
Plotinus, 88, 107, 108, 109, 185
poem,
  what is a –, 85 ff
  as a representative of the language,
  217
poet, 146
  as a maker, 74
poetic,
  function, 2, 3, 4, 9, 15, 16, 69
  composition, 63
  language, 22, 72
  problem, 74, 75
poetics, Chapter 3 passim, 72, 112
poetry, passim
  teaching of, 45

philosophy of, 72
  didactic, 104
  study of, 113
  biography in, 114, 132-135, 144, 145
  in childhood, 146-148
  transforming power of, 146-148, 221
  reading of, 152, 153
  of wit, 80
  structure of, 79
  metaphysical, 81, 82, see also under
    Donne and Marvell
  as an instrument, Chapter 14 passim
  new role of, 215
  popular, 220
  response to, 46, 47, 48
political
  discourse, 22
  speaking, 230
politics, 149
Poole, Thomas, 142, 143
Pope, Alexander, 63, 120, 121, 134
pornography, 21
positivists, 24
Prayer Book, 246
praxis, 193
prediction, 236
print, 69
prose, 216
psychoanalysis, 220, 240
psychology, 26, 71, 72, 75, 144, 167,
  237-239
  depth, 220
Ptolematic astronomy, 91
public opinion, 73
pun, 53, 66
purgation, 198
purposing, 232
pursuit of gain, 22
Puttenham, Richard, 42

Quakers, 128
question, 226, 227
  rhetorical, 227

radio, 149, 150, 162, 207
Ramsey, Frank, 11
reader, 42, 167, 182, 222
reading, 150, 219
  aloud, 148, 153
  beginning, 33, 34
  initial learning of, 150, 160
  poetry, 152
reason, 54, 56, 130, 131, 242, 248

recognition, 197, 211
referent, 2, 3, 9, 11
referential function, Chapter 1 passim
Republic, see Plato
research, literary, 132, Chapter 14
  passim
response to poetry, see under poetry
reverence, self-, 246
reversal, see peripeteia
rewording, see intralingual translation
rhapsodes, 151
rhetoric, 36
rhetorical questions, see questions
rhyme, 41, 217
  scheme, 69
Richards, I. A.,
  at Boston Massachusetts, 212
  at Cambridge, 165, 167, 168, 169,
    178
  in Ghana, 181
  in Hong Kong, 180
  at Harvard, 168, 169, 190, 206
  T.V. Professor at Harvard, 206
  at Moscow, 165
  in Russia, 165, 167, 169, 176, 178
  at Peking, 167, 168, 172, 173, 180,
    189, 205
  at Vancouver, 180
  at Vladivostok, 165
works (includes Richard's main works
  in chronological order, whether
  mentioned in the text or not)
  Foundations of Æsthetics (with C.
    K. Ogden and James Wood) (1921)
  The Meaning of Meaning (with C.
    K. Ogden) (1923), 11, 28, 169
  Principles of Literary Criticism
    (1924)
  Science and Poetry (1925), 168
  Practical Criticism (1929)
  Mencius on the Mind (1931), 168
  Coleridge on Imagination (1934)
  Interpretation in Teaching (1938), 8,
    11, 23
  How to Read a Page (1942), 23
  The Republic of Plato (1942)
  Basic English and its Uses (1943)
  Speculative Instruments (1955), 5,
    150
  Goodbye Earth and Other Poems
    (1959)
  The Screens and Other Poems (1959),
    14

Tomorrow Morning, Faustus! (1962)
Why So, Socrates? (1963), 151, 175,
    192, 207-214, 228
*So Much Nearer: Essays towards a
    World English* (1968), 14, 150
*Design for Escape: World Education
    through Modern Media* (1968),
    150, 168
Poetries and Sciences (1970), 5
English through Pictures (with C. M.
    Gibson) (1972), 31
right, Chapter 17 passim
Rooke, Barbara, 128, 129, 130
Roosevelt, Franklin D., 169
Ruskin, John, 82, 242, 243

Sandburg, Carl, 220
Saporta, Sol, 11
saying, 222
scepticism, 234, 236, 240, 241
science, 73, 75, 132, 134, 168, 236, 243,
    246
Scott, Sir Walter, Chapter 5 passim
screens, 112, 113, 150, 153, 178
sculptor, 146
Sebeok, Thomas, 1, 11
second language learning, 33, 34, 160
Second World War, 169, 177
Sedgwick, Ellery, 59
seeing why, 244, 245
selection, 6, 179, 231
self, 241
Seltzer, Dan, 212
semantics, 22, 27, 36
semantic structure, 46
semiotics, 21, 22, 27, 29, 92
sensory imagery, 45
sentence, 28-32, 222 ff
Shakespeare, William, Chapter 3 pas-
    sim, Chapter 4 passim, 80, 86, 98,
    99, 101, 109, 110, 115, 131, 142, 164,
    172, 173, 192, 195
Shelley, Percy B., 48, 49, 55, 110, 114,
    122, 124, 130, 146, 160, 181, 219,
    221
showmanship, 152
sign, 6, 11, 34
  systems, Chapter 2 passim
  mutual dependence of, 33
  power of, 37
  non-verbal, 25, 26
  iconic use of, 27
signal, 12

signans, 36
signatum, 9, 36
similarity opposition, 26
simile, 43, 191
simplified syntax, 169
sin, original, 244
Sir Patrick Spence, 116
situation, 11, 27, 30, 31, 33, 34, 231
Socrates, see Plato
Sophrosyne, 93, 211
Southey, Robert, 138, 141, 142
space travel, 216
specialized quotation marks, see 'Key
    to Metasemantic Markers' on p. XV.
    Also defined pp. 5, 6, 8
speculation, 236
Spenser, Edmund, 110
Spinoza, Benedict, 134
spirit, 158
stanza form, 220
Steiner, George, 21
Stevenson, R. L., 213
stimulus-response routines, 34
story, 239
subliminal verbal patterning, 43
suicide, 212
Sullivan, Sir Arthur, 101
Swift, Jonathan, 79
synonymy, 36, 217

tape, 149
Tate, Nahum, 155
Taylor, Alfred E., 176, 210, 212
Taylor, Jeremy, 136
teacher, proper task of, 249
teaching, see education
techniques of scholarship, 132
technology, 153
television, 69, 70, 148, 149, 162, 206
tenor, 36, 37
theology, 73, 236
thinking, 25, 82, 129
token, 8, 11, 12, 28, 29, 30
tragedy, 147, 193, 197, 198
translation, 10, 17, 23, 24, 66, 172, 180,
    184, 185, 186, 187, 217
    interlingual, 22, 24
    intersemiotic, 22, 24
    intralingual, 1, 2, 9, 22, 24, 217, 219
    difficulty of translating cultural
        concepts, 172, 173
transmutation, see intersemiotic trans-
    lation

transposition, see translation
tropes, 45
truth, 239, 241, 243
Tusser, Thomas, 99
type, 8, 11, 12, 28, 29, 33
    systems, 33

understanding, 77, 85, 130, 131, 167,
    211, 225, Chapter 17 passim
United Nations, 245
unity, 193, 207
unlettered, Chapter 12 passim
uses of language, see language

value, 18, 230-233, 239, 240
    of literature, 129
Vancouver, I. A. Richards at, 180
vehicle, 36, 37, 112, 113
Vendler, Helen, 152
verification, 236
verse writing, 157
video tape, 150, 151
vividity, 229
Vladivostok, I. A. Richards at, 165

Wedgewood, Thomas, 126, 138
Weiss, Paul, 28
western people, 168, 185
Whalley, George, 116
Whitehead, 182
Whitman, Cedric, 212
will, 241
Winckelmann, 147
wit, 80
Wittgenstein, Ludwig, 71
Wordsworth, Dorothy, 136, 137, 138
Wordsworth, William, 99, 112, 117,
    118, 119, 128, 136-142, 152, 164, 180,
    220, 221
word, Chapter 6 passim, 146, 171, 215,
    217
    order, 225, 226
writing, 30, 31

Xenophon, 212

yantra, 5, 233
Yeats, William, 57, 74, 82, 122